Individ...   A Systematic Study
of Conceptions... and Therapeutic Aspects
by Leopold Bellak, Marvin Hurvich, and Helen A. Gediman

Innovative Treatment Methods in Psychopathology
edited by Karen S. Calhoun, Henry F. Adams, and Kevin M. Mitchell

The Changing School Scene: Challenge to Psychology
by Leah Gold Fein

Troubled Children: Their Families, Schools, and Treatments
by Leonore R. Love and Jaques W. Kaswan

Research Strategies in Psychotherapy
by Edward S. Bordin

The Volunteer Subject
by Robert Rosenthal and Ralph L. Rosnow

Innovations in Client-Centered Therapy
by David A. Wexler and Laura North Rice

The Rorschach: A Comprehensive System
by John E. Exner

Theory and Practice in Behavior Therapy
by Aubrey J. Yates

Principles of Psychotherapy
by Irving B. Weiner

Psychoactive Drugs and Social Judgment: Theory and Research
edited by Kenneth Hammond and C. R. B. Joyce

Clinical Methods in Psychology
edited by Irving B. Weiner

Human Resources for Troubled Children
by Werner I. Halpern and Stanley Kissel

Hyperactivity
by Dorothea M. Ross and Sheila A. Ross

Heroin Addiction: Theory, Research, and Treatment
by Jerome J. Platt and Christina Labate

Children's Rights and the Mental Health Professions
edited by Gerald P. Koocher

D1085143

CHILDREN'S RIGHTS
AND THE
MENTAL HEALTH PROFESSIONS

SPONSORED BY THE SOCIETY FOR THE PSYCHOLOGICAL
STUDY OF SOCIAL ISSUES

One of the goals of the Society for the Psychological Study of Social Issues
(SPSSI) is the sponsorship of books which provide avenues through
which social scientists can apply their knowledge and insights to the
critical social issues of today. SPSSI considers this book to be a provocative statement about such an issue, and is pleased to sponsor its publication.

SPSSI Editorial Advisory Committee

Jeanne H. Block
Institute for Human Development
University of California, Berkeley

Sol Gordon
Institute for Family Research and Education
Syracuse University

Robert Perloff
University of Pittsburgh

Lawrence S. Wrightsman
George Peabody College for Teachers
SPSSI Publications Committee Chairperson

CHILDREN'S RIGHTS AND THE MENTAL HEALTH PROFESSIONS

Edited by

GERALD P. KOOCHER, PH.D.

A WILEY-INTERSCIENCE PUBLICATION

JOHN WILEY & SONS
New York • London • Sydney • Toronto

Library of Congress Cataloging in Publication Data:

Main entry under title:
Children's rights and the mental health professions.

(Wiley series on personality processes)
"A Wiley-Interscience publication."
"Sponsored by the Society for the Psychological
Study of Social Issues.
Includes index.
1. Child mental health. 2. Child mental health
services. 3. Children's rights. I. Koocher,
Gerald P. II. Society for the Psychological Study
of Social Issues. [DNLM: 1. Child advocacy.
2. Mental health—In infancy and childhood. 3. Mental
health services—In infancy and childhood.
WM30 C536]
RJ111.C52   362.7'8'2042   76-16062
ISBN 0-471-01736-1

Printed in the United States of America

10 9 8 7 6 5 4 3 2 1

Contributors

STEVEN J. APTER, PH.D., Associate Professor of Special Education, Division of Special Education, Syracuse University, Syracuse, New York

DONALD P. BARTLETT, PH.D., Assistant Professor, Department of Psychology, State University of New York at Buffalo, Buffalo, New York

HENRY A. BEYER, J.D., Staff Attorney and Research Coordinator, Center for Law and Health Sciences, Boston University School of Law, Boston, Massachusetts

STEPHEN R. BING, LL.B., Deputy Director, Massachusetts Advocacy Center, Boston, Massachusetts

JONATHAN BRANT, J.D., Assistant Attorney General, Commonwealth of Massachusetts, Boston, Massachusetts

RENE TANKENOFF BRANT, M.D., Clinical Fellow in Psychiatry, Harvard Medical School and Beth Israel Hospital, Boston, Massachusetts

J. LARRY BROWN, M.S.W., PH.D., Executive Director, Massachusetts Advocacy Center, Boston, Massachusetts

BRUCE CUSHNA, PH.D., Associate Director, Developmental Evaluation Clinic, The Children's Hospital Medical Center; Principal Associate in Pediatrics, Harvard Medical School; Adjunct Assistant Professor in Special Education, Boston College, Boston, Massachusetts

NORMA DEITCH FESHBACH, PH.D., Professor of Education and Head, Program in Early Childhood Development, University of California at Los Angeles, Los Angeles, California

SEYMOUR FESHBACH, PH.D., Professor of Psychology, Former Director, The Fernald School, University of California at Los Angeles, Los Angeles, California

MARILEE U. FREDERICKS, PH.D., Director, Des Moines Child Guidance Center, Des Moines Iowa

GAIL GARINGER, J.D., Associate Director, New England Resource Center for Protective Services at The Children's Hospital Medical Center and The Judge Baker Guidance Center, Boston, Massachusetts

PATRICIA KEITH-SPIEGEL, PH.D., Professor and Department Chairperson, Department of Psychology, California State University at Northridge, Northridge, California

GERALD P. KOOCHER, PH.D., Supervising Psychologist, The Sidney Farber Cancer Center and The Children's Hospital Medical Center; Instructor in Psychology, Harvard Medical School; Lecturer in Psychology, Northeastern University; Lecturer in Psychology, Boston University, Boston, Massachusetts

ALICE LOCICERO, PH.D., Staff Psychologist, Martha M. Eliot Family Health Center; Instructor in Psychology, Harvard Medical School, Boston, Massachusetts

RODMAN MCCOY, B.A., Research Assistant, Boston University, Boston, Massachusetts

FREDA G. REBELSKY, PH.D., Professor and Director of Training in Developmental Psychology, Department of Psychology, Boston University, Boston, Massachusetts

L. WENDELL RIVERS, PH.D., Assistant Research Professor and Director, Mental Health Specialists Program, University of Missouri, St. Louis, St. Louis, Missouri

STEPHEN E. SCHLESINGER, B.A., Department of Psychology, State University of New York at Buffalo, Buffalo, New York

DAVID W. SIMMONDS, PH.D., Staff Psychologist, Prairie View Hospital, Newton, Kansas

MARK A. STEWART, M.D., Ida P. Haller Professor of Child Psychiatry, Psychopathic Hospital, University of Iowa Medical School, Iowa City, Iowa

ARMIN P. THIES, PH.D., Assistant Professor of Psychology, Department of Psychology, St. John's University, Jamaica, New York

ROBERT L. WILLIAMS, PH.D., Professor of Psychology, Director of Black Studies, Washington University, St. Louis, Missouri

JOHN P. WILSON, LL.B., Associate Dean, Director, Legal Studies Institute, Boston University School of Law, Boston, Massachusetts

Foreword

Children's rights is an issue whose time is now. At the same time "children's rights" remains a slogan in search of a definition. The Society for the Psychological Study of Social Issues (SPSSI) believes that this book illuminates some of the basic concerns of the contemporary movement for children's rights.

One of the missions of SPSSI is the sponsorship of books that reflect the Society's goal of applying knowledge of social science to policy determination. I believe that, taken broadly, this collection reflects SPSSI's goal. The chapters themselves vary in orientation, tone, and content. Some are reviews of the empirical literature; others are more personal accounts of case histories. Some seek to sensitize us to areas of concern; others propose solutions to these concerns. Some are scholarly; others, polemical.

Probably no individual or organization would completely support every view-point expressed in this book. For example, we may decry the lack of research offered to support several of the recommendations proposed here. We may prefer to see other rights—such as the sexual rights of children— examined. Yet the virtue of this book is that it compactly expresses the state of things. Concerned mental-health and legal professionals must speak out, as they do here; actions must be taken, whether research-based guidelines are available or not. SPSSI feels that this book defines our areas of ignorance and hopes that it encourages efforts to provide the necessary knowledge to make wiser decisions in the future.

LAWRENCE S. WRIGHTSMAN
Publications Chairperson

*Society for the Psychological
Study of Social Issues (SPSSI)*

Acknowledgments

At the outset, preparing this volume seemed to be a simple, straightforward project. Simply contact those friends and colleagues whose opinions you value and whose expertise you feel ought to be shared. Ask them to commit their ideas to paper, add some common threads, a bit of organization, and produce an important and much needed statement on the rights of children. At least that was the plan. As I write these words some eighteen months, three revisions, and hundred aggravations later, my naive optimism has long been exhausted. Should some inner masochism ever drive me to willingly volunteer for such a task again, I trust my friends and family will give serious consideration to euthanasia.

I know that all editors take pride in their work, but my special pride lies in the efforts of the 24 contributors to this volume, who are joined in the belief that individuals should not seek to profit from child advocacy. To that end, all of the authors in this volume have contributed their efforts, and monies earned from the sale of this book will be used to support the rights of children under the aegis of the Society for the Psychological Study of Social Issues. I would like to take this opportunity to thank the authors for their generous willingness to donate all royalties from the sales of this book to SPSSI.

Special thanks are also due Ms. Dorothy Markus, whose keen and critical eye helped to polish the manuscript, and Dr. Larry Wrightsman, who offered support, encouragement, and the voice of reason as each, in turn, was needed, as well as constructing the index.

Finally, with grateful affection, I wish to acknowledge the guidance of my parents, Marion and David Koocher, who taught me first-hand a genuine and sincere respect for the rights of children. And to one other who suffered my ill-tempered frustrations in silence and who was always there with the help I needed when it mattered most: thank you Robin—my proofreader, my critic, my inspiration, my wife.

GERALD P. KOOCHER

Cambridge, Massachusetts
April 1976

Contents

An Introduction: Why Children's Rights?

GERALD P. KOOCHER

The main thesis of this book is that in their day-to-day activities mental-health professionals often violate the individual rights of children. These violations can be inadvertent or deliberate, well-intentioned and carefully conceived or executed for the sake of expediency. Some are designed to cut through red tape; others reflect long-held stereotypes that are ingrained in professional training programs. Still others occur as a result of increasing complexities and the scope of knowledge in the mental-health fields. This in turn leads to increasingly intricate issues and a heightened sensitivity to the rights of the individual. Thus the mechanism for these violations is often clouded, and solutions are difficult to implement. Each paper in this volume focuses on a different aspect of the rights of the child-client in situations common to various practitioners within the sphere of mental-health care.

Initially, it is important to clarify the concept of a *right*. The term, as it is used throughout this book, usually does not refer to the powers and privileges guaranteed by statute or by the Constitution. We are not as concerned here with political obligations as we are with moral and ethical considerations. Each mental-health profession recognizes its own special ethical or moral responsibilities routinely due the individuals or the groups that it serves. Most professional associations have drafted and promulgated "codes of ethics" or "ethical standards" to which their members must subscribe. Such documents are generally well-reasoned, responsible, and self-policing beyond the violations covered by statutes. Often, however, the standards of professional associations do not specifically address children as a unique subset of the population. The recognition that children are unique and the attendant special demands on those who work with

1

children and families formulate the definition of the term *children's rights* used in this book.

As adults, it is easy for us to think of children as miniature versions of ourselves; indeed, outwardly they appear to be like us, and they do grow up to be like us. The subtle fallacy inherent in this reasoning is that children are not simply small grownups. Children are unique in at least two important ways. First, a child's basic equipment for adapting and functioning in the world is quite different from that of an adult. Second, at the very least children are constantly subjected to benign oppression and to all the other violations that any under-represented minority group experiences. If this seems to be a strong statement, it is no less extreme than the "business-as-usual" attitude that frequently prevails when children are handled by the adult world. We in the mental-health field consider ourselves professionals and shy away from the thought that we are engaged in a "business." Yet too often we respond in a business-as-usual manner when we meet the child who is brought to our hospital, clinic, school, or office.

The special vulnerabilities of children are well documented in child-development research. The impact of experiences in early childhood on later development and behavior is unquestionable. Intellectually and emotionally (as well as physically), children are not born prepared to survive independently. In fact, the human infant is probably the most dependent newborn in the animal kingdom. The primacy effect of early experiences, developmental stages, and the critical periods of cognitive and emotional growth create potential behavioral influences that exist for life. As mental-health professionals, there is a real need for us to apply our knowledge in these areas sensitively and deliberately in our daily work with children.

The benign oppression referred to earlier is most obvious when we consider the nature of the child and his/her rites of passage in our society. This process, generally known as socialization, usually means that older, bigger, stronger, and more experienced (although not necessarily wiser) people are constantly trying to guide, educate, bully, or otherwise direct smaller, less sophisticated, dependent, and more vulnerable people (*sic* children). Regrettably, the oppression inherent in the socialization process is not always benign or enlightened. We do not contend that the current process of socializing children is evil or in need of a radical overhaul. Rather, our appeal is that children be recognized as a minority group that deserves special and thoughtful consideration from every viewpoint. After all, the rights of any minority must be recognized and protected by the majority.

It has long been known that the potential exists to offer our children more fulfilling, healthier, well-adjusted lives. This view is eloquently stated in the report of the Joint Commission on Mental Health of Children

(1970), which incorporates the concept that children are indeed people who have the right to live in an enabling society. Now it is time for the professionals who applaud that report and its conclusions to begin cleaning some of their own houses in regard to the rights of the children they serve. There are actions and issues that require the attention of concerned professionals, and there are steps in a positive direction that can be taken by responsive and responsible individuals.

However, this book is not intended to be a unilateral attack on existing professional mental-health practices. Rather it, is because we see the sensitive professional as a primary-change agent that we begin here. It is our intent to make professionals in the clinical fields of child mental health aware of crucial current issues in the hope that expediency and past neglect, where they exist, can be replaced by the thoughtful application of alternative procedures. The mental-health professions have long struggled with meaningful issues and problems in child mental health. There are no easy answers, and few universal criticisms can be made with total validity. Here, we hope to shed additional light on the complex questions in the mental-health field and to make examinations of many key mental-health issues.

When I sought contributors for this book, I asked them to explore thoughtfully and analytically their particular issues and then to write in a solution-oriented vein. It is not enough to be a critic. One must be willing to pose solutions and to take affirmative steps. If this book moves one reader to act, then we have succeeded in taking that first step.

REFERENCE

Joint Commission on Mental Health of Children. *Crisis in child mental health: Challenge for the 1970s.* New York: Harper & Row, 1970.

Child Mental Health and Professional Responsibility: A Re-Examination of Roles

GERALD P. KOOCHER

This book contains a variety of articles bearing on the interaction between children, their families, and members of the mental-health professions. Some of these chapters ask professionals in their daily clinical work to respect the rights of children. Others urge the reader to adopt a social advocacy role on behalf of children in need mental-health services. Still other chapters argue for changes in public policy matters that influence the care and treatment of children. The precise thesis and focus of each chapter is different, naturally enough, because the authors are all different people. In gathering this collection, it has been necessary to tolerate differences in style, belief, and emphasis among the many contributors. In some ways this lessens the potential unity of the whole book, a phenomenon endemic to collections of this sort, but in the main it reflects the true state of the field. To imply that there is unity, overwhelming agreement, or consistency across interdisciplinary lines regarding the provision of mental-health services to children would be a gross oversimplification as well as a disservice.

Despite many basic differences, an integral premise and framework provide an underlying foundation that unites the papers in this volume. It is the belief that mental-health professionals are responsible not only for what they do, but also for what they may fail to do for the children they serve. This concept is eloquently developed by Polier (1975), who recognizes four basic areas of concern:

1. The responsibility of the individual professional.
2. The responsibility of social agencies empowered to deliver services.

5

3. The rights of children to receive services in accordance with law and social morality.
4. The professional responsibility of resolving larger social issues that determine the rights and entitlements of children from the standpoint of public policy.

Members of the mental-health professions usually provide services through or in conjunction with social agencies, strive to uphold reasonable standards of legal and moral conduct, and express great interest in particular social issues, making it clear that these areas are not mutually exclusive. Some of the issues raised here may overlap, covering more than one of these four areas, but each chapter in this book is placed in one of Polier's four sections, based primarily on the person or persons chiefly responsible for formulating and implementing policies with regard to the issues raised.

Part One, "Professional Responsibility in Service Delivery to Children," focuses on the individual professional in the service-delivery system. The issues raised bear directly on the actions (or the inactions) of direct-service providers. The changes recommended in Part One are generally within the capability of the individual mental-health professional. In the first chapter, LoCicero discusses the child's right to be informed about clinical evaluations, and the purposes and results of such evaluations. Koocher then explores the rights of children in psychotherapy and the special considerations that the child therapist must address. Simmonds follows with a look at the "identified-patient" status some children earn more as a function of a family disorder than of individual pathology. The professional's role as an "expert witness" in custody battles is examined by Fredericks, who notes traditional role conflicts between the assessment of parental competence and the needs of children caught in legal limbo. Finally, Keith-Spiegel presents a detailed and searching examination of children as participants in research, in which she explores past and current research practices and raises complex issues that are in need of sensitive scrutiny by the would-be researcher. All the chapters in Part One are of direct concern to the individual practitioners and researchers who must face children in these daily situations. The authors call for increased sensitivity to the needs of the child in each context, and suggest steps and attitudes that mental-health professionals must be willing to adopt to safeguard the rights of the children with whom they work.

Part Two, "Institutional Responsibilities and Childrens' Rights," looks at the interface of children's rights with the institutions responsible for the delivery of services in the mental-health field. In the first article Thies addresses the rights of children in residential treatment facilities and notes the dilemmas faced by the individual child therapist as a professional and as an institutional employee, tempering real issues with the responsibilities that must be accepted on behalf of the children being served. Apter then raises the complex issue of training versus service. Respecting the rights of children in institutional settings and maintaining a dual mission of service delivery and professional training is not easy, but Apter notes some moral imperatives of key importance. Children who are different or who are considered as defective in some way have long been institutionalized as a kind of "sanitizing" service for society. Cushna discusses the origins of this problem and outlines the need for constructive changes in the direction of deinstitutionalization. Finally, the thorny issues of institutional records, confidentiality, and the right to access by children and families to records on their treatment or diagnoses are thoughtfully analyzed by Brant, Garinger, and Brant, who suggest some ways in which the rights of both professionals and clients can be safeguarded under a uniform institutional policy of record management. All the chapters in Part Two address policy matters that involve individual professionals but that are generally determined at the institutional level. The authors call for changes in institutional policies, but the people who comprise the staff and governing boards of these institutions must ultimately initiate these changes.

Part Three, "The Question of Due Process in Mental-Health Services to Children and Their Families," addresses the right of children to receive service in accordance with due process of law and moral sensitivity. In other words, it is not enough that agencies *provide* service. Mental-health services must respect the rights of the child and be sensitive to family problems. First, Beyer and Wilson discuss the ways in which a parent may "voluntarily" commit a child to a mental institution, even if the child is unwilling. The child's right to resist so-called "voluntary commitment" and the potential problems in the current system of commitment are examined. The following two chapters raise the issue of parental violence against children in two different contexts. Feshbach and Feshbach take a family-centered view of corporal punishment and the rights of children if this punishment becomes abuse. Garinger, Brant, and Brant consider the manner in which society and the law address the problem of child abuse and suggest the need to approach this problem in new and more constructive ways. Finally, Bing and Brown address the social institution of the juvenile court and discuss the problem of attempting to deliver mental-health services to children under legal sentence or statutory mandate. All the chapters in Part Three examine the delivery of mental-health services in contexts in which service delivery per se may be regulated under law and the receipt of service may not necessarily be welcomed by the particular child or family involved. The rights of children in situations where the legal and mental-health professions often confront one another are of increasing social importance.

In Part Four, "Professional Responsibility in Public-Policy Problem

Areas," addresses professional responsibilities in some broad policy areas that affect children. These areas certainly involve individual-service providers and social institutions, but here the impact of individual behavior is much less important than the impact of the social policy as a whole. In fact, social policy seems to take precedence over the assumption of meaningful responsibility by professionals in such situations. Mental-health professionals in these areas too often have been unable to take a uniform constructive stand. In the first chapter in Part Four, Bartlett and Schlesinger are concerned with the application of labels and the assignment of diagnostic categories to children. The long-term effects of such labeling and some constructive alternative approaches to the problem are presented. Williams and Rivers then examine the subtle effects of language differences between black and white children in the design of standardized intelligence tests, which are biased toward white children. The importance of considering the child's own language system in psychological evaluation and the right of the child to be compared with other children who have the same cultural background are discussed. The last three chapters in Part Four deal with the use of psychotropic drugs in the treatment of children. Brown and Bing begin by noting the potential for the misuse of such drugs to create a kind of societal tyranny against children. Stewart approaches the problem from a different perspective, pointing out that psychoactive drugs can be useful, but expressing concern for the inappropriate applications that have developed. Finally, McCoy and Koocher summarize the main issues of such drug abuse and urge the adoption of a careful and sensitive policy for uniformly handling requests by parents, schools, or institutions for psychotropic drugs to be used in the treatment of certain children. All these areas involve broad questions that must be addressed by a large number of professionals if there is to be any meaningful opportunity for change. Coherent policy by public agencies and professional organizations is necessary if children's rights are to be upheld.

Essentially, the ultimate question raised in this book is to what extent should professional status be immunized from the responsibility to advocate on behalf of children? Advocacy takes many forms and can occur between a single client and a professional as well as in a court of law or before a legislative committee. It is unfortunate that some professionals and professional societies have remained aloof from the advocacy of public policy for children. In such cases, inaction truly represents an abdication of responsibility. Writing about psychologists in particular, Ramey (1974) notes that individuals are frequently called on by government and other public institutions to give advice in matters concerning public policy for children. By the same token, Ramey points out, only rarely have psychologists sought to influence the course of public policy for children through the actions of their professional associations. At the same time, it is clear that a collective and cohesive response by psychologists could have a powerful impact on the formulation of public policy for children's programs.

There will always be opponents to any advocation on the part of a professional body. An outstanding recent example, also drawn from the ranks of psychology, reflects the difficulties faced by professionals who do attempt constructive advocacy on behalf of children. The official proceedings of the American Psychological Association (Conger, 1974) contain a resolution that concludes:

Therefore be it resolved: That the American Psychological Association opposes the use of *corporal* punishment in schools, juvenile facilities, child-care nurseries, and all other institutions, public or private, where children are cared for or educated (p. 632).

Although the resolution was easily passed by the governing Council of Representatives, the record shows that it was passed ". . . with a request that the vote be shown as other than unanimous." Not only is it difficult to comprehend why truly concerned professionals would not wish to support such a bland resolution of advocacy, but it is also incomprehensible that some professionals would try to lessen the impact of such a resolution by taking exception once it had clearly passed.

In the final analysis, the individual professional must be recognized as the key to the assertion and maintenance of children's rights in the mental-health field. As long as professional organizations are responsive only to their members and government and social institutions operate on inertial guidance, children will continue to be an underrepresented minority with no power to advocate for themselves. Change must begin with an initial housecleaning, proceed to advocacy in the professional world, and eventually reach the public forum. This may be a new and an uncomfortable role for many mental-health professionals, but it is a responsibility that they dare not shirk.

REFERENCES

Conger, J. J. Proceedings of the American Psychological Association, Inc., 1974. *Am. Psychol.* **30** (1975), 620–51.

Polier, J. W. Professional abuse of children: Responsibility for the delivery of services. *Am. J. Orthopsychiatry.* **45** (1975), 357–62.

Ramey, C. T. Children and public policy: A role for psychologists. *Am. Psychol.* **29** (1974), 14–18.

Professional Responsibility
in Service Delivery
to Children

Part One focuses primarily on the individual mental-health professional as an agent who delivers services to children and their families. All the contributors to Part I address the individual practitioner, suggesting that past methods need to be reexamined and restructured within a new frame of reference: a respect for the rights of children. The special interests and talents of each contributor are reflected by the chosen topics.

Dr. Alice LoCicero, who received her graduate training at Catholic University, works as a staff psychologist in a family health center located in the heart of one of Boston's poorest public housing projects. Previously an elementary-school teacher, LoCicero is now on the faculty of the Harvard Medical School. Working closely with children and adolescents has made her seriously concerned about the child's right to be informed as well as evaluated.

Dr. Gerald Koocher, the general editor of this book, received his graduate training at the University of Missouri, Columbia. He is a supervising psychologist at the Sidney Farber Cancer Center and The Children's Hospital Medical Center in Boston, and he holds teaching appointments at Boston University, Northeastern University, and Harvard Medical School. Koocher's special area of interest as a clinical child psychologist is the uniqueness of the therapist–client relationship and the child's rights in the context of that relationship.

Dr. David W. Simmonds, who also trained at the University of Missouri, Columbia, completed additional training at the University of Texas Medical Branch in Galveston. He now works on the staff of Prairie View Hospital in Newton, Kansas. Simmonds is especially interested in family process and transactional analysis, and focuses on the psychotherapeutic problem of casting children in "identified patient" roles.

Dr. Marilee Fredericks is the Director of the Des Moines, Iowa, Child Guidance Center, and a past president of the American Psychological Association's Section on Clinical Child Psychology. Fredericks is frequently asked to "give expert testimony" in child custody cases; her recent Presidential Address on the problems such testimony engenders led to the invitation to her to address these issues here.

Dr. Patricia Keith-Spiegel, Professor and Psychology Department Chairperson, California State University at Northridge, has published over 50 professional papers since she earned her doctorate at the Claremont Graduate School. She is active in professional affairs and is a member of the American Psychological Association's Committee on Scientific and Professional Ethics and Conduct. Using children as research subjects hit close to home when Keith-Spiegel was approached for permission to "study" her own child under rather questionable circumstances. She brings the insight of a sensitive parent as well as a thoughtful behavioral scientist to her treatment of this topic.

The underlying theme implicit in each of these chapters is that the individual professional (clinician, teacher, or researcher) must assume many and varied responsibilities if children are to benefit from mental-health services. Part I primarily focuses on the actions and the inactions of individual mental-health professionals that can be crucial to the rights of their child-clients.

The Right to Know: Telling Children the Results of Clinical Evaluations

ALICE LoCICERO

TALKING TO THE CHILD

An 8-year-old girl who had been hospitalized several times for surgical procedures, was undergoing out-patient psychotherapy in a hospital clinic. The girl dramatized a scene in which she assumed the roles of various hospital personnel—none of whom would tell either the sick child or her mother what was wrong with the child. Instead, each person, in turn, gave the mother a piece of paper on containing a scribble and directed them to another department. After the dramatization, the therapist asked the surgeon to discuss the girl's next procedure with the family beforehand. At the following session, the girl correctly explained the scheduled surgery to her therapist. She said the surgeon had given her mother this information in her presence. "But," the girl added, feeling hurt and angry, "he didn't say *anything* to me!"

This girl's dramatization referred to medical personnel, but the analogy to the child-guidance field is inescapable. The child—bright, perceptive and sufficiently in touch with her own feelings—was able to define what actually happened in addition to her own reactions to the situation. Other children faced with the same situation may realize only how anxious, sad, confused, angry, or simply bad they feel. Yet many clinicians (here referring to persons working in the mental-health and child-guidance fields) evaluate children capably, but then do not share the results of their evaluation with the designated patient—the child.

The intention here is not to address the question of whether to accept the designation of a child as the primary patient, although this is a useful and provocative question. In this chapter, concern is expressed for the instances in which the child is evaluated. No doubt these evaluations are and will continue to be made. In Massachusetts, for example, all young people between the ages of 3 and 21 who seem to have special educational needs are entitled to an evaluation of those needs, which commonly include psychological testing.

A distinction is often made between children who come to a clinician knowing that they have problems, suffering because of them, and seeking relief, and children who are brought to the clinician only because their behavior is distressing to someone else, for example, a parent or a teacher (Bornstein, 1949; Chess, 1969; Freud, 1946). It is both possible and advisable to share the results of diagnostic evaluations in some form with children in both categories, although it is perhaps more important as well as more difficult to do this when children are referred for evaluation.

The clinician should directly address the child being evaluated, carefully taking into account the child's level of cognitive and affective development, and applying clinical skill and knowledge to decide what to say to the child and how to say it. This is a difficult task, demanding a knowledge of cognitive and affective development, a thorough acquaintance and a friendly relationship with the child, careful planning and choice of words, attentiveness during the session, and an ability to convey a sense of concern and hope. It is not unreasonable to expect a clinician involved in diagnosing children to exhibit all these capabilities.

THE VALUE OF THE FOLLOW-UP SESSION

It is important to consider the value of a successful follow-up session in terms of the benefits to the child, the parents, and others, including teachers and therapists, who will be working with the child to implement the clinician's recommendations.

The Child

During a session with a child, the clinician should implicitly express an interest in that child as a person with experiences—a person who is separate from, although related to, his or her parents. This is an appropriate indication of respect. Child psychotherapy rests on the assumption that children themselves, with help, can make changes in their own lives. It seems reasonable, then, to share with the child any understanding that might help him or her to make decisions that could contribute to progress in healthy development.

Another message implicit in the interpretive interview—no matter how brief or simple that interview may be—is that the clinician, who now knows the child so well that the parents look to her or him for advice, is not afraid of what has been learned: the truth is not unspeakable. This is especially important when considering the point made by Chess (1969) that children sometimes feel that being brought to a clinician is evidence that they are "wicked" or "crazy"; Some variants on this theme expressed by children I have evaluated are "bad," "wild," "retarded." Thus the reasons children invent to explain their visits and their diagnoses are often worse than the truth. In a brief interpretive session, the clinician clearly should not expect to change a child's false self-beliefs, because the misconception being discussed may have deeper roots. The clinician's silence will not "confirm" the child's beliefs, and by challenging the false idea and raising an alternative, in some cases the clinician can convey the message that a well-respected and knowledgeable adult in the child's life sees the child in a more positive way than the child has anticipated. This realization in itself can be therapeutic, and may initiate the process by which the child eventually achieves a better and a more acceptable view of himself or herself.

Sometimes, of course, children's fear that they are seriously emotionally disturbed or retarded are confirmed by evaluation. In such situations, the clinician helps both parents and child to face the knowledge of the child's problem, to put it in perspective, and to make reasonable plans for treatment.

In addition to indicating respect and questioning misconceptions, the follow-up session gives the clinician an opportunity to discuss recommendations with the child. Thus the child is prepared for the purpose, goals, and procedures of treatment. Such preparation can be of substantial help to the child, who can then mobilize resources to deal constructively with the treatment situation. The clinician must be careful to present the situation realistically to the child and to avoid raising false hopes. The clinician who knows the child can help the child cope with any anxieties regarding the treatment or changes necessary to implement the recommendations.

The point is made (Chess, 1969; Freud, 1946; Sylvester, 1952) that the child's preparation for treatment and the early stages of the treatment itself often seriously influence the course of treatment. Thus a thoughtful follow-up session can benefit a child for months or even years ahead.

The Parents

By indicating respect for the child as an individual with private experiences, the clinician sets an example for parents; in some cases, parents are encouraged to perceive the child in a new way. Further, by talking with the child about the results of an evaluation, the clinician relieves the parents of the possible burdens involved in deciding whether or what to tell the child, issues often cloaked in secrecy. In this regard, it is important for the clinician to convey the same information to the parents and the child, each according to their individual capacities to understand. Further, the clinician should offer guidelines to the parents, if this seems advisable, as to how to answer the child's questions about the problems and recommendations. McDonald (1965) makes a helpful suggestion that results and recommendations should usually be discussed with parents first, so that the clinician knows before talking to the child how receptive the parents have been to the recommendations. Then the clinician knows if it is possible to assure the child that a specific kind of help is actually to be provided.

It hardly needs to be stated that if a child knows the method and the goals of treatment and if the child expects to receive answers to questions about the treatment, the treatment process can be initiated and can progress more smoothly. The well-informed and respected child is in a sense invited to become a partner—an active participant—in the treatment process. Although resistance to treatment is always possible, a healthier aspect is that children who see themselves as active participants in their own treatment are allied with the therapist from the outset, thus enhancing their own development.

SOME GUIDELINES

There is an important distinction between the concepts of honesty and spontaneous openness. The clinician should be honest. Talking to children about serious issues in their lives requires careful thought and planning. The clinician who shares findings spontaneously, without considering what, why, how, or to whom, will rarely help and may even harm the child. The purpose here is to raise points for further consideration and to answer some questions that may have occurred to readers about the content of follow-up or interpretive interviews. Obviously, written guidelines can never be substituted for the judgments made in individual situations by skilled and thoughtful clinicians.

A Paradigm

Much has already been written about discussing the reasons children have come (or have been brought) for evaluation, and to review this here is beyond the scope of this chapter. Such discussions occur routinely, to

facilitate communication, to obtain further diagnostic information, to establish rapport, and generally to assure that the evaluation is made under
ideal conditions that allow the child to communicate freely (Adams, 1968;
Chess, 1969; McDonald, 1965). A great deal of what is said in this context is applicable to follow-up interviews and provides a paradigm for
discussing assessments and recommendations with children. Interpretive
sessions should allow children to feel secure in the knowledge that their
own best interests are being served by the evaluation process, much as the
discussion of the reasons for evaluation allows children to sense that it is
to their advantage to reveal themselves in the evaluation process.

Demystifying the Evaluation Process

In all cases, but perhaps especially when the clinician is preparing the
child for psychotherapy, it is important to let the child know that clinical
methods involve neither magic nor mind-reading, but rather the understanding of the individual child based on the clinician's knoweldge of
many other children who have similar concerns. This enables the child
to enter treatment without fear and with a realistic sense of how he or
she can be helped. When discussing the results of evaluations, the clinician
should focus on the child's experiences, including the experiences the child
has related during the evaluation as well as experiences the clinician can
sense empathetically that the child is likely to encounter. By focusing on
real experiences, the clinician can strengthen the child's sense that the
evaluation process is relevant and related to other aspects of the child's
life.

Dialogue

It is up to the clinician to make every reasonable effort to engage the child
in dialogue, so that the clinician has as clear an idea as possible how completely the child understands what is being said. At times the clinician
may ask the child, "What do you think of that idea?" In this way the
clinician learns more about the child, and the child learns that his or her
questions, elaborations, and disagreements are taken seriously and that he
or she is viewed as a partner in the treatment process.

Interpretation of Unconscious Material

As in all clinical work, it is important in the interpretive session to tell
children only what they can understand, accept, and find reassuring and
helpful. Perhaps the most difficult decisions the clinician faces in sharing
findings with children involve the interpretation of unconscious material.

This problem is illustrated by the following passages (Lippman, 1945), showing the positive and the negative effects that can result from the interpretation of dreams in diagnostic assessments. The first passage illustrates the potential benefits of dream interpretation:

In general, children enjoy talking about their dreams. . . . The young child is rarely surprised when asked by the therapist about his dreams. The older child as he approaches adolescence may wonder why he is being asked to relate his dreams, especially if he has been told that they have no significance. After he is told why the dream material is asked for, he usually enjoys helping the therapist to understand the material, often accepting it as a puzzle that should be solved (p. 234).

The second passage illustrates the potential danger inherent in interpreting unconscious material:

The most effective way to stop a child from telling his dreams is to try early to explain or interpret their content to him; this applies especially to dreams that reflect hostility or sexual conflict. It becomes apparent to him that dreams reveal secrets and it is therefore dangerous to tell them. He may go away from the interview more anxious and disturbed than when he came, and thus be conditioned against the treatment (p. 235).

Initially these passages appear contradictory. However, the first passage implies the unhurried partnership of child and therapist in the attempt to understand the dream material for the child's sake. By contrast, the second passage implies the interpretation of possibly threatening material by the therapist, without the cooperation of the child and before the child is ready to accept and deal with the material that has been revealed. Skill and empathy are required if the clinician is to decide whether or how to interpret unconscious material and whether this material is to be revealed through dreams, projective tests, or dramatic play.

Discussion of Family Problems

Sometimes it becomes apparent to the clinician during an evaluation process that the child's difficulties are actually directly caused by an unresolved problem of a parent or sibling or by relationships among other family members. The question then arises whether it is wise to discuss these problems with the child. Once again, the answer varies in different situations, and the decision can better be made by considering the individual child, the problem, and the family. It frequently suffices to tell children in these situations that their parents have some problems to work out and not to reveal the substantive issues. First, the parents have a right to confidentiality. Furthermore, as Wickes (1966) points out, "The child need not, usually should not, know the actual problem, for often it is one that taxes all our adult understanding to the utmost, and its knowledge would impose far too heavy a burden on the childish mind" (p. 40).

When the Problem Diagnosed Is Severe

In some situations, the diagnosis is that the child's problem is a serious one, such as organic brain damage, mental retardation, or severe emotional disturbance. Here the clinician's diagnostic skill, courage, and honesty are tested. Here, too, however, if the clinician concentrates on the child's experience, speaks in specific terms, maintains the proper perspective, and communicates care and hope, a follow-up session can be beneficial to the child. In discussing his final statements with patients, Sullivan (1954) says "My point is that I try never to close all doors to a person; the person should go away with hope and with an improved grasp on what has been the trouble" (p. 211).

Whether the diagnosis is organic brain damage or something less physically serious such as hyperactivity or a learning disability, the clinician's role in talking with parents and children is not to communicate the diagnostic category, but rather to define carefully which areas of the child's functioning are strong or adequate, which are weak, and what assistance is available. Some children may already sense the problematic areas; it is important to support their ability to maintain perspective, so that their feelings of inadequacy or anxiety do not interfere with their strong areas of functioning.

Thinking in terms of strengths and weaknesses is also imperative when working with a child who is mentally retarded or developmentally disabled. The clinician may point out direct experiences with the child's strengths, such as the ability to relate, friendliness, the ability to express feelings, or whatever qualities emerge during the evaluation. In this context, it is possible to acknowledge the child's continuing difficulty with academic work. It is helpful if the clinician has some practical knowledge of the real-life adjustments and productivity of adults who have been academically retarded in their school years, so that the clinician may express realistic hope.

When a child is only mildly emotionally disturbed, the clinician can help the child to define the areas that cause confusion or worry. If the disturbance is serious and the child is overwhelmed with anxiety much of the time, the clinician should acknowledge what the child already knows and help the child envision how things may be after help is received. For the school-aged child, for example, the clinician can talk about other children who have been worried or afraid most of the time and who could not do their work at school because these worries got in the way. Then the clinician might talk about the kind of help available to such children and the ways in which these children invested their energy after the condition was relieved, for example, in schoolwork, sports or play, or whatever seems appropriately within the grasp of the understanding of the child. A seriously emotionally disturbed child may not respond verbally to such comments. In such cases it is important for the clinician to look for clues to the child's response to clarify what has been said or, if necessary, to allay any anxiety that may have been raised.

Once the treatment plan is known, the clinician may decide to tell the child the specific details, again stressing the child's view of the experience of treatment.

Words

It is important that the clinician choose words wisely. It should never be taken for granted that a child knows the meaning of a word such as "concern," and in some instances the clinician should use two or three words, such as "worries, problems, fears," to be sure a point is clarified. Emotionally charged words should be used carefully and should be chosen deliberately only when it is clear that the clinician and the child understand the words in the same way and that they are the best words to make a point clear and explicit.

Again this is a matter to be considered in view of the knowledge of the specific child being evaluated, but the clinician should keep in mind that some words have meanings that are unique for children because of personal experience—meanings that may not be shared by the clinician, parents, or other people. This point further supports the necessity for the clinician to be attentive to the child's reactions to what is being said.

RESPONSIBILITY

Children and parents may readily accept the results of diagnostic evaluations if they have directly sought the clinician's advice themselves. However, the clinician may have to assume a greater responsibility when discussing diagnostic results with a child who has been referred for evaluation by an outside social agency. The contractual agreement with an agency may require a written report of results. In the instance of public-assistance referrals, it is most beneficial if the child can discuss the evaluation results with a person who understands clinical work and who knows the child well. But the clinician should not leave this matter to chance. The contract with the referring agency should include the interpretive session, or the clinician should work closely with persons in the agency who know the referred child so that they are able in turn to discuss the results of the evaluation with the child directly. The first alternative may be preferable, because it gives the child an opportunity to talk directly with the clinician and to raise questions or issues that are in need of clarification. However, whether the clinician directly discusses results with the child or ensures that a staff member of the referring agency does so, the fact that the clinician considers sharing results to be an essential part of an evaluation of a child teaches, by example, the respect and concern for the personal dignity of even the very young child.

REFERENCES

Adams, P. Techniques for pediatric consultation. In J. J. Schwab (ed.), *Handbook of psychiatric consultation.* New York: Appleton-Century-Crofts, 1968.

Bornstein, B. The analysis of a phobic child: Some problems of theory and technique. *Psychoanal. Stud. Child,* **3–4** (1949), 181–226.

Chess, S. *An introduction to child psychiatry* (2nd ed.). New York: Grune & Stratton, 1969.

Freud, A. *The psychoanalytical treatment of children.* New York: International Universities Press, 1946.

Lippman, H. S. The use of dreams in psychiatric work with children. *Psychoanal. Stud. Child* **1** (1945), 233–46.

McDonald, M. The psychiatric evaluation of children. *J. Am. Acad. Child Psychiatr.* **4** (1965), 569–612.

Piaget, J. *The language and thought of the child.* New York: Harcourt Brace Jovanovich, Inc., 1926.

Sullivan, H. S. *The psychiatric interview.* New York: Norton, 1954.

Sylvester, E. Discussion of techniques used to prepare young children for analysis. *Psychoanal. Stud. Child* **7** (1952), 306–21.

Wickes, F. *The inner world of childhood.* New York: New American Library, 1966.

Yarrow, L. J. Interviewing children. In P. H. Mussen (ed.), *Handbook of research methods in child development.* New York: John Wiley & Sons, Inc., 1960.

A Bill of Rights
for Children in Psychotherapy

GERALD P. KOOCHER

The fact that children in psychotherapy need to have their rights protected simply does not occur to most practitioners. We see ourselves as constantly mindful of the child's best interests with a sincere fervor not totally unlike that of the parent who marches in an antibussing rally or administers a spanking "for the child's own good." Just as we may at times question the assumption that parenthood automatically bestows a knowledge of what is best for one's children, we must also question the glib assertion that child therapists usually know what is best for their patients. It is time to question whether the therapist can always be relied on to protect the child's rights and to work in the child's best interests.

Ross (1974) develops these ideas and argues for a realistic set of principles to guide child therapists. His four basic tenets are:

1. Children have the right to be told the truth.
2. Children have the right to be treated with personal respect.
3. The child-client has the right to be taken seriously.
4. The child has a right to meaningful participation in decision making that applies to his or her life.

A broad range of professionals disagree with Ross' points and express their concern about them elsewhere in this book. The chapters by Keith-Spiegel and LoCicero, for example, touch on these same issues in the different contexts of research study and clinical evaluation, respectively.

At the time of the writing the author was supported in part by the U.S. Department of Health, Education and Welfare, Maternal and Child Health Project No. 928. The constructive criticism of Gary Melton and Barbara Pedulla on an earlier version of this material is gratefully acknowledged.

These recurring themes are not redundant, because each situation requires different considerations on the part of the professional involved, and it is not difficult to see how they can too easily be forgotten.

INITIATING TREATMENT

In his classic essay on "The Art of Being a Failure as a Therapist," Haley (1969) demonstrates the necessity of taking the patient seriously, dealing openly with the patient, and making the patient an ally in the treatment process. While most practicing therapists who work with adult patients readily accept such principles, a similar advantage is not always extended to the child in psychotherapy. A recent study of the effects of preparing children for psychotherapy (Holmes and Urie, 1975) offers an excellent example. The study found that when children were "prepared for psychotherapy" (that is, when they were told in advance what the therapy was about, what to expect from the therapist, and what to discuss with the therapist), premature terminations were less likely to occur, and a high degree of agreement about improvement in "target symptoms" was noted among therapists and parents. The authors use these data to argue for the better preparation of child-clients for psychotherapy, but the fact that such an argument is even necessary is somewhat unsettling.

Unlike the adult, who usually enters therapy as a free agent, children are most often introduced to psychotherapy by their parents. Generally the parents have had prior contact or conversation with the therapist about a "child's problems," and in some ways represent a kind of benevolent conspiracy. While many psychotherapists would refuse to treat involuntary patients, child therapists do so routinely. It may not be necessary to prepare the child in advance for therapy or this preparation may occupy the first few sessions, but too often the offering of such consideration in the form of an explanation and preliminary discussion with the child is simply omitted. This is doubly unfortunate because it not only represents a failure to recognize the child's rights, but it also reduces the effectiveness of psychotherapy (Holmes and Urie, 1975).

Whether psychotherapy is necessary or indicated, what the goals ought to be and how these goals should be approached are thorny generic questions. Most therapists routinely raise these issues with adult clients as part of the basic therapeutic process. Child-clients, on the other hand, seem only to complicate the problem of addressing these issues directly, because of their relative position of weakness, naivete, and submissiveness in the adult world. The child's level of comprehension and emotional immaturity is often invoked as a rationale for omitting these considerations, but such arguments do not seem totally justified. Too often the individuality of the child may be taken for granted in the initiation of psychotherapeutic referrals. It may well be that this problem is more representative of the difficulty many therapists face in communicating these issues to children. It is easier to avoid dealing with the issue than to struggle to produce understandable communications about the need for treatment, the process of therapy, and the issues on which to concentrate. Granted, it is not easy to answer the bluntly searching questions of children when we are not used to considering our normal procedures and approaches to be novel; but psychotherapy with an adult therapist is different from most of the other social relationships that children have and deserves special consideration here. Yet in a basic text on child psychotherapy (Hammer and Kaplan, 1967) the authors state: "Probably all systems or schools of psychotherapy would agree that the one basic and general goal for all children is emotional growth and maturity (p. 1)." The fact that the definition of "emotional growth and maturity" differs qualitatively from system to system and from therapist to therapist does not enter into the discussion. Part of the difficulty is the dilemma of precisely defining who the client is: the parent(s) or the child.

In most cases, the child-client is accepted for treatment at the request of the parents, is not asked to decide what he or she wants, and has little control over the goals of the therapy that the grownups establish in consultation with one another. Ross (1974) cites an illustration of this dilemma: the case of a 7-year-old brought to the clinic by a mother who complains that the child "won't listen . . . won't obey . . . won't hang up clothes after school, and has poor table manners." In the course of an assessment, it is determined that the family's values require that the child be "seen and not heard." Tentative attempts to modify parental expectations are met with objections and resistance; interviews with the child elicit the typical 7-year-old's denial of any difficulty and assurances that "everything's all right." When specifically asked if (s)he would like help with anything, the child responds in the negative.

The problem now becomes a question of what is in the child's "best interests." Does respecting the child's right to refuse help mean that it is in the child's best interests to struggle through a stressful childhood? or, is it better that the child learn to live in this authoritarian home with a minimum of stress and conflict, a possibility that can be offered by helping the child "adjust" to the reality he must face? Still another avenue worth exploring is raised by Simmonds contribution to this volume, which addresses the issue of "identified-patient" status in the family and suggests a need to examine carefully the nature and the sources of complaints brought to the therapist, which in turn may lead to a family-treatment modality.

Even when the need for (or the lack of) therapy can be reliably assessed without question, how should the child's right to self-determination be respected? In the case of a 7-year-old, for example, should the child have the right to override adult judgements and refuse therapy? If the child's right to refuse treatment is asserted, the parents' right to seek help for their child seems blocked. In making a decision the therapist cannot help but apply his or her own set of values to the situation, further clouding the whole situation. Although the therapist may try to arrive at impressions from a detached or independent viewpoint, there is a dual obligation that tends to make this difficult. On one hand, the therapist is ethically bound to respect the best interests of the child-client. On the other hand, the therapist is being paid to act as a kind of parental agent and parents are legally responsible for their children's welfare in most cases. Clearly, there is no simple solution to this array of contradictory considerations. However, a great need exists for the child therapist to weigh these matters carefully whenever a new child-client is referred for treatment.

Yet Ross (1974) notes that it may actually be impossible for a therapist to successfully balance these differing roles, and he suggests that perhaps such situations require an independent child advocate. A child advocate who would not be paid by the parents and would not be a colleague of the therapist, but simply an individual who can ensure that the treatment planned and undertaken actually serves the child's best interests. Ross is correct in raising this issue, but pragmatically it seems unrealistic to expect such advocates to be readily available, paid, and employed workably in the usual therapy situation or even to always know the child's best interests. Nevertheless, some circumstances should require a mandatory outside evaluation of the treatment plan for the child-client.

THE PROBLEM OF AVERSIVE THERAPIES

The best example of a therapy plan that ethically demands review by qualified individuals external to both the family and the therapist is the case of so-called *aversive counter-conditioning*. Aversive therapists generally involve the pairing of a noxious stimulus (usually electric shock) with the behavior that is considered maladaptive or with objects associated with that behavior. There is reasonable evidence to suggest that in some circumstances such aversive conditioning, coupled with the reinforcement or reward of alternative behaviors, can produce adaptive changes in behavior (Blackman and Silberman, 1975; Mikulas, 1972; Sherman, 1973). Most scientific reports on the application of this mode of treatment with children clearly indicate that it has been adopted as a "last resort" to stop self-injurious or destructive behavior that cannot be successfully modified by other less severe interventions. Current thinking seems to hold that ". . . a small number of electric shocks to the extremities, as part of a sound, comprehensive treatment program, can terminate the savage, self-mutilation of some autistic children" (Davidson and Stuart, 1975, p. 756). In some reported cases, however, it is not easy to discern whether the treatment goal justifies the means.

Such an example is presented by Tate and Baroff (1966), who successfully modified the self-injurious behavior of an institutionalized, psychotic, 9-year-old boy named Sam. The youngster reportedly banged his head against hard objects, punched himself in the face, and performed other acts that led to his partial blindness; he was threatened with total blindness unless his behavior was stopped. A paradigm of reward solely for nondestructive behavior was deemed insufficient, and after various less-severe techniques were tried, Sam was treated by a program of rewarding nondestructive behavior with praise and punishing self-injury with a painful electric shock on the right leg delivered by a cattle-prod device. Tate and Baroff reported that the procedure resulted in the complete elimination of Sam's self-destructive acts after *167 days of treatment.*

One American firm currently manufactures a radio-operated "remote shocker," which they boast "can deliver a painful shock from up to 300 feet away." Such products, readily available to any customer willing to pay for them, are touted as useful in stopping such unseemly behavior as "spitting, vomiting, and public toileting." It is difficult to believe that such devices are always, or even occasionally, applied with the thoughtfulness or sophistication described by Davidson and Stuart (1975).

It seems reasonable to insist that when a significant question arises as to the capacity for a child-client to participate meaningfully in the decision to employ a potentially harmful or coercive mode of therapy, an outside advocate must act on the child's behalf in the decision-making process. It also seems appropriate to place the burden of seeking such advocacy on the shoulders of the would-be therapist as a moral imperative. Lest the wolves be sent to watch over the sheep, the best potential source of independent child advocates would seem to lie in the ethics committees of state and regional professional or mental-health associations.

THE QUESTION OF CONFIDENTIALITY

The confidentiality of psychotherapeutic interviews has long been a well-established and a widely accepted principle. How, then, can the conscientious therapist respect the rights of child patients to privacy? In the traditional *child guidance center approach*, the parent(s) see one therapist while the child sees another. This traditional model implies that the therapists consult with one another intermittently, discuss the case with supervisors, and generally share any other information presented to them individually under the umbrella of confidentiality. The issue of how rigidly the patient's privileges must be respected in such circumstances is a key one, especially since the "patient" may be a parent (adult), a child, or both.

While there are probably as many different solutions to these problems as there are therapists, it is interesting to note the evolution of at least one thoughtful professional in addressing this issue. In an early article, Ross (1958) wrote of the prime importance of confidentiality in establishing a trusting therapeutic relationship. Ross suggested that there be no contact between the child's therapist and the child's parents; he urged that the confidential nature of the therapy be thoroughly explored with the child at the start of the treatment, he worried about the child's distrust of the therapist as a person who had conspired with the parents to influence him or her; and he urged that no material from the parents' sessions be introduced into the child's sessions, or vice versa. Some years later, Ross (1966) reconsidered his earlier writings, noting that not all children were suspicious or even chiefly concerned about confidentiality during their therapy and that the basis of patient–therapist trust was far more complex than a pure reliance on confidentiality. In the final analysis, Ross acknowledged that there is no evidence to support the contention that a single therapist cannot successfully treat both parent(s) and child individually.

Ultimately, the message Ross imparts is that truthfulness, personal respect, serious consideration, and involvement in therapeutic goal-setting are far more important factors than confidentiality per se. When the child senses that the therapist is offering these paramount items, then and only then do real trust and growth between patient and therapist become possible. If the child voices concern about confidential issues, the therapist may then respond with honest reassurance. When a parent offers a crucial piece of data in a therapeutic session, the therapist may raise this point to the child when appropriate and be truthful about the source of information. At times when the child expresses a serious concern that may not have been voiced to the parents, therapy may help the child work toward expressing that concern directly to the parents in private or in a joint meeting with the facilitative support of the therapist.

What if the child-client discloses plans to engage in dangerous, antisocial, or self-destructive acts, and then asks for assurances of confidentiality? This is a rare and an extreme example, but it may be the child's

way of testing the therapist's trustworthiness. It is of paramount importance for the therapist to assess the validity of the child's dangerous plans,
but the initial response should be the same even when it is unlikely that
the threatened act will be committed: The therapist must realize that the
child is expressing a very serious concern and must respond with equal
seriousness and respect for the feelings that produced the concern. Often
the therapist's serious effort to help the child-client deal with the distressing matter presented is enough to defuse the situation. When this is not
enough, however, the therapist should be prepared to intervene constructively and to discuss this intervention with the child at the first possible
opportunity.

I am reminded of a 6-year-old girl who perched herself on my window-
sill in an early session and spoke of jumping out (even though the win-
dows were childproof). When I told her that I would not let her jump
and hurt herself and that I did indeed care about her and wanted to help
her, she heaved an audible sigh of relief. It was a test, and I had passed.
I am not certain what I would have done had the child threatened to
jump from a window at home later that night. I suspect that I would
have talked seriously with her about why she felt badly enough to think
of doing such a thing, but in the final analysis I would have felt compelled to take positive preventive steps if she had persisted with con-
vincing threats. Preventive steps are justifiable in that this type of a threat
from a child-client to a therapist is like a call for help to an external
(but hopefully trusted) superego. I would begin by expressing my concern for the child and the dangerous consequences of the intended act,
and I would ask the child to help me think of ways that together we
might prevent the act from occurring. If it became necessary to discuss
precautions with the child's parent(s), I would hope that this might grow
naturally from my talk with the child herself and perhaps permit the child
to directly communicate her distress to her parent(s). The point is simply
that although the therapist must be willing to assume protective responsibility in such a case, this experience can often be changed from the
violation of a confidence to finding a shared solution to a difficult problem.

RECOMMENDATIONS

It is possible to outline some recommendations based on the issues just discussed. First it must be noted that much of the following material focuses
primarily on the child who voluntarily submits to outpatient psychotherapy.
Issues relating to institutionalized treatment are raised elsewhere in this
book; Part One is aimed chiefly at the individual therapist. There is a sig-

nificant overlap between institutionalized and individual treatment, however, and the fact that outpatient psychotherapy is the prime focus here should not lead the reader to conclude that institutionalization per se alters the basic rights of the child-client. If anything, the therapist of an institutionalized child should be especially mindful of the child's basic human rights and sensitive to potential infringements on these rights.

Indeed, the first necessity is for child therapists to recognize that they are morally bound to serve as an advocate for their child-clients. Unlike adults, children in general cannot be their own advocates physically, psychologically, or under statute. To put it bluntly, the therapist must continuously think of looking out for the child. The detached intellectual distance that may work well in initial adult therapy is not appropriate to use with children.

A second significant need is for child therapists to recognize that situations may arise in which their roles as therapists will be in conflict regarding specific issues about goal setting, therapy modality, parent desires, child's needs, and other central therapeutic issues. In such cases, the therapist is morally bound to seek a consultative opinion from a competent independent professional. If colleagues see the need for an outside opinion but the therapist does not, those colleagues must discuss their concerns with the therapist and urge that person to seek an opinion from a party who is not directly involved in the treatment. This is much the same approach that should be taken when there is any initial breech of professional ethics, and colleagues must be willing to speak up when such issues present themselves. Finally the necessary resources for offering such opinions must be established. This can best be done through state and local professional mental-health associations. The increasing number of professional standards review committees should help to facilitate such a program.

A final suggestion concerns the training of student therapists and the continuing education of practicing professionals in the field. The need to be sensitive and responsive to the basic rights of children outlined here must be routinely stressed in professional-development programs for those who will eventually work as child or family therapists.

The essay by Haley (1969) regarding how any therapist can become a failure was not written especially for therapists who work with children. Rather, it seems intended to chide the therapist of any client to respect and become seriously involved in the communications of the person who seeks help. Why should circumstances differ for the child? As Haley notes, these basic client considerations are not automatically granted to adult clients by all therapists. The irony is that child-clients have often been systematically denied such considerations by well-intentioned therapists who treat their adult clients quite differently.

There are those who might argue that truthfulness, personal respect for the client, serious listening, and active client involvement in therapeutic goal setting are related to the personality attributes of therapists and cannot truly be modified. I am inclined to doubt that belief, and have noted over time that the most effective child therapists I know already take these principles into account. Regardless of theoretical orientation, personality, or level of experience, the therapist who most easily wins the confidence and trust of children will be one who has learned to involve them in an alliance based on mutual respect and concern. It is evident that experience is one teacher of such attitudes toward children, but it seems a more effective strategy to include the routine presentation of these concerns in training child therapists. Because much of the real learning of therapeutic technique takes place during supervisory hours, it is important for the supervisor to express at least as much concern about the involvement of and respect for the child as for the "chief complaint."

The problem is not so much that therapists are rushing to trample the rights of their child patients, or even that children are daily being hurt by considerations that are being overlooked. Rather, the key issue is that so much more could be done with greater effectiveness if child therapists recognized their clients' basic rights as a matter of routine. It is easy to be so caught up in the rush to be of help, in the desperation of concerned parents, or in the application of the latest technical knowledge that the child becomes lost in the process. It is not inane to note that children are people and to recognize that they bring to the context of psychotherapy all the uniqueness of individual human beings as well as a special measure of vulnerability. The child therapist must always be mindful of all that this implies.

REFERENCES

Blackham, G. J., and Silberman, S. *Modification of Child and adolescent behavior* (2nd ed.). Belmont, Cal.: Wadsworth, 1975.

Davidson, G. C., and Stuart, R. B. Behavior therapy and civil liberties. *Am. Psychol.* **30** (1975), 755–63.

Haley, J. *The power tactics of Jesus Christ.* New York: Avon, 1969.

Hammer, M., and Kaplan, A. M. *The practice of psychotherapy with children.* Homewood, Ill.: Dorsey, 1967.

Holmes, D. S., and Urie, R. G. Effects of preparing children for psychotherapy. *J. Consult. Clin. Psychol.* **43** (1975), 311–18.

Mikulas, W. L. *Behavior modification: An overview.* New York: Harper & Row, 1972.

Ross, A. O. Confidentiality in child guidance treatment. *Ment. Hyg.* **42** (1958), 60–66.

Ross, A. O. Confidentiality in child therapy: A reevaluation. *Ment. Hyg.* **50** (1966), 360–66.

Ross, A. O. The rights of children as psychotherapy patients. Paper presented at the American Psychological Association Meeting, New Orleans, Louisiana, September 1, 1974.

Sherman, A. R. *Behavior modification: Theory and practice.* Belmont, Cal.: Wadsworth, 1973.

Tate, B. A., and Baroff, A. S. Aversive control of self-injurious behavior in a psychotic boy. *Behav. Res. Ther.* **4** (1966), 281–87.

Children's Rights
and Family Dysfunction:
"Daddy, Why Do I Have to Be
the Crazy One?"

DAVID W. SIMMONDS

Because children do not live in a vacuum, psychopathology in a child may be a manifest expression of dysfunction in the child's family. Why then are children in these cases treated as isolated individuals. Families often ostensibly come to treatment centers to obtain help for a "sick" child. From the viewpoint of family therapy that child is the "identified patient." More and more families are entering family therapy as the treatment of choice when a child who exhibits a behavior disorder is the "patient." The trend in child psychotherapy is increasingly away from play therapy with the child and toward working with the family system in which the child exists.

Problems arise in the administration of family-therapy cases in mental-health delivery systems, where a medical record is often created for one member of the family who is designated as the patient. That one member, often the child, is offered up to the medical-records section as a kind of sacrifice, prepared to be labeled. We know that psychiatric labeling can be prejudicially applied to an individual in future years. Because the child is usually least able to resist the labeling process, parents may totally escape psychiatric labeling during family therapy simply by designating one of their children as the "official" patient.

In the American Psychiatric Association's *Diagnostic and Statistical Manual of Mental Disorders* (1968), there is no diagnostic category for family dysfunction. The closest designation is one for marital maladjustment, a difficulty in the shared relationship between two people rather than a problem that resides in one of the two individuals. Similarly family therapists view family dysfunction as a condition existing within the system (family) and not within the individuals. But there is no diagnostic classification for family dsyfunction. What if there were? Few patients are exposed to a mental-health delivery system who have received a diagnosis of marital maladjustment or other diagnoses within the general category of difficulties "without manifest psychiatric disorder." Why? It is certainly more humane to regard any individual, child or adult, as part of a problem situation rather than as diseased. However, we must consider the position of the health-insurance industry. Insurers typically do not cover policyholders who are treated for conditions diagnosed as "without manifest psychiatric disorder." Health-insurance policyholders are reimbursed for the treatment of mental "illness," and that illness or disease must rest inside the skin of the patient as if it were a cancerous tumor to be excised. As long as such a situation is prevalent in the insurance industry, patients must bear psychiatric labels. In a dysfunctional family, the label is usually placed on a dependent minor who has no recourse.

HEALTH INSURANCE AND FAMILY THERAPY

Just how reluctant are health-insurance vendors to reimburse policy holders for the activity broadly known as family therapy? In family treatment, no individual is labeled; rather, the system in which individuals interact and coexist is viewed as the unit of treatment and focal point for change. According to a survey by Sonne (1973), there was varying reluctance among health insurers to pay for interviews with an entire family, but there was a universal unwillingness to reimburse for a service that was not rendered to a single, identifiable patient or to a group of such patients (who might happen to constitute a family). Sonne observed that a number of his colleagues who dealt with families utilized the latter approach: the treatment of a family was presented for reimbursement as the treatment of a collection of individuals, each having a specific diagnosis.

Apparently dissatisfied with this practice, which violently disrupts the concept of family therapy, Sonne wrote a brief letter to ten health insurers asking if it was their practice to reimburse for treatment of a disturbed family. He received nine replies, the most concise simply being "no." Each of the remaining eight replies reported a willingness to provide compensation if each family member has a specific psychiatric diagnosis. Of these eight insurers, three asserted a willingness to support counseling for the parents of a disturbed child, although one required that the child (the identified patient) be present during such interviews. One of the eight insurance companies supported one or two sessions with family members to help "evaluate the individual being treated." For four of the eight responding companies, payment of claims for treatment of family members depended on their eligibility to meet requirements for coverage "on an individual basis." Sonne commented that he knew of no instance where family therapy was reimbursed by health-insurance carriers, except in cases where family contacts were defined as collateral visits or in cases where each family member was individually diagnosed.

The disease theory of mental illness prevails, or at least holds sway, in the health-insurance industry. However, an increasing number of family therapists are asserting that symptoms in an individual family member may reflect a disturbed family system. As yet, the health-insurance industry appears to be reluctant to support the concept of socially shared psychopathology. This reluctance may not be widely shared by health-care providers themselves. Of the physicians replying to a survey in the Seattle area, 64% agreed that family counselors should be included in health-insurance plans; only 27% were opposed to this opinion (Bennett, 1974). These results suggest that physicians in this limited sample feel that the family is a legitimate unit of treatment and/or that family counseling is a useful, productive form of intervention. The more problems are seen as family problems, the less a child in the family can be forced to carry a psychiatric label.

Assuming that it is wise and humane to divert our children from psychiatric labeling and to protect them from its potential abuses, (1) what evidence can we present to health insurers and to the community at large to prove that family therapy works, and (2) can we offer any support to the basic premise that symptoms can arise from the interpersonal rather than the intrapsychic realm? These two issues will be examined separately in the remainder of this chapter.

THE EFFECTIVENESS OF FAMILY THERAPY

Evidence to support the effectiveness of family therapy as a broadly defined technique for modifying the functioning of the family unit has been encouraging but sparse. Serious criticisms have arisen in the literature concerning many attempts to judge the outcome of the family-therapy approach. Pool and Frazier (1973) reviewed several years of family-therapy literature dealing specifically with the treatment of children and adolescents. A number of these studies claimed success in alleviating symptoms in both children and adolescents. Included were nontraditional models of family therapy, including multifamily therapy groups and crisis intervention. After this review, Pool and Frazier concluded that it is difficult to assess the outcome of family therapy using objective criteria. They found that successes were often defined psychodynamically, a method that has always been difficult to measure, or that successes could have been defined as the authors' subjective evaluations of improvement. Pool and Frazier discounted psychometric data, which might have permitted comparisons to be made among families by utilizing control groups and alternative treatment modalities. Their findings indicate good reported results using family-therapy techniques—results nonetheless based on questionable research methodology in assessing therapy outcome.

A second survey focusing on 20 years of family-therapy outcome studies was reported by Wells, Dilkes, and Trivelli (1972), who defined the goal of such treatment as improving the family's functioning "as a unit." These authors studied psychotherapy-outcome research designs in an effort to specify adequate research methodology to be used in family-therapy effectiveness studies. Having specified a research design of minimum acceptability, Wells, Dilkes, and Trivelli reviewed 20 years of interdisciplinary literature, finding 18 studies that reported specific outcome measures for three or more families treated. These studies were then categorized as employing inadequate, borderline, or adequate methodology. Of the 18 studies, 15 were considered inadequate because of the lack of a control-group comparison. One study was classified as borderline. Two studies were categorized as using adequate research methodology. Both of these studies are related to an extensive research project conducted by Langsley and his associates at the Colorado Psychiatric Hospital in Denver. This important project is discussed later in this chapter.

The survey by Wells, Dilkes, and Trivelli provides data from all the reviewed studies concerning the clinically judged effectiveness of family therapy. The overall rate of improvement for children and adolescents in family therapy was an impressive 79%. These results are subject to research-design problems common to most therapy-outcome studies, but the findings compare favorably with the results normally obtained in individual psychotherapy. Many families produce multiple "patients," who enter individual or group psychotherapies. The improvement of the functioning family unit appears to be an economical alternative to the singular treatment of multiple "patients" in a family. Additional support for the economy of family therapy can be found in a consumer-satisfaction study at the High Plains Community Mental Health Center in Hays, Kansas, in which patients indicated how much each therapy session helped them in solving their problems. Individual, group, and family therapies were considered equally helpful by the recipients of these services. Group and family therapies were viewed as economical (in terms of number of persons served) alternatives to individual psychotherapy (*Innovations*, 1974).

As mentioned previously, a classic study of the effectiveness and economy of family therapy was conducted by D. G. Langsley and associates in

Denver and initially reported by Langsley, Pittman, Machotka, and Flomen-haft (1968). During their project, 150 families seeking hospitalization for an identified patient were randomly assigned to short-term, crisis-oriented, family-therapy treatment. A matched control group of 150 families received traditional inpatient treatment for the identified patient in each family. All family-therapy cases were treated without hospitalization. A variety of objective outcome criteria were established. Both the family-treatment group and the hospitalized group exhibited improved social adjustment and personal functioning at a six-month follow-up evaluation; no differences between the groups could be psychometrically measured. The family-treatment group lost fewer days of normal functioning; 29% of the hospitalized sample were readmitted to the hospital within six months, but only 13% of the family-treatment cases were hospitalized during that period.

The differences revealed by this study are dramatic and compelling in several ways. First, family treatment costs were estimated to be one-sixth as much as hospitalization costs for the obtained sample. Second, the family-treatment sample showed similar or better functioning on the measures obtained. Third, the identified patient in the family-treatment group was not removed from the family, which in itself may have averted further family crises. Finally, the results were obtained by using more adequate research methodology than is usually employed in family-therapy research.

Family-crisis therapy has proved to be effective in keeping acutely de-compensated psychiatric patients out of mental hospitals and helping them to function in society. Separating a "patient" and a family is disruptive. Removing a child from parents and siblings can clearly be traumatic. A treatment methodology that produces good results without inflicting such trauma deserves serious consideration. Family treatment can avoid stig-matization by psychiatric labeling and can preserve and enhance the family unit.

INTRAPSYCHIC VERSUS INTERPERSONAL CAUSATION

We have already observed that family therapy is valuable as a treatment modality for both children and adults. Family treatment is tied to a set of theoretical underpinnings far removed from those of most psychotherapies. Traditional theories generally assume that dysfunctional behavior results from intrapsychic imbalances and faulty coping processes that can be related to the individual's developmental history. Early experiences can trigger the development of stress-response patterns, but in the broad framework of therapy systems theory "maladaptive" behaviors of individuals are viewed as a means to maintain balance in the family system. Symptoms are exhibited when stress is applied to the family system. In the report by Langsley *et al* (1968), families were seen in times of severe crisis. Langsley and his colleagues suggest that such crises seem "far more related to the immediate settings, recent stresses, and current events than to past history" (p. 155).

There has been little substantive "proof" of intrapsychic determination of behavior, but only mechanistic behaviorism has seriously challenged this basic concept. Social-systems theory provides another challenge, and evidence to support this theoretical position has begun to appear. Hadley, Jacob, Milliones, Caplan, and Spitz (1974) detected a positive relationship between family crisis and symptom onset. These authors suggest that symptoms occur during crisis periods and that symptoms can be viewed not merely as responses, but as attempted solutions to a dilemma.

Hadley and his associates studied two types of developmental crisis; the addition (by birth, adoption, or marriage) and the subtraction (by death, separation, or the child's leaving home) of a family member. They surveyed the relationship of these crises and the date of symptom onset in a group of 90 families undergoing outpatient psychotherapy. In this group, 37% of the sample cases experienced symptom onset within nine months after the *addition* of a family member; 27% reported symptom onset within nine months after the *loss* of a member. Eliminating duplications, 61% of the families studied reported symptom onset within nine months after the addition or the subtraction of a family member. The correlation between date of symptom onset and date of crisis was 0.74 ($p < .01$).

The findings in the Hadley study represent a conservative estimate of the relationship between crisis and symptom onset, because only two types of crisis were evaluated. Family moves, job changes, and status shifts are some additional stresses that were not included in the study. However, the Hadley study identified only those crises that preceded the onset of symptoms. Clearly, symptoms can appear in anticipation of upcoming stresses such as marriage, divorce, foreseeable death, moving, job change, and so on. Although the Hadley study does not establish a causative relationship between crisis and symptom, the conservative approach of the study does produce significant correlational data to support social-systems theory.

SUMMARY

A child's rights may indeed include the right not to be a scapegoat, labeled by both the family and the mental-health delivery system involved in treatment. The child is often least able to resist the symptom-bearing and labeling process. Psychiatric labels have not proved to be assets to individuals in their future endeavors. The health-insurance industry has been reluctant to provide reimbursement for the treatment of socially shared psychopathology, so the mental-health delivery system requires the family to designate at least one patient. Family-treatment providers view the entire family system as the unit of diagnosis and intervention. This radical concept is becoming widely accepted, and outcome data point to its effectiveness and economy. Underlying theory has received empirical support.

Let us hope that these trends will continue, so that our children may live in a society that has no need to infringe on their rights not to become mental patients.

REFERENCES

American Psychiatric Association. *Diagnostic and statistical manual of mental disorders* (2nd ed.) Washington, D.C.: American Psychiatric Association, 1968.

Bennett, J. G. Physicians survey shows they feel family life on decline . . . want counselors' insurance plans. *NAFL News* 2(3) (fall 1974), 3.

Hadley, T. R., Jacob, T., Milliones, J., Caplan, J., and Spitz, D. The relationship between family developmental crisis and the appearance of symptoms in a family member. *Fam. Process* 13 (1974), 207–14.

Innovations Now. *Innovations* 1 (1974), 26.

Langsley, D. G., Pittman, F. S., III, Machotka, P., and Flomenhaft, K. Family crisis therapy: Results and implications. *Fam. Process* 7 (1968), 145–58.

Pool, M. L., and Frazier, J. R. Family therapy: A review of the literature pertinent to children and adolescents. *Psychother: Theory, Res, Pract.* 10 (1973), 256–60.

Sonne, J. C. Insurance and family therapy. *Fam. Process* 12 (1973), 399–414.

Wells, R. A., Dilkes, T. C., and Trivelli, N. The results of family therapy: A critical review of the literature. *Fam. Process* 11 (1972), 189–208.

Custody Battles: Mental-Health Professionals in the Courtroom

MARILEE FREDERICKS

The mental-health literature, which addresses almost every facet of the human situation with more than passing vigor, provides only minimal guidance for considering the roles of mental-health professionals in custody disputes. This unusual silence reflects our tradition of resistance to involvement with children when their parents are divorcing.

Simultaneously, the legal profession's literature about custody cases (Inker and Perretta, 1971; Podell, Peck, and First, 1972) calls for an increased reliance on the testimony and advice of psychologists, psychiatrists, and other experts in the fields of human behavior to ensure that the needs and interests of children are brought to the attention of the courts.

These two fields would appear to be on a collision course. At best, a collision could result in embarrassment for mental-health experts for refusing to help children. At worst, it could ensnare children in yet another debate between adults.

It is disappointing, but not surprising, that mental-health professionals have been late in developing a more assertive, child-oriented stance relative to custody disputes.

Much of the attention of mental-health professionals has been drawn to those children who are already disabled. Although troubled, most children who are the subjects of custody disputes are not disabled. We have been protected, both by our "busyness" and by the divorce laws, from exposure to the experiences of children whose parents are engaged in this particular brand of struggle for their own psychological survival. Kept busy attending to the behaviors of husband and wife, the courts have failed to press for information about parent–child issues.

41

THE IMPACT OF "NO FAULT" DIVORCE

Changes in law, making possible the dissolution of marriages without the establishment of wrongdoing or blame on the part of either marriage partner, have had a major impact on both the court and the mental-health profession. The court, without its usual simple guideline for establishing custody—(that is, to determine which parent is the "good guy" in the marriage), is forced to give more thoughtful attention to the childrens' needs and is given the opportunity to do so. The major work of the court in no-fault divorces is the equitable distribution of the couple's property. Thus the law in such divorce cases has had the additional impact of casting a harsh light on the status of children, who are regarded as property rather than as persons.

No-fault divorces also rob mental-health professionals of two major justifications for resisting involvement with children during divorce actions. Prior to the passage of no-fault divorce law, children could be considered grounds for divorce. Attorneys and their clients sought the services of mental-health professionals in their efforts to establish wrongdoing on the part of a client's husband or wife. We were asked to verify that the child was disturbed and to pinpoint the behavior of the offending spouse as the source of that disturbance. Given these conditions, mental-health professionals could (and did) argue that their involvement would compliment the parents' need to perpetuate and encourage a child's problematic behavior. By further refusing to support the consideration of children as grounds for divorce, the actions of mental-health professionals could not make real the childrens' fantasies that they were the cause of the divorce.

In retrospect, these attempts to protect children seem naive. They may have been irresponsible because they were based on judgments that were obviously made without seeing the children themselves and therefore without regard to what their needs might or might not have been.

Whatever the current assessments of those justifications for inaction during the divorce process, no-fault divorce changes the picture. With no need to search for ways to establish fault to end a marriage, there is no need to consider a child's problems as grounds for divorce, and mental-health professionals need not fear that their actions will add to a child's burden. Moreover, no-fault divorces, where the only battle is defined in terms of "who gets the children," are a mixed blessing for children. When clearly the object of the struggle, no child with adequate reality testing can escape some experience of feeling responsible for the parents' unhappiness. Fears that the involvement of a mental-health professional during the divorce process might add to a child's burden must be superseded by the possibility that such an intervention could lighten that burden.

With some justifications for avoiding contact with children whose parents are divorcing negated by the changes in divorce laws, there remains the oft-stated concerns about the limits of the mental-health professional's knowledge regarding the relative merits of different patterns of custody. A careful examination of this source of resistance to involvement in custody disputes brings to light some curious inconsistencies in the behavior of mental-health professionals.

In private offices, clinics, and mental-health centers, mental-health professionals regularly make judgments and develop recommendations that affect children's futures. As a result, for example, children may be placed in residential treatment centers or kept in what have been destructive home-family situations with promises that efforts to improve these situations will be successful. Or children may be shifted from one school to another on the grounds that a new environment will better meet their needs. When asked to participate in custody determinations, many of these same professionals refuse, giving as a reason the uncertainty that available methods can predict what will be a helpful or nonhelpful social and emotional environment for a child. That uncertainty appears to increase in direct relationship to how open to public view and to systematic challenge mental-health professionals expect their recommendations to be.

Respect for and awareness of the boundaries of knowledge is a quality to be prized. However, when those boundaries are presented as fixed in one situation (custody disputes) and as fluid and subject to thoughtful expansion in other situations, mental-health professionals must wonder at their quiet acceptance of this ignorance.

We know that children sometimes do not learn how to do things or deny knowing how to do things because they will then be expected to do them. As mental-health professionals, we must acknowledge the possibility that our reluctance to become involved in custody disputes is not prompted by our limited knowledge, but rather that our limited knowledge is prompted by our reluctance to become involved in custody disputes.

We are left with one minimally acknowledgeable basis for our tradition of resistance. Simply put, court appearances make mental-health professionals nervous, and giving testimony is an expected part of working in the child-custody arena. In the courtroom, we are working beyond our usual physical and interpersonal environment. Our discomfort with custody disputes may be more related to that than the fact that we are working beyond our usual guidelines for assisting children.

We can make the effort to get to know that strange environment only when we believe that our purpose for being there is to *assist the children* who are the subjects of custody disputes. In the process of assisting children, we also assist the courts. However, that is not our reason for becoming involved, and it should not determine the directions of our actions or recommendations. At times, our testimony can make the work of the court more difficult (raising some issue that complicates decision making), and the *primacy of our responsibility to the child* must be articulated.

Mental-health professionals for whom court appearances are made more palatable because they serve as a friend of the court should reexamine their position. This is not to suggest that we should be unfriendly, but our stance as a friend of the court has outlived its usefulness. It originally served as our only way of indicating that we were not working on behalf of either custody seeker. Now maintaining the position that we serve as friends of the court perpetuates the idea that the child is not a party to the dispute. Moreover, it may influence (albeit subtly) the form and scope of mental-health work.

THE TRADITIONALIST VERSUS THE EXPLORER

Until this point, mental-health professionals have been discussed as if we hold common views and behave in common ways relative to the dissolution of marriage and custody proceedings. Actually, our differences are pronounced. Two extreme positions in mental-health practice—those of the traditionalist and the explorer—may be used as a framework to examine these differences.

These two models operate from quite different experiential and attitudinal bases. We would expect to find traditionalists among mental-health professionals who primarily serve adults. Explorers (so designated to indicate the wilderness quality of the custody arena) would be expected to concentrate their services predominantly on children and families. Child mental-health practitioners are in a position to witness the effects of post-divorce emotional battles on children with alarming regularity, and should be in a state of readiness to explore constructive divorce, custody, and visitation planning. Indeed, J. C. Westman, one of the few writers on this topic (Westman, Cline, Swift, and Kramer, 1970; Westman, 1971), is a child specialist.

Not all mental-health professionals who work with children and families are explorers. Influences other than experiences with children—such as the relative "open-ness" of the setting in which the individual practices; the range and closeness of the practitioner's contacts with the community's children, parents, and child-serving agencies; and the practitioner's self-perceived level of competence—may be more important.

The settings in which a traditionalist practices are less likely to permit open-door referral policies than the settings in which the explorer practices. Open doors allow all manner of situations to cross our experience threshholds. Open doors and varied contacts with the community also let us see what is going on outside. What is going on outside is a rapid increase in divorces and in the numbers of very young children whose lives are being affected by divorce (U.S. Department of Health, Education and Welfare, 1969).

Perhaps the central determinant of whether a mental-health professional remains a traditionalist or becomes an explorer is self-perception of level of competence. Traditionalists are irritated by and fearful of any situation in which their thought processes must be exposed to public questioning. Explorers accept as their responsibility the importance of keeping their views and thinking open for review.

Related to general level of self-comfort are the differing reactions of the two models to court orders and subpoenas. Court orders are distressing to the traditionalist, who defines them as attempts to control his practice. Despite this claim, even when the order specifies an action that contradicts his opinion about what should be done, the traditionalist usually follows it to the letter. In contrast, the explorer contacts the judge who issued the order if something seems to be amiss. The explorer knows that court orders related to custody disputes are not intended to impose boundaries on how he carries out his work. He knows that court orders are prepared by attorneys who do not know his language any better than he knows theirs. He also knows that to follow a court order that does not permit the development of his best opinion would be unfair to the child, to the court, and to himself.

The explorer establishes the conditions under which he will work. This is not done in the spirit of communicating that he, rather than the court, is in charge. It is a matter of recognizing some realities: (1) within the limits of his knowledge and skills, the explorer wants to do the best possible job; (2) if his knowledge is going to expand, the explorer must develop experiential norms; and (3) the explorer cannot develop experiential norms if he does not set up some standard conditions.

The subpoena represents a special problem for both the traditionalist and the explorer. If a subpoena calls for a court appearance to present opinions and recommendations developed as a part of custody-determination studies, this does not present a major problem—at least not to the explorer. In each contact in which custody is at stake, the explorer clarifies to all concerned that he is working for the child and for no one else.

If attorneys or their clients seek custody opinion outside the boundaries of formal legal procedure, the explorer makes explicit her or his intent to place the child's interest before theirs and points out the possibility that if the recommendations developed contradict their case, they could be subject to subpoena.

There *is* a problem, however, if the subpoena calls for testimony and recommendations for one purpose (establishing custody) but the information has been gathered for a different purpose (psychotherapy with the child and the parents).

In this case, the explorer reviews the record and contacts the judge and/or attorney. The explorer must explain that these are not the best possible data for determining custody, admit to any bias held, and offer to arrange for more useful studies to be conducted. Again, the explorer will behave in keeping with the belief that the court is interested in obtaining meaningful information. The traditionalist, on the other hand, may be expected to react with anger but to take no corrective action. Instead, he may secretly pledge to "get even" from the witness stand.

The traditionalist tries to avoid contacts with children whose parents have taken legal steps to terminate their marriage. He may have contact with the divorcing couple as a conciliator. For the most part, he defines conciliation narrowly as marriage counseling directed toward preserving the marriage and not toward helping the couple to separate emotionally as well as legally. Counseling is terminated when the couple or one party verifies a firm intention to dissolve the marriage. The traditionalist is adamantly opposed to court-enforced conciliation. Having translated "conciliation" to mean "counseling," it is predictable for the traditionalist to voice the practical and ethical problems involved in court-enforced counseling.

The explorer feels a strong sense of urgency to participate in divorce and custody planning. He believes that divorce is a family affair and that the children must be seen and heard in a divorce case. Thus when a divorcing couple has children, the explorer defines "conciliation" as "consultation" and has no difficulty in accepting court-enforced participation in conciliation. The thrust of the explorer's work as a conciliator is directed toward helping the couple formulate guidelines for the conduct of their post-divorce parental partnership. The explorer knows that he cannot serve as a conciliator in this broad sense unless he knows the children who are involved in the divorce.

If the traditionalist agrees to participate in custody determination, he places major emphasis on determining the relative personal strengths or weaknesses of the custody seekers. They are the objects of his study, and he endeavors to obtain data about their functioning. When examining the child, the traditionalist usually scrupulously refrains from inquiring about the child's views of the custody dispute and rarely actively seeks to determine the relationship between the child and the custody seekers. Some traditionalists, apparently in explorers' clothing, entirely discard their normal methods of getting to know children and accede to an attorney's suggestion that a visit to the home will provide a good basis for understanding the family's relationships. (This may be true, but not for someone without experience in home observation.) The traditionalist has a single goal: to gather data to present to the court.

When the battle lines are drawn and custody is at stake, the explorer focuses on the child and does not confine his activities to mere data-gathering for the court. The explorer believes that studies that turn attention away from the custody seekers' rights and wishes may help to shift attitudes that have grown rigid and narrow as the legal machinery worked. Within the context of the explorer's work, the child is again seen and heard as an individual with needs, wishes, and interests of his own; and the custody seekers are again seen and heard as parents instead of as plaintiff and respondent.

The explorer imposes a structure on clinical interviews with the custody seekers that reflects his intent to refocus their attention on the child. The first segment of the interview consists of gathering information about the child: getting to know the child through the parents' eyes. Only when the explorer is sure that they—and he—have the child firmly in mind, will he invite the parents to share their reasons as to who should have custody of the child (how will the child be better served by living with each parent?) and to share their perspectives about what went wrong with the marriage.

Many custody seekers, armed with tapes and diaries detailing their spouses unfaithfulness or malicious behavior, resist this unexpected reordering of priorities. However, the explorer perserveres. The explorer does not hesitate to make suggestions or advise the parents about the child and the possible interpretations of the child's behavior. The explorer is careful to include a discussion of the parents' post-hearing plans, for them as well as for the child.

Finally the explorer listens and learns. When a mother, who is present specifically as part of a custody dispute, lashes out at a society that forces mothers to seek custody whether they want it or not (or be considered freaks) and adds that it is time that women did not "get stuck with the kids," the explorer assumes that the women is making a personal statement. Further, when her child in the course of a conversation about his frequent earaches says that he and "Daddy sit up and rock" until he stops thinking about his ear, the explorer begins to draw some conclusions about the behavioral correlates of such vague parenting concepts as nurturing and protecting.

The explorer speaks openly with the child about the parents' divorce, the custody dispute, and about the explorer's own role in that action. He will use the methods and materials he usually uses in examining children. The child's hopes, ambitions, fears, worries, views of himself and his accomplishments and of himself in relation to others, and views of his parents, are no less matters of interest than they would be if the child were referred to the explorer for a reason other than a custody proceeding. After the standard part of the examination, the visit becomes a supportive treatment session. Again the explorer has the additional aim of setting stress-reducing processes in motion. To this end, the explorer uses the time to reinforce the child's sense of himself as a separate and competent person with affairs, concerns, choices, and interests apart from the parents.

CASE EXAMPLE

The following sample situation encountered in my own work illustrates the importance of focusing attention on child-relevant issues. It also illustrates the plight of children who are involved in custody disputes and the confusion that surrounds making a custody decision.

The natural parents were young when they married; they immediately had children. The parents fought, the father changed jobs frequently, and neither parent took very good care of the children. The father finally enlisted in the service. Just before he went overseas, the marriage was dissolved and the mother was awarded undisputed custody of the children.

Shortly after the father left the country, the mother voluntarily entered the psychiatric unit of a local hospital, leaving the children (2 years and 10 months old, respectively) with her mother. The grandmother, not unlike many noncustodian caretakers, placed the children (with the help of a local human service worker) in a 24-hour babysitting home. During the next two and one-half years, there were eight such babysitting home placements for these children.

As soon as he learned of his former wife's hospitalization and of the children's first placement, the father secured a hardship discharge from the service, returned to his hometown, and, with his new wife, instantly instituted proceedings to gain custody of the children. At that time, the children (now 2½ and 1 year old, respectively) had been in three foster homes.

For two years the attorneys and the court "thought it over," while the children moved in and out of five more foster homes, visiting the father, mother, and grandparents at regular intervals. In the meantime, the natural mother, who still had legal custody of the children, had disappeared and reappeared twice, had remarried and divorced, had had another child and had abandoned the baby, and had finally relinquished custody of the two children in question. The mother's place as a custody seeker was taken by the grandmother.

At this point, the father's attorney contacted me, seeking an evaluation of the situation. I set forth the conditions under which I would work. These included such basics as having authorization of the children's guardian ad lietum and freedom to share my recommendations, whether in favor of his client or not, with the guardian ad lietum. With my conditions accepted, I began to review two years' worth of depositions. The depositions contained prolonged discussions about a local night spot, the father's employment history and the ups and downs of his hourly wage, the first marriage, the natural mother's activities, and the grandparents' history and work status.

References to the children and to their odyssey through eight different foster homes were virtually absent. For two years after the father's request for custody, the children—at critical ages—had been "homeless." When the older child began exhibiting behavioral problems after the fifth move, no one put that into the context of the living situation. Instead a local physician prescribed medication for hyperactivity.

Although the father's hourly wage was less than the grandfather's, no one had noted that the father's annual income was well above the average income generally considered adequate for a family of four. No one had noted that the job father's job changes exhibited a pattern that led to the development of a sellable skill and that he had not been without a job for more than two days during those two years.

The guardian ad lietum, who was supposedly appointed to protect the children's rights, had taken no observable steps to press for a less nomadic existence for the children. In addition to the physician, two human-services experts had been involved in the case. One, the worker who had arranged for all eight of the foster homes, testified that she was deeply concerned about the father's capacity to *provide a stable environment for the children.* The other, a traditionalist, had observed the children with their mother shortly before she disappeared. He reported only that the children, because they were young, should remain in their mother's custody.

The confusion, inaction, and lack of attention to the children—all ostensibly in their own interests—in this situation is not unusual. Only a traditionalist would think it was.

Of special note is that these children were represented by counsel on paper but not in spirit. The explorer joins other childrens' rights advocates in applauding the movement toward appointing an attorney to serve as the child's guardian ad lietum. However, the explorer knows that these attorneys approach such work with varying levels of knowledge, skills, and enthusiasm. The legal profession, too, has its traditionalists and its explorers. The explorer assumes responsibility for providing guidance for attorneys as they try to apply their personal experiences and their private beliefs about what constitutes a "good parent" into a broader and more disciplined context of parent–child relationships. Above all, the explorer remembers that his work in specific custody disputes is directed toward helping the child and not toward verifying the opinion of the guardian ad lietum.

PRESENTATION OF FINDINGS

Reports written by the traditionalist read either like a catalog of technical "results" or a brief note about a casual visit, only more vague. Many times the traditionalist does not formulate a recommendation regarding custody on the grounds that his job is only to provide the court with information that it may or may not use to make its recommendations. The explorer writes reports that include a minimum of technical language and that leave little room for the interpretations or guesswork of others. In addition to a description of data sources and of the child's general functioning, these reports include a statement from the explorer's perspective of the crucial issues to cover or questions to answer. The explorer then addresses those issues or responds to those questions that are within the framework of his observations and experiences. He may also raise questions which he cannot answer or state what kinds of information would reduce his confidence in his opinion. Finally, the explorer states his recommendation and adds a mildly proselytizing statement. The exploer *does take a side* in a custody dispute: he is working for the child.

On the witness stand, the traditionalist testifies in a detached manner, making no effort to be understood or to persuade. This detached manner in itself may be viewed with favor. However, the traditionalist loses this detached manner under cross-examination, becomes stubborn and argumentative, and can be easily led into areas in which he is not knowledgeable. In defense of his statements, the traditionalist loses sight of the child and of the purpose of his own testimony. He forgets, or does not understand, the two-directional nature of communications in the courtroom.

The explorer knows that the real targets of—or intended receivers of —an attorney's messages and, via his questions, the messages of a witness are the judge and the transcript. The witness and the attorney are facing each other and are engaged in an exchange, but both attorneys are speaking to the judge and for the record. The explorer on the witness stand knows that he must talk to the attorney, to the judge, and for the record, simultaneously.

On the witness stand, the explorer makes an effort to be understood and always remembers his purpose in being there. He finds cross-examinations neither exhilarating nor especially disconcerting. In many respects, the explorer appreciates custody seekers' attorneys who take their work seriously. The explorer know that it is in the child's best interests that there be a thorough review of all aspects of the situation, including his own contributions.

The explorer becomes acquainted with the custody seekers as well as the child. Frequently, custody seekers have been the victims of grave injustices, questionable legal advice, destructive counseling, or just circumstances. Even for the explorer, viewing parents or other custody seekers with a sense of fairness is an ongoing struggle. Most child mental-health professionals, whichever extreme position they take, professionally believe that any action that is unfair to a parent has the potential to negatively effect the children. The explorer knows that custody decisions are never "fair" to everyone—if indeed to anyone. Thus seeing his primary role as trying to piece together what is fair for the child, the explorer can derive comfort from observing that the attorneys for the custody seekers are looking after their clients' rights.

FOLLOWING THROUGH

Differences between the traditionalist and the explorer tend to disappear after the hearing. Helping children to understand and to deal with their feelings relative to the partial loss of a parent and to continue the business of living and growing is an integral part of child mental-health practice. The traditionalist confines this work to instances when the child exhibits overt signs of stress. The explorer prefers to remain in touch with the child and with both parents as a "parents and child consultant," even when the child is not exhibiting specific indications of problems.

Differences reappear when post-divorce visitation disputes or post-divorce challenges to the original custody occur. Once again the prospect of involvement in litigation leads to resistance on the part of the traditionalist. Because of this resistance, the traditionalist is spared from a full awareness of the almost never-ending state of uncertainty in which many children live. The most controversial concept in *Beyond the Best Interest of the Child* (Goldstein, Freud, and Solnit, 1973) of "final unconditional disposal" appeals to the explorer, largely because of his exposure to post-divorce disputes.

If all parents were expected to meet the standards of perfection that are considered basic in some custody hearings, few children would be living with their parents—or with any adult. Likewise, if all mental-health professionals were expected to be instant explorers, few children would have the benefit of the considerable skills possessed by most practitioners in the field. Nevertheless, the challenge of assuring that a child's own interests are represented when making decisions that will affect his entire life requires that explorers increase in number.

A word of warning is in order here. In some instances, the mental-health professional may find that he is the solitary voice expressing a given viewpoint in an atmosphere in which that viewpoint contradicts all the customs, beliefs, and expectations of any other participant except the child. Who is fit to influence and guide the young is a subject akin to religion and politics in the intensity of feeling it inspires. It is a subject that each custody dispute touches on, even though each dispute involves individual children in individual circumstances. A publicly stated recommendation which challenges the predominant value system of the community may raise doubts as to the credibility of the mental-health professional. We must be prepared to take that risk—and to make that recommendation—or none of our other recommendations will be meaningful. We must avoid becoming the "window dressing" in custody disputes. The safeguards against this can only be a thorough and an independent study of all aspects of each custody dispute; a constant thesis that we are working for the child; and an approach to each situation as if our professional integrity is at stake—for it is.

REFERENCES

Goldstein, J., Freud, A., and Solnit, A. J. *Beyond the best interests of the child.* New York: Free Press, 1973.

Inker, M. L., and Perretta, C. A. A child's rights to counsel in custody cases. *Fam. Law Q.* 5(1) (1971), 108–70.

Podell, R. J., Peck, H. F., and First, C. Custody: To which parent? *Marquette Law Rev.* 56(1) (1972), 51–68.

U.S. Department of Health, Education and Welfare. National Center for Health Statistics. Monthly vital statistics report. Washington, D.C.: U.S. Government Printing Office, 1969.

Westman, J. C., Cline, D. W., Swift, W. J., and Kramer, D. A. Role of child psychiatry in divorce. *Arch. Gen. Psychiatry* 23(5) (1970), 416–20.

Westman, J. C. The psychiatrist and child-custody contests. *Am. J. Psychiatr.* 127(12) (1971), 1687–88.

Children's Rights
as Participants in Research

PATRICIA KEITH-SPIEGEL

The regulation of human and animal experimentation in general and the protection of human research subjects in particular have generated increasingly vigorous attention in recent years. In the best of all worlds, scientific inquiry, the "social good," inalienable individual rights, progress, and humanitarian ideals coexist in harmony. Yet when these concepts are superimposed on each other, ethical dilemmas arise. As examples, progress in conquering the unknown implies an element of risk; in some instances, the needs of a society may be deemed more important than the rights of its individual citizens; scientific inquiry may be executed poorly, its implications may be applied inappropriately, or it may move in directions that offend sensibilities or cherished values. The use of human beings in research studies involves the complex intertwining and often inextricable combination of all these sprawling issues.

Although it is a somewhat simplistic breakdown, three basic types of sample populations are utilized in the behavioral sciences: nonhuman organisms; "free-agent" adult humans; and a variety of other human beings who by virtue of some characteristic (such as age, institutionalization, physical illness, mental disability, or the like) need special consideration and protection.

The ethical considerations involved in performing research on the first two categories are complicated enough. Without question, investigators who use animal subjects (particularly the domesticated dog and cat) often are forced to prove that what their research reveals is far more important than the degree of discomfort presumed to be experienced by

Adapted from a paper delivered at the 82nd annual meeting of the American Psychological Association, New Orleans, 1974.

the animals during the course of these investigations. With "free-agent" adult humans, the population that most current guidelines are intended to accommodate, questions of adequate protection of the subjects' rights and welfare raise a staggering array of complex issues. The most salient of these include informed consent, the protection of privacy and confidentiality, the risk to the subject weighed against the potential benefits of the research results for the subject and/or others, and the thorny questions of how to decide these matters within the parameters of individual projects and how to monitor the investigators to assure that the welfare of the research participants is indeed protected.

When research involves the third study population, human beings who require *special* categories, the issues become so complicated that even the most rational mind begins to boggle. Yet the irony is that the research participants most in need of protection—by virtue of some characteristic that renders them relatively powerless, more vulnerable, or less able to make decisions for themselves—receive the *least* attention in terms of defining the conditions under which they may or may not participate in research experiments.[1]

We largely restrict ourselves here to a discussion of the ethical issues involved in conducting nontherapeutic behavioral research on child subjects. At the outset, I must express a personal dilemma that all child and developmental psychology researchers face when discussing the rights and welfare of research subjects. Most of us embraced this field with the firm conviction that a thorough understanding of human behavior rests largely on a thorough understanding of the etiology and development of behavior. To stifle or to unnecessarily impede such research would violate personal, lifetime commitments. On the other hand, however, there looms the necessity of tempering professional, personal, and perhaps even humanitarian zeal with an acute sensitivity to the needs and rights of those in a position to provide the knowledge we so enthusiastically seek.

ISSUES: FROM THE CHILD'S PERSPECTIVE

Because of considerations of physical, mental, legal, and social power in concert with the protective stance our society officially sanctions toward the young, children are viewed as both quantitatively and qualitatively inferior to adults. Although the present thesis is that the abilities and competencies of children are greatly underrated, current realities remain that warrant the special attention of researchers who use children as subjects.

The Minority Status of Children

To appreciate the special considerations child research participants must receive, it is necessary to understand the extent to which children are powerless vis-a-vis society. By virtue of their smaller physical statures and less mature mental capabilities, children are usually at a distinct disadvantage in the presence of any person who is older than they are. It has been persuasively argued that minors constitute the *most* discriminated category in terms of legal rights and access to decision-making powers over their own destinies (Keith-Spiegel and Spiegel, 1973). The child brings his "minority status" with him into the research arena, providing the basis for the need for special considerations.

Voluntary and Informed Consent

After considering whether a study using child subjects should be conducted in the first place, the issue of "voluntary and informed consent" is one of the most difficult aspects of child research to resolve adequately. If the statement from the Nuremburg Code had been strictly sanctioned and extended to the behavioral sciences, any research involving minors would be precluded:

The voluntary consent of the human subject is absolutely essential. This means the person involved should have legal capacity to give consent . . . and should have sufficient knowledge and comprehension of the elements of the subject matter as to enable him to make an understanding, enlightened decision (Beecher, 1970, p. 227).

Children are not only presumed to be less capable (depending on their age and mental ability) of understanding what they are agreeing to do, but their legal status in decision making is practically nonexistent. Although most recent guidelines specify that a minor's consent is to be obtained if at all feasible, this point is more a courtesy than a legal obligation.

There are those who maintain that the implications for children inherent in the Nuremburg Code should prevail, except perhaps when an experimental procedure may benefit the child after all known measures of remedying his illness (or other problem) have proved unsuccessful. Jaffe (1969) disagrees with the idea that persons who are unable to comprehend the risks or nature of the experiment, and who are therefore incapable of giving truly "informed consent," should not be used as research subjects. Jaffe feels that reasoning of this sort

. . . improperly makes consent an ultimate or absolute value irrespective of the interest that consent is designed to protect. A rule forbidding experimentaion on a given class of persons may exclude experimentation of value to that class (p. 423).

Current research using child subjects is not discouraged because of the problems related to informed consent, but because the procedures for obtaining that consent are becoming increasingly elaborate. Yet the problems of defining the terms "voluntary" and "informed," especially as they apply to the more vulnerable and intellectually less capable, will continue to be baffling no matter how specific the procedure for obtaining informed consent becomes.

A particularly interesting feature of the policy draft guidelines issued by the Department of Health, Education and Welfare (1973) is the requirement that the child be more involved in the consent procedure than has been previously specified. The consent of child subjects (excluding infants) is to be sought, even if they can only understand that they may refuse to participate. This decision, even by a small child, can be interpreted as withholding consent, whether or not this consent is truly "informed." In this instance, then, we may lose a subject for seemingly irrelevant reasons: bad mood, distaste for the investigator's beard, fear of strangers, resentment of an observer in the home, dislike of the noise of a testing machine, or the like. However, the major ethical principle behind the consent requirement is that it is essential for the subjects themselves to decide to enroll in a participatory system they have not designed for themselves. Thus the basis for a decision *not* to engage in an experiment cannot be questioned.

Knowing how to present the features of a study to a child subject when consent is being sought presents its own set of problems. The intellectual maturity and comprehension level of the subject, interfaced with the nature of the specific project, are important determinants of the procedure to obtain consent. But the researcher must, simultaneously refrain from any temptation to take advantage of the subject's immaturity while seeking consent.

"Obey Thy Mother and Father"—and Anyone Else Bigger Than You Are.   Current ethical guidelines for the conduct of research with human beings stress "freedom of participation." The subject should feel free not only to refuse to engage in the research project, but also to discontinue participation once the study is begun.

Even very young children should be able to comprehend this freedom if it is communicated at the appropriate level: "Jimmy, I want you to know that you don't have to do this if you don't want to, and once we get started you can quit if you want to at any time." However, many children, even when they become stressed or unhappy, may fail to signal a desire to terminate their participation in the experiment. This probably happens because children are socialized to follow orders from any source perceived of as authority. Most children find it difficult to question, defy, or fail to implement a request from an adult (or even from an older child). Noncompliant behavior has probably produced disciplinary actions in the past, and most children usually learn the hard way that their chances of escaping these consequences are relatively low.

Safeguarding child subjects with regard to their "freedom of participation" may then require special sensitivity and responsibility on the part of the investigator. But it should also be noted that regulating the degree of force with which the researcher asserts authority is not confined solely to child subjects, as Milgram's now classic study (1963) has so dramatically revealed.

What's in It for the Child?

Parsons (1969) notes that the most important reward (although not necessarily the only one) that human research subjects receive as a result of their participation in an experiment is qualitatively the same as the reward for the investigator: satisfaction derived from contributing to the advancement of knowledge, and a corresponding recognition of that contribution. Assuming for the moment that an investigator would not undertake a project unless he believed that it would yield valuable information, this symbiotic mutual payoff seems most satisfactory to all parties concerned.

But it can be legitimately debated whether child subjects are capable of perceiving and/or receiving their part of such an abstract reward. Although we cannot reconcile the fact that the "ultimate glory" of contributing to science may not be directly experienced by younger research participants, we should recognize the probable difference that exists between the adult's and the child's perceptions of participation in a research project.

Is there any other feature about being a research subject that might provide some measure of satisfaction to a child? It has been suggested that "captive" research populations in institutions derive personal satisfaction from the special attention they receive as participants in an experiment. Breaking the monotony of an otherwise routine life may be welcomed as something different to do, a new person to talk to. Although noninstitutionalized children could conceivably experience these same satisfactions, it is more likely that their sense of what is novel and attention—getting is environmentally broader than may be the case, for example, for prisoners or residents in homes for the aged.

What about offering the child a more concrete reward—something the child can directly perceive and enjoy? A dollar or a candy bar may be as pleasant an aftermath to the experimental treatment for a child as the final publication of the research data is for the investigator. One colleague, who routinely hands a lollipop to his diminutive data sources after their contributions, likens this practice to that of the friendly neighborhood dentist or doctor, adding, "I want them to think of me as a nice man." But many researchers may be reticent to turn science into a game of common bartering. Certainly this issue has received attention in the context of "enticement to participate" (as opposed to the "post hoc surprise lollipop" example just cited).

It is not uncommon to offer subjects money for their participation in an experiment, even though determining the appropriate sum (which should be enough to offset inconveniences incurred by the subject, but not enough to encourage participation solely for monetary reward) is a controversial issue. But payment for subject services becomes especially complicated when it is applied to persons with restricted access to the rights of free enterprise. Children (as well as prisoners and other special-category subjects) could probably be "bought cheap," thus adding a distasteful element to the research issue of participant remuneration. Moreover, remuneration for a child subject is *not* given directly to the child but to the guardian of the consent. It is true that the adult in charge of the child is often inconvenienced as a result of the child's participation the guardian must drive to the place of investigation, wait while the child participates in the experiment, and so on), but there is something disquieting in the fact that the conscripted subject does not directly receive the contractual reward.

Returning to our search for a source of pleasure or satisfaction for child research subjects, it appears that unless the experimental treatment is fun or interesting, we have little else to offer child participants.

"Step into My Lab . . ."   Adults have mastered the adaptive feat of interacting with strangers in a complicated and impersonal world, and they bring that adaptation with them to the research laboratory as experimental subjects. Unless the experimental manipulation is bizarre, adults are likely to take the experience in stride, as if they were discussing personal finances with a loan officer. But most children (especially very young children) have a rather narrow "world view," and are anxious in unfamiliar places and with strangers. Their home, their immediate neighborhood, and (for older children) their school may comprise the extent of their sphere of social comfort.

Most researchers are sensitive to a child's reactions to the investigator and to any "strange" surrounding (which, to a child, can even include an office), in most instances, these researchers can take appropriate measures to relax and comfort the child. But perhaps a more significant feature of novel experiences for the young is that they may have a considerably greater impact than adults may realize. Even the most routine "treatment" can be quite significant to the child—one he may recall (complete with any affect generated by the experience) for some time. Although in most cases these experiences are not negative, when experimental procedures involve surprises that may be unpleasant, some cause for concern seems warranted. Thus it is important for researchers to consider the restricted "world view" of the child during the design phase of the experiment and to make every effort to minimize any risk relevant to its possible effects.

ISSUES: FROM THE PARENTS' PERSPECTIVE

Because parents are legally responsible for all matters pertaining to their children, by definition parents are drawn into research procedures when their children (if they are minors) serve as subjects. Parental consent to permit children to participate in a study is mandatory in research ethics codes. Moreover, some parents may have other interests in the research project, raising additional ethical dilemmas that often involve the issue of confidentiality.

Informed-Consent Problems Related to Parents

It is not unusual to find parents who refuse to allow their children to participate in even the most innocuous study for any of several reasons: a distrust of scientists in general or of psychologists in particular; not wanting strangers to talk to their children; an unwillingness to endure any inconvenience to themselves, and the like. However, the opposite phenomenon can also occur and should be cause for concern. Most if not all child and developmental psychologists repeatedly endure parental requests for help and advice as to how to handle some problem related to their children as soon as "what we do" has been ascertained. Complete strangers are often willing to describe the most intimate details of their family lives to an "expert." This phenomenon has two implications for researchers during the informed-consent phase in an experiment. First, parents must understand that we are requesting—not *demanding*, as one more legitimate authority to which the welfare of their children has been consigned—the participation of their child in a research study. The parent who is insecure in her or his parenting ability is particularly vulnerable here, and we would not take advantage of such a situation. Second, care should be taken not to permit the parent to misinterpret that benefits to the parent or the child are ensured as a result of the child's participation in the research study, unless some feature of the particular project guarantees that probability. Yet even here promises are extremely risky and probably never justifiable when experimentation by definition has inherent unknowns. One principle in the Society for Research in Child Development Guidelines (1973) touches on this general problem: "Because the investigator's words may carry unintended weight with parents and children, caution should be exercised in reporting results, making evaluative statements, or giving advice."

It has been suggested that parents may not be that much more capable of giving informed consent for their children than the children are themselves. Parents may have the same difficulties in understanding the information supplied by the researcher as they would if they were being requested to volunteer for the experiment themselves. But the problem can extend beyond achieving an adequate understanding of the study. Just because an adult is the parent of the child does not mean that the parent will make the best possible decision regarding the child's welfare. As stated in the provision of the World Medical Association, parents should be completely free to make decisions on behalf of their children:

One may even question the moral legitimacy of such freedom, and, in the light of present knowledge of the way in which parental responsibility is sometimes discharged, this could sometimes be of little value in protecting the human rights of the individual (Katz, 1972, p. 982).

Lasagna (1969) questions whether relatives can be trusted to be objective when giving their consent. Speaking specifically of the mentally ill, who are judged to be incompetent to decide whether or not to participate as research subjects, Lasagna states, ". . . one has the feeling that relatives of the insane are often almost as disturbed as the patients" (p. 459). This concern may be widened to include research on "problem children." How often do we hear psychologists say, "Show me an emotionally disturbed kid, and I'll show you an emotionally disturbed family!"

What should be apparent here is that researchers cannot lull themselves into a state of ethical bliss simply because they have managed to meet one of the strongest ethical-legal requirements of child research by managing to obtain parental consent.

Confidentiality Problems Related to Parents

Another important consideration related to parents involves the limits of confidentiality. Respecting the privacy of experimental participants by keeping the details of their participation confidential is an important feature of ethical research codes. However, this issue becomes especially complicated when the research participants are minors.

Parsons (1969) discusses the delicate connection between consent and privacy, pointing out that ". . . consent to participate [in research] actually constitutes consent to relinquish certain areas of privacy that might otherwise have been enjoyed and protected" (p. 352). This means, that participants often consent to what is tantamount to allowing their privacy to be invaded. Here the ethical question becomes not so much whether privacy is actually invaded, but how privacy can be protected. This important distinction presents a special dilemma with child subjects, because we may not be able to obtain truly informed consent from them and instead we may have to rely on a secondary source (usually the parents) for consent. Complicating the matter further is that holders of legal consent often feel that they are *entitled* to access to the details of the individual child's performance in an experiment. Moreover, parents or other secondary sources of consent (school authorities, institution personnel, and the like) have been known to specify sharing specific knowledge about child subjects with them as a *condition* of granting initial consent for the child to participate in the project.

These ethical dilemmas currently plague many nonresearch psychological activities that involve children, most notably test-score results and other assessment evaluations and psychotherapy-process information. How much and under what circumstances should significant knowledge be shared with significant others? Where should the thin line be drawn between compromising confidentiality and upholding the best interests of the child? In nontherapeutic behavioral-science research, however, the issue may not be this complicated. In such experiments, it is unlikely that there would be any need or reason to share the details of the child's performance with anyone else. Any information the child provides in such studies is held in the strictest confidence, and this can be stated at the onset of the project. Even if this means losing some subjects, the investigator is assured that the participants' rights are protected. However, it should be mentioned that knowledge of a subject's performance can be shared with others at the subject's consent. But with child subjects, all the consent problems previously discussed pertain here. It should also be noted that even during a routine experiment the investigator may sometimes feel obligated to deliberately disclose information to others for the subject's welfare.

ISSUES: FROM THE PERSPECTIVE OF THE INVESTIGATOR

Some people may regard scientific researchers with great awe, but researchers are merely human beings with their own biases, motivations, needs, values, and vulnerabilities. These idiosyncratic characteristics fol-

low the researcher into the laboratory. Even the "rigorous empiricist" described by Brymer and Farris, 1967)—who believes that values should
not affect scientific research and who therefore views ethics as inevitable
problems of strategy rather than morality—reveals a strong value orientation that greatly influences the nature of his inquiry.

In this section, we discuss some aspects of the *personal* qualities of
researchers that might influence attitudes toward and the conduct of child
research.

Implications of Investigators' Views of "Children's Natures"

During a seminar several years ago the students broke into a particularly
colorful and intense verbal battle over the propriety of a particular study
in which child subjects were exposed to experiences of failure. One faction felt that it was unfair to manipulate the situation in a way that could
cause the child possible unhappiness and loss of self-esteem. Another
faction felt that these complaints were unfounded, because the manipulation was not intense and was probably analogous to the failures children
experience every day. It soon became clear that the argument was not
as much over the merits or demerits of a particular research technique as
it was a basic disagreement over the nature of children. Those who objected to the study characterized children as vulnerable, highly impression-
able, and particularly sensitive to negative experiences. Those who
supported the study described children as tough, resilient, and able to
take most experiences in stride.

Similar differences in opinion as to the strengths and weaknesses of
immature human beings exist among developmental psychology researchers.
It is probable that views or theories about the nature of children influence
(at least to some extent) what experimental procedures are considered
appropriate. Orientations could range from absolute detachment, where
children are viewed as akin to laboratory rats, to a conviction that developing human beings are so fragile that any experimental introjection into their
lives must be executed with great caution. It is likely that such extreme
views are rare but that many less dogmatic variations of both of these
views exist among researchers. I know one developmental psychologist
who believes that it is wrong to force a child to clarify, through verbal
responses to direct questions, attitudes that may still be forming, because
such induced affirmations may "set" these attitudes prematurely in the
child's mind and stunt the course of natural discovery. I know other psychological researchers who believe that to obtain the most valid information possible from children, you must ask what you want to know in the
most simple and direct manner. Clearly, such differing views are revealed

in various research designs; if an open discussion on this point were to be held, questions of ethics would surely arise.

The dilemma inherent in this issue, which makes impossible to fully resolve the matter at this point, is that we do not yet know a great deal about the nature of children—that's what continuing research is all about! But it does seem fair to conclude that research utilizing child subjects should be designed and conducted with a sensitivity to the very possible vulnerabilities of the immature human being.

Investigators' Responsibilities Toward Their Subjects

Encouragement and support for experimentation is a relatively recent historical phenomenon. Freund (1969), for example, cites a court decision of two centuries ago that held the physician *personally* responsible for any negative effects that resulted from deviating from the accepted method of treatment. This, Freund notes, is in marked contrast to present practices, because most contemporary medical therapy is considered to be "experimental."

The shift in emphasis to the sanctioning of experimentation as a means to improve knowledge carries with it one obvious pitfall: the personal responsibility of the investigator to his subject is diminished, because inherent in the definition of the term "experimentation" is the implication that the investigator may not know, nor need he pretend to know, exactly what he is doing. In fact, it is not uncommon to find the use of exculpatory provisions by investigators (although these are now expressly forbidden in the new Department of Health, Education and Welfare guidelines).

Whereas the value of experimentation is not being contested here, we are now faced with the myriad dilemmas that surround the definition and enforcement of sound ethical experimental procedures. But with all subjects, and with child subjects in particular, the investigator's personal quality of caring for them, of respecting their feelings and rights as people, and of taking special steps to ensure that no ill-effects befall them as a result of their participation in the project are crucial. The guidelines issued by the Society for Research in Child Development (1973) specify that the investigator is responsible for maintaining ethical practices not only for himself but for his collaborators and staff as well. Moreover, whenever research procedures cause undesirable consequences that were previously unforeseeable, the investigator should employ appropriate measures to correct these consequences and should consider redesigning the procedure.

Identifying a Subject with a Problem Unrelated to the Research Purpose. An acute dilemma that has serious implications for the issues of privacy and confidentiality involves uncovering an indication that a subject has a problem that the investigator feels deserves attention during the course of the research process. In the case of child subjects, should the parents, teachers, or others be made aware of the investigator's concern? The guidelines of the Society for Research in Child Development (1973) state:

> When, in the course of research, information comes to the investigator's attention that may seriously affect the child's well-being, the investigator has a responsibility to discuss the information with those expert in the field in order that the parents may arrange the necessary assistance for their child.

Although this statement seems both rational and humanitarian, it is necessary to discuss its inherent pitfalls in the context of the subject–experimenter consent contract. On one hand, the investigator who discovers a potential area of difficulty for a child and who delves far enough into the dilemma in an effort to determine what to do about it, deserves commendation for his sensitivity to the child's welfare. But if we adhere to the objective features of the implicit or explicit subject–experimenter contract, there are usually no provisions in nontherapeutic behavioral science research beyond the prescribed collection of data. Is any further intrusion into the participant's life ethical, strictly speaking? Is it feasible to extract the child's permission to relay this unforeseen state of affairs to others?

This is not to suggest that investigators remain myopic, concerning themselves exclusively with study requirements and each subject's welfare only as it pertains to data gathering, and be blind to all other aspects of the subject's well-being. But it should be recognized that deliberate disclosure, which may well involve a deviation from some of the ethical procedures already discussed, is a complicating factor in research. It represents one of those agonizing situations in which social responsibility and routine ethical procedures are pitted against one another.

Professional Needs versus Subject Welfare

Research is a competitive business. The typical investigator is usually not seeking monetary gain, but he is apt to be driven by a desire to discover something important—to be a hero in the War for Knowledge. The hope for recognition probably provides another incentive—to win a medal for being a hero in the War for Knowledge. It is feared that human subjects are more likely to become "compromised casualties" when scientific zeal is overpowering. Will the investigator pause to assure that the subjects' rights and well-being are being fully protected?

Another aspect of this problem is the "publish-or-perish" philosophy under which many academics and professionals must operate to advance in rank or at times merely to retain their jobs. It may well be time to consider that doctrine as an ethical issue. It seems probable that many investigators conduct research only because they *must*. Again are ethical considerations fully regarded under this circumstance? Barber, Lally, Makarushka, and Sullivan (1973) present some rather shocking documentation indicating that one category of researcher, designated as the "mass-producer" type (who publishes often but whose research is rarely cited), tends to approve study designs that have questionable features with regard to the protection of human subjects.

These concerns are particularly critical for investigators who use child subjects, because children are less able to muster adequate defenses against a "soldier" who may be fighting the War for Knowledge for the wrong reasons!

Role of the Investigator as Teacher

Sensitivity to the rights of human participants in research is not spontaneously generated, nor is it the natural outgrowth of a firm grasp of the subject matter of science in general (and developmental and/or child psychology in particular) and a sound training in research design and procedure. Yet we appear to have greatly underemphasized research ethics and the rights that should be extended to experimental subjects in our educational curriculum. This may be caused in part by a relative paucity of available published material (particularly material pertaining to the use of children in research) and by the perpetuation of generational ignorance (we never learned much about such matters ourselves and therefore do not teach them to our students). Aside from the recommendation that this omission in educational training be remedied immediately, there is a compelling reason for students to be well sensitized to ethical considerations in research. Because universities are the gatekeepers of future researchers (it is highly unlikely that anyone without post-secondary training would be in a position to conduct psychological experiments), we can be sure that tomorrow's researchers are exposed to the issues. The findings of Barber and his colleagues (1973) that only 13% of the medical-researcher population surveyed reported having had, as students, a seminar, a lecture, or part of a course dealing with research-ethics issues well illustrates the scope of the problem. But a solution is close at hand if the academic training personnel will only assume the responsibility. An encouraging trend is that a number of recent child-development textbooks devote at least a few pages to the ethical implications of research involving children (Ambron, 1975; Munsinger, 1975; Mussen, Conger, and Kagan, 1974).

A second important service the teacher-investigator must perform is to see that students learn a great deal about children by extensive observations of and interactions with them. Even though adults by definition have already lived through all the previous developmental stages we are concerned with here, it is not true that they thereby fully understand persons who are now where they once were. It is my impression that students often begin interacting with children as *experimental subjects* rather than as *people.* Aside from the fact that complete familiarity with the population to be studied is prerequisite for the design and implementation of sound research, this point has ethical implications as well. Treating child subjects with respect and dignity results largely from knowing them in their own right—not merely as objective little data givers.

ISSUES: EXPERIMENTAL DESIGN AND STUDY TECHNIQUES

Unfortunately, the requirements of the appropriate scientific procedure in a given experimental design and the rights of the human subjects to be used do not always effortlessly mesh together. Also, on occasion either necessity or ignorance produces an experimental plan that lacks precision or is inadequate. Critical ethical dilemmas arise in both cases.

The Experimental Design as an Ethical Concern

The questions of adequate experimental design, analysis procedures, and interpretation of results are often considered qualitatively different from ethical issues. But what needs to be considered and emphasized in the training of future researchers is that these two categories are hardly distinct, regardless of how appealing and convenient it may be to separate "science" from "values." Rutstein (1969) put it this way:

. . . When a study is in itself scientifically invalid, all other ethical considerations become irrelevant. There is no point in obtaining "informed consent" to perform a useless study. A worthless study cannot possibly benefit anyone, least of all the experimental subject himself. Any risk to the patient, however small, cannot be justified. In essence, the scientific validity of a study on human beings is in itself an ethical principle (p. 254).

It is also during the period of formulating the research question and the experimental design that ethical problems must be anticipated.

The consequences of conducting and reporting poorly designed studies extend beyond the inappropriate use of human subjects or even the failure to advance knowledge. The results of such research can be misleading and can even cause injury to the entire population from which the sample was taken for use in the study. For example, one media-publicized "study" on adult, male murderers found that they could not spell well, nor could they spell well as children. The investigator concluded that an inability to spell predicted murderous tendencies! Aside from the obvious shortcomings in the experimental design (biased sample of murderers who were caught and imprisoned, lack of a control group, and the like), imagine yourself the scientifically unsophisticated parent of a child who is a poor speller or a teacher who is looking for a scapegoat to hide your inability to teach!

Even when experiments are well designed, the "significance" of inferential statistical analyses must still be translated into some stated interpretation. As desirous as it may be to make the most impact with the widest possible generalizations, this interpretive boundary is often overstepped. One example of the critical step from a mathematical probability statement to interpretation involved a study of mechanical-aptitude score differences between boys and girls in which the boys were favored at a .05 level of significance. These findings were interpreted as supportive of the *innate* superiority of the mechanical ability of males.

Most researchers should probably be encouraged to think a "little smaller" and/or to consider *many* possible interpretations of their findings. This should not be viewed as downgrading the importance of research work or as an advocation of wishy-washy conclusions, but rather as a means of establishing more responsible and creative science.

Ethical Considerations in Longitudinal Design Research

Tracking the same subjects across time is immensely important to the field of developmental psychology, because this provides the best means of truly assessing behavioral correlates of change. In addition to some basic difficulties inherent in this study method (expense, task equivalency at various ages, appropriate analysis techniques because order effects cannot be balanced, effects of history and an inability to control the environment between testings, test-sequence effects, and the like), there are some ethical considerations.

The major feature that distinguishes longitudinal research from most other types of research is that the subject–experimenter relationship exists for an extended period of time, sometimes many years. What additional ethical obligations the investigator incurs here, particularly if the study involves creating subject dependency (such as providing food or special training), are not very clear. If investigators are responsible for the well-being of their subjects for the duration of their participation in a project (which, for most behavioral research, is a period of an hour or two), how is this obligation to be modified, if at all, for investigators who engage in longitudinal research?

Another ethical concern involves confidentiality. The identity of subjects cannot be immediately destroyed, because the longitudinal design by definition necessitates finding the same subjects again and again, so that each successive set of data can be matched appropriately. Coded systems (where the actual identities of subjects are locked in a file to which only authorized personnel have access) are the most common method of maintaining confidentiality.

Losing subjects from a longitudinal study is viewed as something of a disaster. Cohort mortality, for whatever reason, is one of the investigator's greatest concerns, because subjects cannot be replaced once the study is underway. Losses of time, money, and effort from previous measurements add to the distress of losing longitudinal research subjects. Thus on many occasions, the "freedom to participate" ethic can cause the longitudinal researcher to despair. The researcher may find it especially difficult to resist inclinations to pressure a subject to remain actively engaged in the study.

Ethical Concerns in Controlled Experimentation

The use of *control groups* for comparison purposes with regard to the group(s) receiving experimental treatment is an accepted, even an essential, feature of much contemporary scientific research. Rutstein (1969) documents the many pitfalls of uncontrolled medical research, including the quick acceptance of "cures" that fade into disuse and the ultimate discovery that the "cure" is more harmful than the disease. Rutstein concludes that "controlled studies, when indicated, impose fewer ethical problems than uncontrolled human experiments" (p. 533).

The critical ethical issue in controlled experimentation is withholding what is believed to be a useful treatment or experience from participants who are in need of some benefit of such treatment. The most acceptable resolution to this dilemma in both biomedical and psychological research is to use the *best known treatment* for the control group condition and to compare it to the effects of the experimental treatment.

Unfortunately, this solution cannot be applied to every controlled experimental design that is potentially beneficial to subjects. A common design involves treating one group and *leaving the other group alone*, except for measurements of the dependent variable(s). Responses to inquiries regarding the propriety of such research might be: "Our only introjection into the subjects' lives is in the form of trying to *possibly* benefit *some* of them. The controls remain as they would anyway, but the results may ultimately benefit the control-group members." However, not all critics of all studies may be comfortable with this rationalization. Confounding nontreatment controls with such factors as study duration and previous established knowledge about the effects of the independent variable quickly muddles the issues again. For example, a three-year study comparing the effects of poor diets on cognitive development between grant-funded, nourished (experimental-group) children and "naturally" poorly nourished (control-group) children may well raise ethical questions, especially because the deleterious effects of malnutrition on intellectual development have already been established.

The American Psychological Association guidelines (1973) suggest that if an experimental treatment proves beneficial, it should be made available to the control-group participants. The APA also suggests that the researcher's responsibility to subjects does not necessarily terminate once the data has been collected, especially when dependencies and expectations have been established. Thus investigators are being asked to think beyond data collection per se, even if this requires additional involvement with their subjects, after the research is complete.

Finally, it should be noted that much controlled experimentation in developmental or child-behavioral research does not present the benefit/no-benefit dilemma directly. Although almost any research finding may shed light on what *can* be applied in a beneficial manner, (a better way to teach children how to read, for example), the original study question may not have been designed to attain this goal. Thus a known benefit is often *not* being withheld from a control group; the experimental treatment has simply not yet been identified as beneficial.

Risks and Benefits to Child Subjects

Assessing risks for a behavioral-research subject is extremely difficult. Often we simply do not know what the risks may be, and differences in individual subjects provide an array of potential reactions to a given research technique. But the new Department of Health, Education and Welfare guidelines (1974) hold investigators responsible for assessing not only *physical risk* but *psychological harm* and *social injury* as well. Although no investigator would want the effects of these seemingly formidable terms to befall any human research participant, it is not yet clear how these terms will be operationally defined.

The draft of HEW's policy for researching child subjects is particularly stringent with regard to potential risk. This draft states that unless previous research has been conducted on animals or adults that provides sufficient knowledge as to the risk involved, then the research should not be conducted on children. The draft further states that even if information from experimentation with animals or adult humans suggests that potential risk to children is sufficiently low, other unknown factors must also be considered. These include differences in response patterns between children and adults, the possibility of the delayed expression of injury in children, potential effects on developing organs (particularly the central nervous system), and the possible misuse of data by institution or school personnel. Clearly, investigators should apply research procedures from experimentation involving animals and adults whenever possible. In behavioral research, however, the analogue studies may not be available or the results may be misleading when applied to children. Biomedical researchers are voicing the same concerns, fearing that if HEW's draft guidelines hold, research on conditions that are "uniquely pediatric" will be greatly hampered.

Fortunately, most behavioral-science research involves exposing the child to neither physical nor psychological risk. The American Psychological Association guidelines (1973) discuss what risks might be involved at great length (pp. 58–87). "Mental stress" is probably the most likely state some investigators induce purposely or accidentally. However, the APA guidelines are strict regarding the use of any procedure that may cause physical or mental discomfort in human subjects of *any* age. Further, investigators who can justify the exposure of subjects to some mental or physical stress are admonished to ensure that there are no discernible aftereffects.

It can be argued whether children should ever be used in nontherapeutic behavioral-science studies in which *any* risk might be present. Carrying this argument even further, some feel that children should not be involved in experimentation unless there is no risk *and* unless the potential for some direct benefit to each subject is present. On the other hand, some behavioral-science research utilizing temporary mental-stress techniques with children have begun to pave the way for long overdue cultural reforms in the traditional socialization techniques used by parents and the educational system that may ultimately benefit individual research subjects as well as childkind. Yet, even if a study is deemed sufficiently significant to allow children to be exposed to some temporary discomfort or distress and no alternative procedures are feasible, the vulnerabilities of children (less ability to manage their emotions, weaker or less developed defenses and stress-coping mechanisms, and so on) heap added ethical responsibilities on the investigator to preserve the ultimate welfare of the subjects.

Deception, Concealment, and Debriefing with Child Subjects

Behavioral scientists have never received much sympathy, sometimes even within their own ranks, for their frequent concealment (withholding information from the subject) and deception (misinforming the subject).

Aside from a general impression of fraudulence, the ethical implications arising when deception or concealment is interfaced with "informed consent" are obvious and profound.

The unfortunate fact remains, however, that just as biomedical researchers have requirements for the "state of the body" of their subjects, psychologists have requirements for the "state of the mind" of their subjects. At times, it is absolutely essential to the validity of the research findings that the subject's mind be "free" from direct knowledge of what is being investigated. Yet special responsibilities are inherent in this requirement. First, it is difficult to defend deception (or concealment) unless it is absolutely necessary to the integrity of the research question. And the research question itself should be a very important one; deception and concealment can in these regards, be likened to the concept of risk. Second, provisions must be made for informing the subject of the research investigation when it is complicated:—the so-called *debriefing session*. In most cases, debriefing can be accomplished with relative ease and, hopefully, the subject understands and is satisfied. At times, however, total debriefing seems indefensible on ethical grounds, because the subject could become so upset or outraged that an explanation of the procedure would cause psychological harm in and of itself! A volume could be written on this issue alone, but the confinements of space here preclude the thorough discussion it certainly deserves.

The use of deception or concealment with children can cause certain additional dilemmas. Less mature persons may have great difficulty understanding any subsequent explanation of their treatment, especially in the context of switching stated realities. In the end, the child may be confused rather than enlightened.

Ironically, the American Psychological Association's guidelines (1973) implicitly condone *additional* deception during debriefing sessions with child subjects. The APA document states that the primary objective of the post-investigation clarification procedure is to ensure that the child leaves treatment subject to no undesirable aftermaths. To accomplish this, the APA suggests that certain misconceptions should not be removed (for example, if a child was previously led to believe that he performed better than he actually did) or even that additional misconceptions should be induced (the experimenter may try to convince the child that he did better than he actually did).

How complicated the issue of debriefing becomes when objective ethical principles are placed in one pan of the scale and human kindness and consolation in the other. But what should be obvious here is the particularly awesome responsibilities that investigators who use child subjects must face and the balance they must strike between their research interests and the welfare of their research participants. The ideal experimental design would be a study in which the requirements of answering the research question and an honest relationship with the research participants are not diametrically opposed.

The Search for Antecedent or Predisposing Factors

An interest shared by most developmental psychologists involves the discovery and understanding of how what happened or how people behaved earlier in their lives relates to what happens to them or how their behavior is affected later. Sometimes this research is longitudinal; sometimes it is based on "working backwards" by reconstructing life histories.

Often these inquiries are conducted with the most humanitarian intentions. Frequently, they involve searching for predisposing factors that are likely to produce unhappiness or severe maladaptive behavior (mental illness, criminality, and the like) in the hope of discovering clues early enough to permit preventive intervention. The Joint Commission on Mental Health of Children, for example, specifically stresses the need for and the high priority of programs designed to prevent emotional and mental disturbance (see Hamm, 1974). Indeed there seems to be an increasing recognition of the facts that many people are not turning out as well as they could and that perhaps we should try to correct this earlier in their lives instead of focusing exclusively on the often ineffective remedial attempts to mop up the damage later on.

However, critical ethical concerns are inherent in researching antecedent and predisposing factors of behavior patterns judged as maladaptive or unproductive. A major ethical issue is the effects of *labeling* a child as "at risk" prior to a full manifestation of the problem. That dilemma becomes particularly acute if confidentiality is compromised. The knowledge that a child has been dubbed by a researcher as "*pre*delinquent," "*pre*homosexual," "*pre*violent," "*pre*failure," "*pre*crazy," could exacerbate the adjudged incipient problem. How the child is then regarded and treated by people who "know" and how the child then begins to perceive himself or herself can even lead to a self-fulfilling prophecy. In such instances, investigators would mistakenly consider themselves successful in predicting a problem when, in fact, they have been causal factors in bringing about that problem!

Another serious criticism being voiced more frequently is that this study approach singles out individual children who seem to exhibit some incipient deviance and then focuses its efforts on bringing them back onto the right path when the crux of the problem actually lies *outside* the individual—society's attitudes toward homosexuals, the competitive educational system, racism or sexism, and restrictive views of what constitutes "normal" or "socially desirable" behavior are examples. It is also true that most target populations chosen for study and "remediation" contain children of poor and/or ethnic heritage. This has led to the concern that white, middle-class values are simply assumed to be desirable and are to be forced on other cultural groups. Finally, because these projects are very expensive and in most cases require the support of government funding, some researchers have expressed the fear that "human engineering" patterns will be established by the political powers, who will decide what behaviors are to be "corrected" and "controlled."

However, in an exceptionally thoughtful article, Gray (1971) clarifies the ethical concerns that emanate from research involving planned intervention into the life of the child. Despite criticisms of such programs, Gray argues convincingly that the appropriate goal of intervention research is to make more life options available to the individual than would otherwise be available. For example, poor children may learn the behavior necessary to survive in poverty; but their behavior may also be maladaptive in terms of ever moving out of their environment.

It remains difficult to quarrel with action research that may improve the quality of life for our nation's children and thus enhance their chances for a happier and more fulfilled adulthood. But researchers must also be acutely aware of the social forces contributing to individual development and must remain especially sensitive to the political issues involved in what they do.

Ethical Questions Surrounding Study Techniques in Child Research

Several study methods and treatments used by behavioral scientists have been debated within the discipline. Two techniques that have received much attention recently are the use of intelligence tests and behavioral modification. With regard to children, the concern is that both methodologies can be easily misused to the detriment of the subject. IQ test scores can lock youngsters into their "place" or be used to reinforce and perpetuate racist stereotypes. Behavior modification not only frightens people, but causes great concern among those who believe that it is wrong to impose behavioral control over another person. The popular social philosophies of the counterculture ("do your own thing"), the women's liberation goal of shattering sex-role behavioral expectancies, and the emphasis of "humanistic psychology" on the uniqueness of each person, all augur that we be increasingly vigilant for signs of forces that may be interpreted as violating the "freedom to control our own minds." In this context, imposing behavior patterns on children can be interpreted as denying them their basic freedom to develop as individuals. Such debates will probably continue, and researchers who utilize these types of procedures must be prepared to face controversy.

I informally surveyed nearly 100 published articles describing experiments in which children were used as research subjects. In general, most of the studies provided no apparent cause for ethical concern. When "taking the role of the child," most of the studies involved playing "games," manipulating toys or other intriguing objects, looking at pictures, or discussing some "fun" topics. In many other cases, the children were probably unaware of anything unusual because they were simply observed. With some exceptions, these experiences were probably pleasant (or at least not unpleasant) for the children. When "taking the role of the mother," I found only a handful of studies objectionable—usually for idiocyncratic reasons.

"Taking the role of the developmental psychologist" was most difficult, primarily because the articles themselves generally contained too little information to make ethical evaluations. Even in questionable studies, I felt that if the parent and the child both gave their consent that the study was acceptable. Unfortunately, the methods of obtaining consent (if it was obtained at all) were rarely specified. Even when consent was obtained, I often wondered how "informed" it was. If the researchers told the parents *all* of the relevant facts about their child's participation (for example, "Your child has been placed in the passive-underachieving group by her teacher, and I want to interview you to see if I can figure out what it might be about the way you treat her that makes her that way.") I wonder how many of the studies would have been completed at all! Deception and concealment were common practices in the sampling of studies I reviewed, but both were usually relatively benign and a quick debriefing probably counteracted any negative aftereffects. Once again, however, details were usually lacking in the published reports. In making more sweeping ethical judgments, I did find some studies were objectionable on the grounds of poor design, inadequate study techniques, or causing too much fuss by comparison to what the study was worth. Others may disagree with me here or conversely may have found much more than I deemed questionable.[2]

In sum, it was encouraging to find that the vast majority of studies I reviewed presented little or no cause for concern in ethically related matters. Perhaps most researchers use the rule-of-thumb suggested by Mitchell (1964):

...When deciding whether an experiment is justifiable, the old question, "Would you subject your own child to this?" is still a good yardstick for most moderately minded people. [But Mitchell continues] It should be remembered ... that some zealots may be prepared to submit their own families to indignities that the average man would consider excessive. The experiment . . . in which Oliver injected his own son with a crude extract of endocrine glands is a well-known example (Katz, 1972, p. 998).

When should children not *be used as research subjects?* Of course, certain research questions should not be answered using any human population. It is unnecessary to cite examples from the Nazi experimentation era to illustrate this point. Other obvious conditions precluding the use of children as research subjects include studies in which the physical or psychological risks are assessed to be substantial or for which appropriate and/or legal informed consent cannot be obtained. Here we discuss a few of the more subtle, less clearcut issues that are probably more prevalent than the extreme cases that all men of good will would consider undesirable and ethically indefensible.

Should children ever be used as research subjects if the fact that the subjects are children is irrelevant, or at least unessential, to the researcher's interest? The American Medical Association Ethical Guidelines provide that minors be used in nontherapeutic research only when the nature of the investigation is such that mentally competent adults are not suitable subjects (Katz, 1972, p. 975). It therefore seems reasonable to suggest that child subjects not be used in behavioral research unless a primary component of the study is the behavior of immature humans.

One reason children may be frequently utilized as experimental subjects is that they—and some other populations that are abundant in more or less captive groupings (prisoners or college students are other examples)—are often more convenient to obtain for study purposes than those elusive adults who, wandering about of their own free will, comprise the majority of behaving humans. At this point, we can ask if it is appropriate to conduct research *primarily* on child subjects simply because this population is convenient to study. Instances have been observed in which a population of children becomes available and an investigator *then* designs a study based on that particular population. Here we may not be arguing research ethics in its strictest sense, but rather the issue of the quality of scientific inquiry. It can be argued that creative and important work occurs when both the research question and design *precede* the pragmatic consideration of what subjects are to be researched. It is unfortunate that practicalities and convenience often supercede scientific ideals.

There are persons who, in combination with one or more characteristics other than chronological age, require additional special considerations prior to their utilization in research studies. Research subjects who are simultaneously in two human-participant "special categories" (mentally retarded minors, institutionalized delinquents, autistic children) are not uncommon. Then there are children who, because of the socioeconomic circumstances of their families or some other distinguishing characteristic such as racial heritage, may be rendered even less powerful than the Anglo-Saxon child with a middle-class background. Banning research on children in special categories would not be in the best interests of the participants themselves; thus investigators studying such sample populations have scientific and ethical responsibilities far above the commonplace.

WHERE ARE GOING FROM HERE?

The public sector appears to be waking up after a relatively long period of leaving the driving of society to the "experts." Research regulatory agencies seem to be in a similar frenzy of activity, as new policy guidelines regarding research procedures and standards are pronounced. Although at this point the ramifications of these newer developments are not clear, it is probably safe to venture the opinion that the days of sovereign and self-governed scientists are passing.

The New Social Consciousness and Research Ethics

Scientific investigators who use human subjects should increasingly feel the effects of the "new consumerism." Among the questions that are asked more and more frequently: "Exactly what are you doing? What are you trying to prove? Why? What are the implications of your findings? Will your findings be implemented in a way that will affect me? If so, how?" Organizations that are composed of or are advocates of persons who are frequently chosen to be research subjects (prisoners, women, various ethnic minorities, and the like) are becoming especially sensitive to the intentions of researchers. McKinnon (1974) has developed what could be called a "Research Participant's Bill of Rights" that advocates the right to be different, the protection of emotional privacy, the community monitoring of experimentation, and the consensus between the scientific and consumer communities that knowledge sought falls within the public concern, that publicly funded project information should be made available to the public, and that investigators should be accountable to both the experimental population and the general public.

Behavioral researchers who study children should be prepared to have their work challenged in ways rarely experienced before. As examples, the experimenter who is interested in developing behavior-modification techniques to facilitate toilet training may be asked, "Why do 2-year-old children *have* to be toilet trained? Why should scientists contribute to the perpetuation of a cultural hangup that forces our young to be uniform in bathroom behavior?" The investigator who wishes to assess the effects of drugs on the adaptation of "hyperactive" children in the classroom can now expect to be questioned, "Why focus on drugging active children to fit into the restrictive and abnormal atmosphere of an outmoded educational system? Why not focus your inquiry on the *school's* inability to hold the child's attention and its failure to teach the child?" Instead of continuing research studies that prove or examine why black and brown children score lower on intelligence tests, the new critic may investigate the validity of the measurements used and/or the studies demonstrating what strengths and abilities minority heritage children have that the traditional assessment techniques fail to measure. The list of such investigative challenges is endless.

Who Should Protect Children's Rights as Research Subjects?

The merits and the demerits of strict centralized regulations regarding the protection of human subjects—professional self-regulation, peer review, local monitoring committees, and other regulatory mechanisms—have been considered at great length (Katz, 1972; Etzioni, 1973; Barber et al., 1973). Options are diminishing for many federally funded research projects as firm policies are being rapidly established. It is important to note that the ethical principles themselves are not being altered drastically and are largely repetitive of earlier codes. The major exception here is that the social acceptability and impact of the research project is beginning to be considered during the evaluation process. However, the most significant feature of the new policies is an emphasis on mechanisms to ensure that the ethical principles regarding the protection of human subjects are practiced by the investigator.

The policy draft of the Department of Health, Education and Welfare pertaining to the special protection of child research participants (1973) holds researchers to particularly intense consent requirements, review, and monitoring. Investigators who study minors are to be scrutinized by up to five committees, depending on subject–risk assessment. All proposals are to be examined by the Ethical Review Board (at the sponsoring HEW agency) and by the Protection Committee (at the grantee institution). The Ethical Review Board is to receive proposals from the Primary Review Committee and to evaluate these proposals in terms of "ethical issues and questions of societal acceptability in relation to scientific value." This review board is to be composed of 15 persons, no more than one-third of whom may be engaged in research, development, or demonstration activities that involve human subjects. The Protection Committee is responsible for the welfare of the actual research participants and judges the reasonableness of the consent procedure, oversees the process of subject selection, monitors the subjects' continued willingness to participate, and designs procedures to permit intervention on behalf of child subjects. The Protection Committee is to be comprised of at least five members who are "competent to deal with the medical, legal, social, and ethical issues in volved in research, and to represent the community from which the subject population is to be drawn."

A colleague, upon considering all that may be logistically involved in continuing his career as a child-development researcher, facetiously lamented:

I can just see it now. My proposal will be reviewed by 4316 people, none of whom will agree with any other and most of whom will know nothing about research or else they wouldn't have been allowed on the committees. After 72 rewrites, something will miraculously pass even though it will have been changed from an investigation of mathematical ability development from infancy to adolescence into a study of arithmetic scores in the 6½-year-old. In the meantime, I shall have been twice an inpatient for the treatment of paranoia. Then my Protection Committee composed of community representatives —a real-estate salesman, a mother of seven, a gay activist, a Red Cross volunteer, and a junkie—will approve of six kids I can use if I substitute one procedure which they said constituted a high risk; the pencil used for filling out the arithmetic test might poke their eyes out. So I'll switch to a crayon—nontoxic, of course. Then I'll go about getting all of my consents—from the kid, his mother, his father, the school superintendent, the school principal, and the teacher. All of the parties will give their approval in one case. And that child will walk in, kick me in the shins, and run away. You know, in the old days when dissection of corpses was disallowed, anatomy students robbed bodies from graves at night. Kidnapping never appealed to me before, but now. . . . Either that, or I could always drive a cab.

Some have expressed concern in a very serious manner that strict blanket policies will unnecessarily hamper the process of valuable scientific inquiry. Worse yet, too-strict policies could tempt the dedicated and determined investigator to seek ways of getting around the barriers which would undermine the very safeguards the policies are attempting to effect.

It has been argued that professional self-control is the appropriate mechanism for upholding ethical standards, because peers possess the specialized knowledge necessary to fully comprehend and to judge a given research plan, its procedures, and the value and implications of its findings. However, it has also been argued that to the extent that the research process and its implications affect many people outside the scientific realm as well as society in general, control should not be left exclusively in the hands of the scientific community (Barber et al., 1973). Furthermore, scientists may be so absorbed in rational processes that they may not fully perceive the impact of the many nonrational components involved in making individual or social decisions (Edsall, 1969). Finally, because professional self-control means that the peers of the experimenter and not the peers of the subjects have the decision-making power, bias and nonobjectivity may operate during the evaluative process (Veatch and Sollitto, 1973).

However, any debate as to who can best monitor investigators' ethical behavior may overlook two important underlying points. First, regardless of the source of the standards, we must consider the problem of effectively implementing them. The "American way" seems to be to approach any problem by appointing a committee. Certainly, we have all served on enough committees to experience the cumbersome and often unproductive manner in which they operate. Second, much research is not funded or is funded by sources that do not specify or carefully monitor human-use guidelines. Some funding sources have a vested interest in the research projects they support, raising the question of whether truly objective and ethical procedures are expected from their investigators.

Thus we have come back full circle to the ethical stance of the individual investigators: if human concern does not emanate from within, then all other action is virtually negated. We can ill-afford the complete scientific detachment illustrated by a comment attributed to a famous rocket scientist: "I just build them; it's not my responsibility where they land." Nor can we tolerate the Nazi (or Watergate) mentality: "I was just following orders."

Those of us who work with children have an especially awesome responsibility for what we do, and we must dedicate ourselves—each in our own conscience—to doing it with care, with compassion, and with humility. These qualities can neither be abrogated in the name of objectivity nor dictated to exist by fiat.

NOTES

1. The Department of Health, Education and Welfare is busily issuing experimental subject-use policies and has to date completed policy revisions for animals, humans (but these fail to translate easily into use with human subjects in special categories), and aborted, live fetuses. The final policy on child use will be among the last to be issued (it has been circulated in draft form only as of this writing). The American Psychological Association has recently redeveloped its own human-use guidelines (1973); however, its coverage of special considerations for child subjects is far from exhaustive. A more focused set of princi-

ples, *Ethical Standards for Research with Children,* has been issued by the Society for Research in Child Development (1973); although not detailed, this does contain a number of important points that are referred to throughout this chapter.

2. It has been suggested that all matters pertaining to human subject participation (consent methods, risk assessment, debriefing procedures, and so on) be published in detail with the article. Journal editors often refuse publication of papers that do not conform to acceptable ethical procedures. However, it has not been fully explored whether they would accept the responsibility for such censorship.

REFERENCES

Ambron, S. R. *Child development.* San Francisco: Rinehart, 1975.

American Psychological Association. *Ethical principles in the conduct of research with human participants. Washington D.C.:* American Psychological Association, 1973.

Barber, B., Lally, J. J., Makarushka, J. L., and Sullivan, D. *Research on human subjects.* New York: Russell Sage, 1973.

Beecher, H. K. *Research and the individual: Human studies.* Boston: Little Brown, 1970.

Brymer, R. A., and Farris, B. Ethical and political dilemmas in the investigation of deviance: A study of juvenile delinquency. In G. Sjoberg (ed.), *Ethics, politics and social research.* Cambridge, Mass.: Schenkman, 1967.

Edsall, G. A positive approach to the problem of human experimentation. *Daedalus* **98** (1969), 463–79.

Etzioni, A. *Genetic fix.* New York: Macmillan, 1973.

Freund, P. A. Introduction: Ethical aspects of experimentation with human subjects. *Daedalus* **98** (1969), vii–xiv.

Gray, S. W. Ethical issues in research in early childhood intervention. *Child.* **18** (1971), 83–89.

Hamm, N. H. The politics of empiricism: Research recommendations of the Joint Commission on Mental Health for Children. *Am. Psychol.* **29** (1974), 9–13.

Jaffe, L. L. Law as a system of control. *Daedalus* **98** (1969), 402–26.

Katz, J. *Experimentation with human beings.* New York: Russell Sage, 1972.

Keith-Spiegel, P., and Spiegel, D. The minor. In D. Spiegel and P. Keith-Spiegel (eds.), *Outsiders U.S.A.: Original papers on 24 disadvantaged groups in American society.* San Francisco: Rinehart, 1973.

Lasagna, L. Special subjects in human experimentation. *Daedalus* **98** (1969), 449–62.

McKinnon, M. Issues in human experimentation: A consumer point of view.

Paper presented at the American Orthopsychiatric Association Meeting, San Francisco, 1974.

Milgram, S. Behavioral study of obedience. *J. Abnorm. Soc. Psychol.* **67** (1963), 371–78.

Mitchell, R. G. The child and experimental medicine. *Br. Med. J.* **1** (1964), 722–26.

Munsinger, H. *Fundamentals of child development.* New York: Holt, Rinehart & Winston, 1975.

Mussen, P., Conger, J., and Kagan, J. *Child development and personality.* New York: Harper & Row, 1974.

Parsons, T. Research with human subjects and the "professional complex." *Daedalus* **98** (1969), 325–60.

Rutstein, D. D. The ethical design of human experiments. *Daedalus* **98** (1969), 523–41.

Society for Research in Child Development. *Ethical standards for research with children. Chicago:* Society for Research in Child Development, 1973.

U.S. Department of Health, Education and Welfare, and National Institutes of Health. Protection of human subjects: Policies and procedures. *Fed. Regist.* November 16, 1973 (draft for public comment).

U.S. Department of Health, Education and Welfare, and National Institutes of Health. Protection of human subjects. *Fed. Regist.,* May 30, 1974.

Veatch, R. M., and Sollitto, S. Human experimentation: The ethical questions persist. *Hastings Cent. Rep.* (June 1973), 1–3.

Institutional Responsibilities and Children's Rights

Part Two shifts in focus from individual mental-health professionals per se to the mental-health institutions that serve children and their families. After all, institutions are made up of individuals, yet the anonymity offered in the guise of "institutional policy" can dole out a good measure of tyranny to the child in need of mental-health care. As agents of society at large, institutions often perform functions that we would prefer not to have to think about. The chapters in Part Two are designed to encourage professionals to examine these often troubling issues.

Dr. Armin P. Thies earned his doctoral degree in clinical psychology at the University of Missouri, Columbia, and learned some "facts of life" about residential treatment facilities for children while working at the Children's Village in Dobbs Ferry, New York. Thies has taught at the University of North Dakota, and is now Assistant Professor of Psychology at St. John's University in Jamaica, New York. His chapter presents some hard issues to be considered by professionals who practice in residential treatment facilities for children.

Dr. Steven J. Apter received a Ph.D. degree in clinical psychology from Syracuse University, where he is now Associate Professor of Special Education. He also directs a psycho-educational training program for troubled children at the Institute for Community Development in Syracuse. Because of his interest in professional training and children's rights, Apter was invited to contribute his thoughts on the special circumstances of service delivery to children in a teaching institution. He addresses the issue of simultaneously casting children as clients and teaching tools.

Dr. Bruce Cushna received a doctorate from the University of Chicago, and taught at the University of Iowa before becoming Associate Director of the Developmental Evaluation Clinic at The Children's Hospital Medical Center, Boston in 1967. Cushna holds faculty appointments at both Boston College and Harvard University, and has been professionally active in national and regional planning for children with developmental disabilities. His chapter addresses the use of institutionalization as a "sanitizing" mechanism that society uses to isolate the retarded person, and argues for an affirmative deinstitutionalization program as the right of handicapped children and adults.

In the final chapter in this part, three uniquely talented people address the issue of institutional record-keeping practices and patients' rights. All three authors are members of Phi Beta Kappa and have achieved distinction in their chosen fields. Mr. Jonathan Brant, a practicing attorney and Harvard Law School graduate, served as Counsel to the Massachusetts Governor's Commission on Privacy and Personal Data. He is now an Assistant Attorney General of Massachusetts. Ms. Gail Garinger, a graduate of Indiana University and Harvard Law School, is a practicing attorney and Associate Director of the New England Resource Center for Protective Services through The Children's Hospital Medical Center and the Judge Baker Guidance Center in Boston. Dr. Rene Tankenoff Brant is a graduate of Harvard Medical School with postgraduate training in pediatrics and adult and child psychiatry. She is a Fellow in Psychiatry at Harvard Medical School and at Boston's Beth Israel Hospital. It is not often that mental-health professionals and members of the legal profession combine their thinking on an important issue in the way that these authors have done.

The chapters that comprise Part Two are all united in their focus on institutional problems in the delivery of mental-health services to children and their parents. Although each chapter examines a different facet of the interface between the institution and the child, all the authors call for the respect that institutions and society at large should grant child-clients and their families. Each chapter offers general suggestions and appropriate directions as to what constructive social action can be taken.

The Facts of Life:
Child Advocacy
and Children's Rights
in Residential Treatment

ARMIN P. THIES

As Rodham (1973) points out in her discussion of children under the law, the needs and interests of children will become legal rights when they are accepted as enforceable claims against other persons or institutions. There is, however, a difference between meeting the needs of children and protecting them from the actions of powerful others. The former denotes positive action for the benefit of children, whereas the latter merely prevents the exploitation or abuse of children by others who are attempting to meet their own needs or interests. In community systems of mental-health services, legal protection for children does not guarantee that services are available to meet a child's particular needs. It is increasingly apparent that advances in children's legal status seldom lead to improved services for children. When social services are flooded and overcrowded, either desperation follows or a seller's market develops. Under such conditions, mere legal or administrative safeguards become impotent and may even lead to other abuses.

THE LAW VERSUS THE CHILD

New York City provides a more than adequate model for the problems that develop when social services are inadequate to meet the needs of the community. New York City has an estimated 20,000–40,000 mentally ill children and another 160,000–200,000 children with serious emotional problems (Office of Children's Services, 1973A). In contrast, the same report notes that there are a total of 175 beds in municipal hospitals for the emergency psychiatric treatment and short-term care of children. Other child-care agencies are so overcrowded that conditions have reached tragic proportions (see Citizen's Committee for Children of New York, 1971, for additional discussion).

Nationally, the greatest advances in the campaign for children's rights have been the extension of constitutional rights and guarantees of due process to children in juvenile- or family-court proceedings. Invalidating the assumption that the needs and interests of children coincide with the needs and interests of their parents or of the state was no small victory for advocates of children's rights. In the Family Court of the State of New York, law guardians are assigned to all children who come before the court as delinquents or "persons in need of supervision" (PINS). PINS children are predelinquents who are found to be "habitually truant," "incorrigible," or "out of lawful control." The function of the law guardian is to protect the interests of the child against both parents and state. The law guardian is supposed to ensure that due process is accorded the child through the requirement of proof beyond reasonable doubt for any petition brought before the court (Office of Children's Services, 1973B). On the surface, such a court process appears to encourage justice. However, in courts with enormous case loads, proof beyond a reasonable doubt becomes a principle by which law guardians dismiss petitions *before* the fact-finding session to lighten the court's unbearable case load. Such a use of this principle does not appear to be consistent with the spirit of recognizing the needs of children.

Although the Family Court, which has contact with these children, may not be in the business of providing social services, no one else seems to be providing such services either. Thus children whose cases have been dismissed before trial receive no consideration concerning needed intervention. In most of these cases, some intervention does seem necessary. A survey of PINS petitions between June 1971 and May 1972 indicated that 65% of the petitions were instituted by the child's mother and that another 27% were instituted by close relatives or the school (Office of Children's Services, 1973B). In these cases, a troubled relationship between the child and the child's primary caretakers evidently required therapeutic intervention.

Similarly, under conditions of inadequate resources for social services, the law guardian may come to view his role not as a protector of the special interests of the child against the state and parent but rather as a protector of the child against placement.

In practice, when various judicial regulations governing the conduct of the Family Court were made without regard to improving the services available to the Family Court, the Court was placed in the position of proceeding expediently but ineffectually or proceeding illegally. The New York State Family Court Act provides for at least two hearings, a fact-finding session, and a disposition session on each petition brought before the Court. For children in detention, two adjournments of not more than ten days each are permitted between the fact-finding and disposition sessions. For children returned home or remanded to a municipal hospital, the Court may adjourn for a reasonable period, not to exceed 60 days. In the same sample of PINS petitions cited above, the time that elapsed between the two court sessions was over six months for 44% of the cases and from three to six months for another 27% (Office for Children's Services, 1973B). For those children who required placement, much of the time was expended seeking treatment facilities to accept the child. If residential treatment is judged appropriate for the child, psychological and psychiatric evaluations are required by the voluntary treatment agencies. Applications for admission must then be made to agencies in seriatum. Each agency may spend several weeks "considering" the application before rejecting the child for admission. Although the law is designed to prevent the prolonged detention of children without treatment, the lack of adequate referral resources either forces the Court to return the child to a destructive home environment or to ignore the lawful time limits placed on court sessions. Once again, well-intentioned legislation designed to protect the interests of children is defeated by the lack of adequate treatment resources.

Many other examples exist in which the law has failed not only to fulfill but even to protect the rights of children. Laws requiring the court to proceed through evaluation centers in municipal hospitals before placing children in state hospitals were designed to prevent inappropriate referrals and custodial care of children in state mental wards. Instead, the procedure has produced "turnstile" children who are shuffled from court to hospital to community and back to court on new charges (Office of Children's Services, 1973A).

As another example of this antithesis between the intent of the law and the resulting effect on children, the New York State Court of Appeals ruled *In re Ellery C.* that PINS children could not be confined with delinquent children. In effect, the ruling prevented the Family Court from placing PINS children in state training schools. Again, this seems to be an apparent step forward in meeting children's needs, particularly their need for treatment. However, there are not enough placement resources for PINS children, and judges are becoming more reluctant to dismiss delinquency petitions against children in favor of PINS petitions, because the court does not want to limit its placement resources (Office of Children's

Services, 1973B). Thus inappropriate remanding to custody replaces improper placement in mental hospitals.

Much of the new emphasis on children's legal rights appears to emanate from the frustration inherent in dealing with huge, poorly functioning bureaucracies. The force of law is seen as the only way to deal with these power-oriented systems. However, the fundamental right on which all other rights of children in trouble depend is the right to treatment; that is, the right to have their special needs fulfilled. For children with emotional problems, child advocacy becomes a mental-health service rather than a legal service. In view of the poor results in constructing systematic guarantees, the particular needs of a child can apparently only be assured to that child through the efforts of individual child advocates.

For the purposes of this discussion, a broad interpretation is made of Rodham's (1973) definition of a child's rights as enforceable claims against others. Thus the rights of a child are not restricted here to the child's special needs and interests that are legally enforceable. They are extended to include those needs and interests that are enforceable as claims against others by virtue of administrative authority or by virtue of the influence exerted by mental-health workers who assume the role of child advocate. In particular, the basic function of any residential treatment center is to provide treatment. Within such a setting, children have a right to expect therapy appropriate to their needs.

The law deals with the rights of treatment only in the negative sense of requiring due process in court hearings where a child is remanded to "treatment" facilities that actually do not have treatment programs but that only offer juveniles custodial care and confinement. Within institutions that do offer therapy programs, a child's right to treatment must compete with the needs of the institution and staff who are in positions of authority and power. The low salaries usually offered to primary caretakers in residential centers for children substantially increase the probability that individuals whose needs conflict with those of the residents fill therapy-delivery positions. In such a situation, the mental-health professional must assume the role of the child's advocate.

In the courtroom, the child advocate is also the adversary of others who attempt to meet their needs at the child's expense. The law guardian functions within very structured rules of conduct and is protected in the role of child advocate. In contrast, mental-health professionals, who assume the role of child advocate within a residential treatment center, become the adversaries of fellow employees and administrators. Because of the possible adverse consequences of these conditions, the self-appointed child advocate must understand how the institution functions and must proceed with caution.

THE STAFF VERSUS THE CHILD

Many institutions develop a familial attitude toward the treatment of children. That attitude is perhaps more characteristic of older institutions with a large percentage of nonprofessional or semiprofessional staff. The family model of treatment is characterized by paternalistic administrators who attempt to control the personal lives of the staff members and to protect them from charges of misconduct by professional supervisors. Such institutions also contain staff members who implicitly view children in their charge as in some way "their children" and who become parental surrogates.

Such a model of treatment affords employees certain advantages that motivate staff members to perpetuate the model. The most obvious advantage to staff members is job security. Personnel problems are not handled by dismissing or vindicating a staff member, but an attempt is made to deal with any difficulties that may arise "within the family." Case dispositions are determined by personal influence rather than by evidence of misconduct. Such protection, moreover, often extends beyond the humane and professional consideration that individuals deserve and tends to perpetuate contacts between the children and incompetent staff members. Such a situation is often intolerable for more competent or qualified personnel, who are usually independent and interested in improving services. Under the family-surrogate model, individuals who commit intolerable abuses are bribed into resigning with the promise of a good recommendation. This practice permits incompetent individuals to "make the rounds" of treatment agencies in a particular geographical location before moving to a new area.

Children with whom a staff member forms an affectionate relationship benefit from having a surrogate parent in that the staff member frequently makes inordinate sacrifices for the child and spends his or her own time and money to be with that child. Implicit in such a relationship, however, is the absence of actual legal or familial ties between the child and the staff member. In contrast, those children who for some reason are not acceptable to staff members may acutely feel the effects of rejection. Not only are they denied the same positive regard that they see other children receiving, but they may actually be neglected if much of the staff member's motivation to care for the children is derived from the satisfaction received in acting as a parent rather than in behaving as a competent therapist.

Mental-health professionals who are new to these institutions find it particularly difficult to function effectively as child advocates. The new staff members quickly learn that their professional qualifications do not influence others to follow their recommendations. Since diverse services must be provided to children in residential treatment, the staff of child-caring agencies is often composed of individuals with a wide range of education, experience, and personal skills. In addition, nonprofessionals and semiprofessionals are frequently threatened by highly trained experts. Conflicts between these two types of mental-health workers center on the relative value of training versus experience. To relatively untrained staff members, experience refers not only to the amount of previous contact with disturbed children, but also to seniority in terms of length of employment in the institution. Those who embrace the family model of treatment view seniority as a measure of loyalty to the institution and as an indication of personal influence among other staff members. Under such conditions, mental-health professionals may find their educational training openly viewed as irrelevant "book work." In addition, highly mobile professionals are seldom able to accrue seniority to increase their own influence.

Professionals who assume that they can rely on their professional qualifications and academic degrees may become frustrated when confronted with the necessity of demonstrating their competence while nonprofessionals are not required to meet the same requirement to be accepted. In addition, nonprofessional staff members frequently use their experience as an excuse for disregarding treatment recommendations that interfere with their own needs. Thus the conflict in values over experience versus training can lead to a polarization between professionals and nonprofessionals. However, because nonprofessionals are usually the primary caretakers and have the most contact with the children, professionals cannot ignore the needs of nonprofessional staff members if they expect to contribute to the effective treatment of the children.

Mental-health professionals in such situations are unable to enter the institution's covert power structure merely on the basis of their education and training; they must therefore demonstrate that they are a valuable resource rather than a threat to other staff members. The self-esteem and self-confidence of nonprofessionals can be raised by recognizing the legitimate value of experience as well as the real limitations of applying education to a specific situation. On the other hand, professionals increase their own value as resources by continually demonstrating that their training has acquainted them with many alternative methods for reaching treatment goals. In addition, nonprofessionals need to be reminded that experience can limit perspective because experience implies a method of finding "what works." The criteria for determining the effectiveness of an experientially based method of treatment may be the rewards the staff members receive as a result of implementing the method rather than the benefits the children receive.

THE CHILD'S OWN BEHAVIOR

Thus methods can frequently develop that maintain the status quo (prevent inconvenience to the staff) and that are repressive in nature. Such a condition is exemplified in the boasts of employees who refer to themselves as "strong" staff because of their control over the children, a control that frequently involves physical discipline. The arguments of these staff members are particularly impressive when they point out the failure of "weak staff" to maintain order, especially immediately after the strong staff leave for the day. Weak staff are often those who attempt to grant children some freedom of behavior to encourage them to control themselves and who attempt to build self-esteem in these children by respecting their rights. Predelinquent children tend to take advantage of a situation to the extent that they have not developed internalized self-control. In this respect, the methods employed by strong staff members ironically train children to depend upon external authority and defeat treatment. In contrast to the repressive measures employed by the supposedly "strong" staff members, methods that attempt to develop internal self-control are viewed by the children as cues to totally disregard the rules of proper conduct.

The behavior of the children also often tends to promote conditions that not only undermine treatment but the protection of their own human rights. When a child reports that he has been abused, the behavior of the child frequently compromises the credibility of the report. Such complaints are frequently made when a child is about to be disciplined for a serious infraction of the rules, such as running away from the institution. The child may attempt to distract others from his offense or to excuse the offense by reporting previous incidents of abuse against himself or other children by particular staff members—usually the same people who are to administer the restrictions to be imposed for the child's present misbehavior.

Anyone who assumes the role of the child's advocate in this situation is placed in triple jeopardy. First, investigation of the charge may undermine the authority of the primary caretaker who is accused, because the child may interpret any inconvenience experienced by the staff member as evidence of the child's own power to cause trouble for others. Second, the child needs to be protected from retaliation until the facts are, if ever, determined. Finally, the accused staff member may also interpret any inquiries or removal of the child from his care as evidence of distrust or personal attack. Such a reaction by the accused staff member would certainly undermine the cooperative working relationships that had been formed. Protecting the child's rights may occur at the expense of weakening the therapeutic elements in the milieu.

Under these conditions, it is advisable for persons who become aware of the child's complaints to refer the child to the supervisor of the accused staff member. That referral does not relieve the staff member of the responsibility of assuming the role of child advocate, nor does it guarantee that appropriate action will be taken. However, at least the proper authorities have been notified and have not been alienated by capricious independent action.

PREPARING THE STAFF FOR ADVOCACY

On occasions when supervisors fail to take appropriate action, the self-appointed advocate of the child must follow through with considerable risk to his or her professional efficacy in the institution. Therefore, it is highly desirable for mental-health professionals to spend a sizable proportion of their initial effort after entering the institution in cultivating personal and professional relationships with other staff members. Nonprofessional staff are far less likely to view a confrontation on children's rights in terms of objective criteria or detached judgements. They are also, however, more likely to "forgive" a clinician for aggressive advocacy for a child if that clinician has previously supported the staff member by providing information that has helped the staff member to perform more competently or by demonstrating respect for those strengths that the staff member does possess.

Thus much of the therapeutic effort of clinical or casework staff, who are in an advisory or a consulting relationship rather than in a supervisory relationship with primary caretakers, must be directed toward modifying the behavior of coworkers and colleagues. In this regard, clinicians do not usually use the methods that they encourage others to employ through their therapy recommendations to clients. Providing positive reinforcement and support for the desirable activities of other staff members is infrequently practiced by many professionals, who rely instead on the weight of educational authority or reason (usually their own) to influence others.

In addition, the rights of children are often violated by staff members as a side-effect of efforts to avoid censure by supervisors for failing to maintain order or to work efficiently. Although a caretaker can be punished for abusing a child's rights, professionals frequently fail to provide alternative behaviors that caretakers can perform to better meet their responsibilities. Through these two methods of providing support to other workers, the mental-health professional can develop cooperative working relationships that will not collapse if a confrontation over the abuse of a child's rights occurs.

For professional staff who function in a supervisory capacity, the use of power over other staff in terms of economic sanctions becomes optional. However, administrative power is limited in its ability to promote the interpersonal relationships that are crucial to even behaviorally oriented therapies. Just as laws and judicial decisions can only establish the conditions that would promote therapeutic interactions between adults and children (Goldstein, 1974), administrative edicts can do nothing to force such interactions to occur. The threat of dismissal or loss of promotion may force staff members to conform to institutional rules or to the structure of a treatment plan, but the resulting discontent may sabotage the substance of the therapeutic program.

An administrative practice that also compounds the disadvantages of experience in the absence of training is hiring previously institutionalized residents as primary caretakers. This practice ensures the repeated use of old treatment methods that have become obsolete or unacceptable. In the absence of evaluation and in-service training or formal education, these individuals are also inclined to bring personal conflicts into the present setting. Considering the severity of maladjustment usually associated with residents in institutions, placing former patients in therapeutic roles appears unwarranted, especially when they are not provided with a great deal of supervison and support. Continuing to help such staff members work out their personal problems while providing services to more severely disturbed children may be impossible in view of the limited resources available to most institutions.

However, former residents, if they are reflective, can be more understanding toward children with problems similar to their own than other staff members may be. In addition, former residents undoubtedly have had intimate experiences with some of the conditions and variables that foster the disturbed behaviors observed in institutions. Such staff members are certainly in a better position than many professionals to determine the treatment goals that would ensure the best chance for continued adjustment after the child returns to the community. However, understanding and experience by themselves do not guarantee effective treatment. Unless former residents can demonstrate flexibility, the ability to adopt alternative therapy techniques and to cooperate with other professionals, their understanding and experience may be put to better use in some other role than that of primary caretaker. In any institution, the needs and rights of children are best protected when there are few needs and rights of staff members that interface with treatment.

THE INSTITUTION VERSUS THE CHILD

In addition to competing with the needs and rights of individual staff members, children in institutions must also compete with the more general needs of the institution itself. These needs are enforced collectively by a group of staff members or by supervisors through their administrative authority. The child's rights to privacy, freedom of expression, choice of activities, protection from adults and peers, possession of personal items, communication with others, freedom of movement, and especially the right to treatment are encroached on by decisions that can be termed "administrative" rather than "treatment."

Administrative decisions are actually based on "hidden agendas" but are justified on the compelling logic of three arguments:

1. For children to receive treatment, the institution must survive.
2. An institution that is efficient and functions smoothly can provide better services.
3. An individual child may be denied special treatment because limited resources exist and other children are also in need of treatment.

Whether a decision is merely administrative or actually therapeutic is frequently difficult to determine. However, the characteristics of administrative decisions are defined by the action taken based on the three previously stated arguments. The first argument is merely a variation of the basic assumption that the needs and interests of children coincide with the needs and interests of their parents or the state. In fact, the needs and interests of institutions do not always coincide with the needs of children. An administrative versus a treatment decision based on the first argument is made when an action is to be taken that will benefit the institution in some way without demonstrable therapeutic value to the individual children affected by that action. The institution needs to earn money and therefore must have good public relations. Thus the need for the institution to survive may justify delaying patient discharges to maintain the census. Or may justify eliminating off-campus privileges as a reaction to infrequent community incidents caused by individual children. Such occasions provide opportunities for advocacy.

With regard to the second argument, desiring to maintain a smoothly functioning institution seems contrary to the realities of treating disturbed children, especially predelinquent or delinquent children. Most systems of psychotherapy require that disturbed behaviors be exhibited before they can be modified. Some controlled disorder with continual problem solving seems a more appropriate environment in a residential treatment center.

Control is the principal issue in attempts to make disturbed children behave normally while institutionalized. For some reason, many staff members assume that if emotionally disturbed children exhibit behavior problems, the staff is not doing a good job and treatment is not occurring. Because problem solving requires effort, staff and administrators may be motivated to avoid problems through methods of control that are of dubious therapeutic value.

Action taken by staff members that appears to be for their convenience is the primary indication of an administrative rather than a treatment decision. Thus justified by the need for an ordered institution, children may be escorted to and from school to ensure their attendance, but may have no escort when they return to a truly dangerous community. The doors to children's lockers may be removed to enable staff members to more easily inspect the neatness of personal belongings or to expose stolen items and weapons. Partitions for privacy in dormatories are not provided to reduce sex play and fighting.

Finally, the last of the three arguments that justify administrative decisions is perhaps the most difficult for a child advocate to refute. Few if any objective criteria exist to determine whether additional therapeutic efforts on behalf of an individual child will yield results commensurate with the expenditure of additional resources. In clinical practice, decisions regarding the allocation of therapeutic resources are often professional judgments based on expert opinion. Therefore, it is difficult to martial evidence in support of a position as the child's advocate.

The inconsistency with which this argument is applied is the best indication that hidden agendas are involved in the decision process. Ironically, a child's advocate may actually oppose special treatment programs in favor of referring a child to a more appropriate environment. For example, a severely disturbed child who requires intensive, individual attention and who frequently absconds from an open institution would benefit from a closed psychiatric setting. However, administrators or other staff may oppose such a referral, despite the common recommendations of several clinical staff members, by rationalizing that everything possible should be done for the child before a referral is made. Implicit in this concern are two assumptions: (1) that no other institution can provide treatment of equal or better quality, and (2) that a referral indicates failure. It is not surprising that when the child continues to be a major behavioral problem, political pressure develops to have the child removed from the institution. The child's advocate then must oppose inappropriate arbitrary referrals and must support the original recommendation that may require more time to implement. In view of such erratic behavior, a child's advocate may well question the motivation behind decisions to deprive other children of special or individualized treatment programs when such programs can be instituted and when they seem appropriate.

In conclusion, systems, rules, and laws in themselves will never adequately protect children's rights or fulfill children's needs. In the institution, as in the courtroom, children must rely on adults to speak for them. Anyone, including law guardians, who is involved in decision processes regarding the welfare of children cannot be totally without personal interests. Mental-health professionals must remain aware of the conflict between their own interests and the interests of the children whom they seek to protect. However, child advocacy is a professional responsibility that must be assumed. Ultimately, the rights of children in residential treatment may depend on it.

REFERENCES

Citizen's Committee for Children of New York. *A dream deferred: Child welfare in New York City.* New York: Citizen's Committee for Children of New York, 1971.

Goldstein, J., Freud, A., and Solnit, A. J. *Beyond the best interests of the child.* New York: Free Press, 1974.

Office of Children's Services. *Desperate situation: Desperate service.* New York: Office of Children's Services, Judicial Conference of the State of New York, August 1973A.

Office of Children's Services. *The PINS child: A plethora of problems.* New York: Office of Children's Services, Judicial Conference of the State of New York, September 1973B. *In re: Ellery C.,* 32 New York Second District, 588 (1973).

Rodham, Hillary. Children under the law. *Harv. Educ. Rev.* 43 (1973), 487–514.

The Rights of Children in Teaching Institutions

STEVEN J. APTER

According to Knowles (1968), the teaching hospital represents the interface between the acquisition of knowledge and the utilization of that knowledge to provide high-quality medical care and to prevent disease. While all hospitals are concerned with the care of sick and injured people, the teaching hospital has additional responsibilities, including the conservation and expansion of knowledge through education and research. Thus while it attempts to provide the best possible care for patients, the teaching hospital is also charged with teaching medical students, training interns and residents, providing support services for schools that train nurses, dieticians, medical librarians, physiotherapists, and technicians, offering inservice education for practicing physicians, and disseminating information pertaining to clinical experience and research findings through publication and lecturing.

Although Knowles agrees that the teaching hospital environment—characterized by constant scrutiny of procedures, questioning of conventional wisdom, and application of the scientific method—is likely to produce an optimal level of patient care, he cites a number of issues raised by the inherent conflicts between the goals of education and service. One problem area in the United States, where health is viewed as a citizen's right, concerns the responsiveness of the teaching hospital to the service needs of the community. The interface between the acquisition and utilization of knowledge in a teaching hospital, Knowles feels, must lean more toward active service.

GENERAL NEEDS OF PATIENTS

Richmond (1961) is also concerned with the reactions of patients in hospital situations involving teaching and research. In an attempt to define the kinds of problems patients face as they enter the hospital for treatment, Richmond states: "In the setting of the vast physical structure of the modern out-patient department and hospital, the patient often enters with some degree of depression, anxiety concerning separation, and certainly considerable preoccupation with himself (p. 349). On that basis as well as on his clinical experience, Richmond sees *respect* as the basic need of patients— respect for their identity, privacy, and time. Richmond stresses that patients for the most part relate to the people on staff (not to the institution), and that respect for patient needs can be increased by example. Thus if faculty members in teaching hospitals show sensitivity to patients' needs, so will students. What students in teaching situations often need is the "permission" to be friendly; faculty can provide this permission by example. In so doing, faculty members also help to provide the sensitive patient care that should exist in spite of the complexities of a teaching hospital.

WHAT ABOUT THE CHILDREN?

A review of the literature in this area reveals a curious lack of attention to the rights of children in teaching institutions, especially with regard to the psychological treatment of children. Yet the need for concentrated focus on the mental-health needs and rights of children seems clear. This chapter specifically examines the rights of children in teaching situations. These rights can be categorized within any number of equally appropriate dimensions. Here children's rights are discussed in terms of four major issues: assessment, treatment, confidentiality, and consideration of the child as a whole person.

A Child's Right to Appropriate Assessment

The major work in the area of assessment is reported by Mercer (1974). Discussing the results of a long-term study of school and agency classification procedures, Mercer concludes that current psychological-assessment procedures are in violation of at least five specific rights of children: (1) the right to evaluation within a culturally appropriate, normative framework; (2) the right to be assessed as multidimensional human beings; (3) the right to a complete education; (4) the right to be free of stigmatizing labels; and (5) the right to cultural identity and respect.

Ross, DeYoung, and Cohen (1971), in their discussion of the newly emerging phenomenon of legal opposition to special class placement, identify four major arguments that child advocates often voice against such placement procedures. These arguments have obvious implications for children's rights to appropriate assessment; they include: (1) testing, which does not accurately measure the learning abilities of many children; (2) administering tests incompetently; (3) failing to give parents an adequate opportunity to participate in the placement decision; and (4) programming special education inadequately. The personal harm created by improper placement under any or all of these circumstances is irreparable.

Institutions that teach psychological assessment do just that. They rarely teach students to combat the many vagaries and ambiguities that stem from evaluation procedures; rather, students expect and are expected to learn the proper administration, scoring, and interpretation of specific psychological tools during their teaching hospital experience.

Unfortunately, the experience of learning to perform psychological assessments has become functionally autonomous: we do it because it's there! Such an attitude is an obvious violation of a child's right to a complete, personal, and considered assessment. A two or three hour visit with a psychology intern that includes a brief interview, an intelligence test, and a projective technique is not necessarily an appropriate assessment. A series of four or five interviews behind the one-way mirror of a child psychiatry unit cannot be considered an appropriate assessment. Nor does the addition of 15 or 20 "in-depth" interviews with the child's parents necessarily facilitate a proper evaluation.

The point is that the rights cited by Mercer should hold even in a teaching-hospital situation. When these rights are disregarded, the potential dangers to which Ross, DeYoung, and Cohen (1971) refer often become facts. Children are multidimensional people who have had a variety of experiences and who come from a wide range of cultural and family backgrounds. They have a right to be assessed in that context. Moreover, the results of psychological-assessment procedures can have an incredible impact on a child's life, and children have a right to be assessed with this fact in mind.

Finally, teachers and students in teaching-hospital situations should be aware of the potential distortion that may arise from becoming so enmeshed in pathology that they are blind to the concept of health. Children have the right to be assessed in an atmosphere that looks for—and is able to recognize and report—healthy psychological adjustment as well as psychopathology.

A Child's Right to Treatment

Children have the right to psychological treatment that is comprehensive, continuous, coordinated, and compassionate. Here we examine some specific qualities of teaching institutions that may impede the delivery of this kind of treatment.

The Child's Right to Treatment versus the Child's Potential Value as a Training Case.   This is a long-standing problem in teaching hospitals. The time and energy that the staff must expend in teaching, supervision, and related duties preclude providing treatment to all children in need of service. Consequently, many teaching hospitals accept a limited number of treatment cases, usually on the basis of their teaching potential.

This poses a problem for children who need tretament but who do not meet the established criteria required to be accepted as training cases. The criteria themselves can often be confusing; children may be refused treatment because they are not likely to benefit, too likely to benefit, too similar to patients currently being served, or not similar enough to patients currently being served. Thus, at times, teaching hospitals identify children in need of service and then find it necessary to refuse them treatment, thereby creating an obvious conflict between a child's right to treatment and an institution's viewpoint as to treatment potential. Usually, the individual loses this kind of battle.

There is another solution, however. If staff members (faculty and students) agree to provide treatment for all children who need it, the staff would not necessarily have to be solely responsible for this treatment. A hospital could offer treatment itself when appropriate, and could assist in redirecting patients to some other local treatment setting when necessary. In this way, the hospital could provide the services it has to offer to children and a more complete learning experience for students, as well as respond to the right of every child to be treated.

The Community's Need for Service versus the Hospital's Limited Resources.   This issue is the same as the one just discussed, but broader in scope. The solution could be similar, too. Does the teaching hospital have a duty to be responsive to the right of children in the community to psychological treatment? The development of programs to meet community needs either in-house or at other settings would be a valuable teaching and learning experience.

The Insularity of the Teaching Hospital versus the Child's Right to Comprehensive Planning.   Children who are fortunate enough to receive treatment still find some of their rights jeopardized. It is important for child therapists to remember that children have lives outside the clinical environment. Often, however, the emphasis on teaching in-hospital skills almost by definition excludes participation in planning a comprehensive treatment program. Even a well-supervised process of therapy does not constitute adequate treatment if the remainder of a child's life is ignored.

The report by the Task Force on children out of school in Boston (1970) cites the common finding that mental-health agencies tend to ignore the role of the school in the child's environment. Consequently, staff members in these agencies remain uninformed about major areas of a child's interpersonal world. Instead, they can only continue to view a child from a very narrow perspective, thus decreasing the likelihood that the child will receive truly adequate treatment.

The Teaching Hospital's Need for Access to Patients versus the Child's Right to Service that Provides the "Least Drastic Alternative" and the Quickest Return to Normal Community Life. At times, the need for patients to be accessible for teaching purposes combined with the isolation of a teaching-hospital staff keeps patients in more intensive treatment programs than might otherwise be necessary. The vast amount of literature on the negative effects of institutionalization does not need to be repeated here. The conclusion that, whenever possible, persons should be treated outside the hospital environment and provided with services in their own communities no longer seems contestable. Therapists must not only provide treatment for children in need; they must also avoid unnecessary treatment when no need exists.

The Child's Right to Continuity of Treatment versus the Hospital's Policy of Service Rotations for Students. Treatment that is continually disrupted by service rotations and other administrative and scheduling complexities is likely to be ineffective. In fact, the continual changing of therapists may well cause additional problems for the child patient. Children have a right to continuous therapeutic relationships with a minimal number of people. Teaching hospitals should maintain sufficient flexibility to ensure that this most important need is met.

The Child's Right to Treatment as an Individual. In addition to the five major conflicts between the rights of children and the specialized needs of teaching hospitals just discussed, other rights of children (especially the right to treatment as an individual, not as a case) are sometimes violated in teaching-hospital situations and in other environments as well. The legal right to treatment (Morris, 1970) and the legal rights of children (Marker and Friedman, 1973) are well established at this point, however. Hopefully, violations of a child's right to treatment will also disappear soon.

A Child's Right to Confidentiality

McGuire (1974), examining the issue of confidentiality in child psychotherapy, drew three major conclusions from his study:

1. No clear, consistent, unified set of principles seems to exist with regard to this issue.
2. A general lack of awareness exists (at least in some psychologists) concerning the content and applicability of the existing APA Code of Ethics (1963).
3. A tendency seems to be developing for mental-health workers to operate according to the unwritten principle that children should be given the same rights of confidentiality as adults.

On this last point, McGuire calls for renewed professional consideration. This discrepancy may be found in the APA Code of Ethics (1963). Principle 6, "Confidentiality," draws no distinction between adults and children. Principle 7, "Client Welfare," states in part that a psychologist should allow personal information to be divulged only after ". . . the responsible person is fully aware of the purposes of the interview, testing, or evaluation and of the ways in which the information may be used." Principle 8, "Client Relationship," states in part: "When the client is not competent to evaluate the situation (as in the case of a child), the person responsible for the client is informed. . . ."

The dilemma for the teaching hospital seems clear: who should be consulted—the parent or the child? This is an important conflict, because so many issues pertain to confidentiality and the invasion of privacy in the treatment of children in teaching hospitals (the use of a one-way mirror, audio and video taperecordings that are later played back to large numbers of people, interviewing children in front of groups of students, and the like).

One possible solution is to inform and seek consent from both parents and child in each appropriate case. Even if the APA Code of Ethics (1963) and the laws concerning informed consent seem to favor the adult, as they clearly do at the present time, no reason has yet been advanced for withholding this information from the child. Certainly, we must respond to the child's rights as well as those of the parents. Otherwise, the parents and the mental-health professional find themselves involved in a manipulative scheme to achieve their own ends while ignoring the child's right to know.

The child's right to know extends beyond the actual mechanical arrangements that are necessary to meet the ongoing teaching responsibilities of the teaching hospital. If outside persons are in contact with the therapist, if the therapist must report information to anyone, if there are requests for information from persons or agencies influencing the life of the child— if any or all of these conditions prevail, the child has a right to know.

A Child's Right to Be Considered as a Whole Person

This may appear to be a somewhat unusual right when compared with the rights previously discussed, but it does merit careful attention. Children are whole, unique individuals and are entitled to be treated accordingly. The right to consideration as a whole person assumes many forms. We examine some of the major ones below.

The Right to be Different. Kittrie (1971) presents a comprehensive and solidly based argument for the right to be different. Kittrie's main concern is the ever-approaching therapeutic state, whereas our concern here is the current state of therapy in the teaching hospital. Nevertheless, the right to be different remains, and psychologists must be willing and able to accept some individual differences as nonpathological. In this regard, Denzin (1971) points out the tendency of some mental-health professionals to develop a self-serving version of treatment that seems to consider lower-class, nonwhite, ethnic groups most in need of service. Denzin cautions: ". . . one should keep in mind the moral and 'scientific' perspective of social workers and physicians who act, in a sense, as moral entrepreneurs in the *production* of deviant parents" (my emphasis) (pp. 28–29).

It is the production of deviance that the teaching hospital must guard against. The need for psychopathology for use as teaching material can overwhelm the child's right to be different. Here, too, we must keep in mind the vast amount of research (Rosenthal and Rosnow, 1969) on the effects of expectations on outcomes. Surely we will produce deviance if we begin by assuming it is present. Just as certainly, we will deprive children of their rights to uniqueness and individuality that are so crucial to their psychological devolpment.

The Right to Be Seen as Whole. When we see a child in a teaching hospital, we see only one part of a very complex person. It is essential that we overcome the insularity of the teaching-hospital environment and find ways to see the child as a total person. Witter (1971) discusses the need to consider variations in socioeconomic status, ethnic-group membership, and specific school environments when attempting to define and treat a child's pathological behavior. The ecological psychologists have shown us that the disturbance is not always or solely to be found in the child, but rather that it lies more often in the complex interaction between the child and his or her environment. It follows, then, that the treatment must not always focus solely on the child; this is the caution for the teaching hospital. Accepting children who are referred for diagnosis and treatment makes it difficult to see more than pathology in a child and anything at all outside the child. We must make a conscious effort to see the whole child and the child's whole picture.

The Right to Be Seen as a Person.   We do not see children as people with all the rights and duties thereof. All the recent work on children's liberation (Farson, 1974; Gottlieb, 1973) points to our denial of rights to children. Politically, economically, legally, and sexually, we have double standards for adults and children. Often these standards are set "for the child's own good." Usually, however, the end result of the double standard is not what was originally intended.

Who represents the millions of children in the government administration? Who will conduct the basic research that is needed to make programs out of the never-ending stream of White House conference proposals and mental-health committee reports? Why are children being incarcerated today for offenses that would not be considered crimes if they were committed by adults? There are many more questions than answers to be found here, but one overall conclusion seems to be that although we like to see ourselves as a child-oriented society, we really are not.

Zigler (1972), in discussing the evaluation of children's programs, points out what is perhaps the most surprising way in which we fail to treat children as people:

It is something *later* that we are shooting for. It is this kind of insidious thinking that I am here to attack; when we talk about the quality of the lives of citizens in this country, we seem to always be talking about the quality of the lives of adults, so that when we mount a program for children we always want to assess its future results (p. 3).

Staff members of the teaching hospital must beware of this trap. It is important to treat children with regard to their future lives, but not exclusively. Children are people now, and our policies and procedures and methods must take that fact into consideration. Sometimes, again, the mission of the teaching hospital makes it difficult to respond to the here-and-now needs of the children it serves. We are more oriented toward the long-term result—the effect on the adult that the child will become. That is not enough; children have a right to be treated as people now.

SUMMARY AND CONCLUSIONS

We have examined the rights of children in teaching institutions with regard to assessment, treatment, confidentiality, and consideration as a whole person. These categories are far from mutually exclusive, and our discussion contains a considerable amount of overlap. These issues are designed to serve as a general and flexible outline of the rights of children in teaching institutions; they are not to be regarded as a rigid code of laws.

At this point, I would like to offer a few thoughts that occurred to me as I wrote this chapter as tentative conclusions:

1. Although teaching institutions have additional responsibilities, they share the burden of patient care with other hospital settings and must be equally responsive. Children's rights should not be diminished when they move from a nonteaching to a teaching institution.

2. "Teaching" in an institution must become more functional, more oriented toward problem solving. Perhaps this is the area where the interface between the acquisition of knowledge and its utilization can be most improved.

3. The kinds of psychological-assessment and treatment procedures identified here as being deficient and in violation of the rights of children almost by definition also constitute poor teaching. There does not have to be a conflict between teaching and service. If we really examine our policies and want to change, teaching and service to children can both be improved.

REFERENCES

American Psychological Association. Ethical standards of psychologists. *Am. Psychol.* **18** (1963), 56–60.

Denzin, N. K. Introduction: Wednesday's child. *Trans.* (July/August 1971), 28–29.

Farson, R. E. *Birthrights.* New York: MacMillan, 1974.

Gottlieb, D. (ed.). *Children's liberation.* Englewood Cliffs, N.J.: Prentice-Hall, 1973.

Kittrie, N. N. *The right to be different.* Baltimore: Penguin, 1971.

Knowles, J. H. (ed.). *Views of medical education and medical care.* Cambridge, Mass.: Harvard University Press, 1968.

Marker, G., and Friedman, P. R. Rethinking children's rights. *Child. Today* (November/December 1973), 8–10.

McGuire, J. M. Confidentiality and the child in psychotherapy. *Prof. Psychol.* (1974), 375–79.

Mercer, J. R. A policy statement on assessment procedures and the rights of children. *Harv. Educ. Rev.* **44** (1974), 328–44.

Morris, G. H. (ed.). *The mentally ill and the right to treatment.* Springfield, Ill.: Thomas, 1970.

Richmond, J. B. Patient reaction to the teaching and research situation. *J. Med. Educ.* **36** (1961), 347–52.

Rosenthal, R., and Rosnow, R. L. (eds.). *Artifact in behavioral research.* New York: Academic Press, 1969.

Ross, S. R., Jr., DeYoung, H. G., and Cohen, J. S. Confrontation: Special education placement and the law. *Excep. Child.* **38** (1971), 5–12.

Task Force on Children Out of School. *The way we go to school: exclusion of children in Boston.* Boston: Beacon Press, 1970.

Witter, C. Drugging and schooling. *Trans.* (July/August 1971), 31–34.

Zigler, E. F. Children's needs in the 70s: A federal perspective. *J. Clin. Child Psychol.* **1** (1972), 3–6.

They'll Be Happier
With Their Own Kind

BRUCE CUSHNA

> "But the children of inferior parents,
> and all defective children that are
> born to others, shall be put out of
> sight in secrecy and mystery, as is
> befitting."
>
> *The Republic,* Book V
> Plato

A judgment expressed about other individuals often conceals the beliefs of the person or social group making the statement. The segregationalist viewpoint that any group is of such great difference that it cannot be mingled with the majority or with presumed higher-ranking groups is a familiar rationalization. The same logic is being applied with widespread social acceptance at this time to groups labeled mentally incapable.

Probably the worst present abasement is to be called mentally retarded. This classification not only incorporates all the derogation of being called "stupid," but also connotes the weighty sophistication of a judgment of mental incompetence that evokes many affective reactions, among them rejection, pity, and/or anxiety over responsibility for the individual so labeled. The label is also, so readily accepted as necessitating such extreme forms of confinement and residence patterns, that only in the 1970s has

The author was supported in part at the time of the writing of this chapter by the U.S. Department of Health, Education and Welfare, Division of Developmental Disabilities Project No. 50-P-05163 and Maternal and Child Health Project No. 928. For the discussion, reflection, consideration, and constructive criticism of the points outlined here, I appreciate the contributions of Allen C. Crocker, John M. Shlien, William E. Kiernan, Jean M. Zadig, Marie Cullinane, Elizabeth Zausmer, William A. Granville, and my wife, Elizabeth Ryan Cushna.

the general public recognized the de facto effect of denying large numbers of citizens their constitutional rights. It is well known that such labeling has permitted thousands of persons to be incarcerated in concentration-camp environments. The misery, suffering, and dehumanization of individuals who are labeled mentally retarded is receiving increasing publicity. However, the popular inclination that allows such practices to become so widespread deserves deeper consideration here.

HISTORICAL PERSPECTIVES

Human societies always appear to have had their ostracized elements. Most histories of the mentally retarded focus on the middle of the nineteenth century as the period of awareness that spawned institutions for the retarded. However, the tendency to dehumanize "retardates" and to treat them as outcasts seems to stem from deeper currents within western culture.

The common historical timing of the Industrial Revolution and the origin of institutions for the retarded is no coincidence. As the social class system on a mass scale became more rigid, the problems of dealing with incompetents became a greater social issue. It is logical that a society organized on a mass-production basis would become more concerned with those members who could not efficiently fit into this model. The classification of "moronic" or "feeble-minded" became a necessary feigned alibi, blaming a presumed individual fault or defect, rather than recognizing the actual causes of this failure to be within the social system.

The distinction between authentic and adventitious types of retardation originated as part of this logical sequence. The authentically retarded exhibit conditions that can be explained on a physical, genetic, or so-called "endogenous" basis. The adventitiously retarded are the exogenous social rejects, the "six-hour retarded children," the environmentally reprived, the bulk of those institutionalized due to "unknown causes," the culturally impoverished poor. This is the group that Braginsky and Braginsky (1971) recognized as "social debris," with the contingency: "This does not mean that poverty alone can account for the putative personal defects or the incarceration of individuals, but it appears to be a necessary condition" (p. 161).

SOCIOECONOMIC CORRELATIONS

Some theorists interpret the current compounding of intellectual deficit with economic impoverishment to mean that social limitations, lack of learning opportunities, and restrictions of mobility thwart curiosity and mental growth. Others take the more fixed viewpoint that the poor are poor because they lack the ingenuity and the wherewithal to overcome their individual limitations. The latter view can be reduced to a genetic-inheritance theory: those who remain poor have simply failed to benefit from the probabilities of meiotic shuffling and later matching of parental inheritable traits. Such a position is closely correlated to the viewpoint of predestination. Regardless of where we take a stand on this theoretical spectrum, we must be careful not to confuse or to contaminate this stand with racial bigotry. There seems to be an inescapable linkage between socioeconomic status and the scores from ability-measuring devices compiled to date. This linkage demonstrates the effect and possibly the means by which the poorer elements, particularly of North American social groups, are being outsmarted by the richer elements. Perhaps worse than that, viewing the extremes of the situation and following the Braginskys' (1971) arguments, it can be seen that the poorer social groups are not only being taken advantage of but are actually being victimized at the present time.

Various rationalizations indicate that the poor are not merely stupid. Most of them center around troubling emotional aspects that vary from middle-class standards. It is said that with greater tolerance, variant family patterns will eventualy achieve greater acceptance. A greater incidence of father absence and broken homes should not be subject to value judgments. More open aggression and even a preponderance of child abuse as well as physical assault are to be understood as reactions to the frustrations of a particular way of life. It is being said that the poor have their own, more personal systems of language. The poor have their own lessons of survival that they master well. Nevertheless, such rationalizations only serve to avoid the issue that the economically disadvantaged segments of American society are not provided with the learning experiences or the greater cultural exposure that would allow the younger members of these social groupings to decide whether they want to remain where they are. These arguments also conceal the social operation that denies younger members of a disadvantaged segment supported access to and/or orientation toward consistent learning experiences that could lessen their probability of remaining in a vulnerable social position.

The poor are deprived of opportunity. The poor are abased and called stupid. The result of the correlation between socioeconomic standing and mental abilities appears to be a reflection of the fact that the stupid members of a society are defined as those to whom least financial resources are allocated. This distribution of earning power is built into the societal class structure. The educational system, as John Dewey (1959) so clearly recognized, is merely the reflection (and the tool) of the greater society that supports it.

Social Class and Special Classes in School Systems

From this point of view, the educable mentally retarded classes were relegated to failure. The two disparate social elements (the mildly authentically retarded and the adventitiously deprived populations) resisted common educational placement. Poor children were segregated because they exhibited behavior problems that modeled aggressive or acting-out behaviors prevalent in their homes. This exclusion procedure was legitimized in expectedly low, although often admittedly unmotivated, IQ scores. But the poor children did not like being called "retarded." Even if the word "stupid" was not used in classification, it was openly applied among peers and in the functional structure of the school. The rebellion and the frustration of the lower socioeconomic children assigned to these classes only heightened their outbursts and behavior problems.

Middle-class parents, on the other hand, were dismayed by the associates of their (for the most part authentically impaired) mildly retarded children. These parents resented the social implications that children in retarded, special-education classes were rowdy, unmannered, and unclean. These two components of the educably mentally retarded classes in public school might have been viewed from the beginning as too disparate to be maintained in a common setting. The only common characteristic of the two groups was that their prior teachers had acknowledged that they were unable to teach these children or to help them assimilate the expected body of knowledge prescribed in the standard, middle-class, elementary curriculum. The two groups were alike in that they were both excluded. But they were more unlike than alike in terms of being educationally grouped to undergo a common learning experience.

DEVIATION AND ABASEMENT

Exclusion has always been a means of dealing with deviates who do not meet societal norms. The social advantage of maintaining an unsophisticated, unlearned, cheap, unskilled labor pool by excluding the poor from educational opportunities should be obvious. What is not as readily apparent is why those "deviates" are not just accepted as occupying a denigrated place in human society. Why are they as ruthlessly and viciously abased as exposés on mental-retardation institutions reveal (Blatt, 1966, 1973)?

Perhaps this phenomenon can be explained by simple metaphor that something is wrong with these people. Something is "defective." If this cannot be diagnosed as a physical disease, then it must be a "mental defect"—something so basically wrong that those afflicted cannot be helped. In fact, this is probably the historic relationship between the mentally retarded and their placement in "homes for incurables."

It should be recognized that by the mid-twentieth century all public institutions for the retarded in the United States were commonly regarded as "homes for incurables." These were the places where the "vegetables" were kept. Even in terms of pre-nineteenth century residential facilities, certain institutions were always maintained for people who were clearly beyond hope. There were always out of the way places where individuals who were significantly different could be ignored and "hopefully" forgotten.

EARLY HISTORICAL PRECEDENTS

The situation of those camps or colonies, those warehouses, those homes for incurables, can be compared in part to the ancient biblical consideration of the "unclean." Strict laws ordered diseased individuals to live outside the community, away from relatives and friends, and to declare themselves unclean to any who might approach. These rules might have contained a modicum of rationale in terms of avoiding contagion or spread of disease. However, the utter, unempathetic banishment of the sick when care and nursing were so direly needed requires deep emotional origins to explain the degree and severity of this ostracism.

The early Hebraic laws of cleanliness centered around life-and-death issues. In Leviticus, where most of the laws of cleanliness are expounded dead bodies were definitely regarded as unclean. The religious cult seemed to have an aversion to closeness to the dead. For example, the most sacred priests, the Nazirites, were forbidden to take part in the burial of even their closest relatives; those persons who did participate in laying the dead to rest subsequently underwent prescribed periods of uncleanness. Care was also taken to assure that the flesh of animals was taken for food only at the time of their death. The so-called unclean animals ate other dead animals and consequently were considered contaminated. Food was essential to maintain life, and thus needed to be differentiated from death. Clean food was in this way dissociated from death. The laws regulating sexual activity were also related to this distinction, the early Hebrews being one of the first societies to recognize paternity. Tribal awareness that sexual intercourse was linked to creating life, brought sexual activity under the regulation of cleanliness. Sexual cleanliness restrictions were designed in regard to the creation of life, because life and the sacred were intrinsically related. The laws of cleanliness clearly involve life-and-death issues.

Consequently the ostracism of the diseased may be seen as an approach to death, but closer scrutiny reveals more extreme emotional reactions. The diseased were actually driven from the community and barred from any contact with the sacred. The diseased were thus disowned by the community of the living. It should be clear, then, that to be unclean, to be forced to bare one's head, rend one's clothing, and warn against potential contact with the community of the living, meant that the victims were no longer considered members of the living community. In effect, they became a community of the living dead. The fear and anxiety incorporated in their rejection and ostracism reflects the attitudes of the awesome belonging to the living dead, of living in a position that is clearly designated as being beyond hope. This orientation and its emotional awe and powerful aversion seem remarkably akin to reactions in the mid-twentieth century toward institutions for the retarded.

NONCOMPETITIVE SUBHUMAN BEINGS

In present social contexts, mentally retarded persons are the most misunderstood and are subjected to the most discrimination of any social grouping. This reflects the achievement ethic that pervades North American, middle-class culture where poor acknowledgment is given to those who do not live up to the competitive model. Children must *earn* good grades in school to prove they are learning. Adult success is measured by the accumulation of goods and positions of status and recognition. Persons whose ability to compete for these goals is limited by physical, sensory, or mental impairment become objects of pity and social avoidance. Individuals with physical or sensory handicaps can still "earn their way," can be trained to "compensate," and may still live "productive and useful" lives. Some prejudicial preference may be indicated that their place in society be to one side of the mainstream of competition—perhaps that the disabled work at designated centers or in their own homes rather than in urban areas or in competitive industry or commerce. However, it is beginning to be recognized that people with physical or sensory handicaps deserve a more prominent place in society. Similarly, the mentally retarded have too long been considered noncompetitive or too limited to produce high enough returns from rehabilitative training. They were prejudged as too far below the considerations of conventional "education" or as custodial objects to be wished out of sight and out of mind.

Another area of grave concern is the domiciliary controversy as to whether retarded children belong in their natural homes. The rejection of so many retarded children from their homes can be directly attributed to the force and strength of the false beliefs that previously compelled many professionals to support this complicity. At times, it seems hard to believe that the human infantile need for maternal nurturing were so readily dismissed. Wolfensberger's (1972) account of the designation of the retarded as "subhuman beings" seems to adequately account for this situation. From the viewpoint of the "professionals" who recommend the banishment of a child from a family setting, the only further accountable explanation seems to be their denial (perhaps unknowingly) of the child's basic human needs. Fortunately, most warehousing institutions are now predominantly closed to young children. Foster homes have become more common for all children, and smaller nursing-home settings are available for children with complicated physical problems. These institutions must be carefully monitored to prevent them from becoming dumping grounds for babies who are more unwanted than incapacitated. In this respect, present concern seems to require that some attention be given to the process by which previous conditions ever came to be.

BANISHMENT FROM FAMILIES

The extremes of banishment and the inability to accept mental handicaps are reached when retarded children are denied the opportunity or the right to be reared in normal family constellations. That denial appears to be the ultimate insult. At a time when most institutional living arrangements were being questioned and most were considered undesirable, retarded children were still being warehoused and subjected to subhuman living conditions. Again rationalizations were rampant: "Families cannot stand this kind of burden." "Think of the normal siblings." "The parents won't let the child be placed in a foster home. We need an institution." Little thought was given to the fact that more intensive and earlier investments would help the child overcome obstacles or compensate for deficits. Immediate partial remedies with too little consideration for ultimate plans and resolutions, were too expediently accepted.

Within the past few years, some advancement toward reversing this unfortunate attitude has been achieved. This may be attributed to the understandable potential injustices of possible measurement errors in the use of basically unreliable infant-assessment devices. The frequent advice to "put them away before you become attached" remains familiar because it was so frequently given in the not too distant past. For example, on the birth of a child with Down's syndrome, the parents were told that such a child would never be able to be happy and given myriad misinformation such as: "He may never walk." "He will never go to school." "Other children won't accept him." "People of your status or standards just don't keep a child like that." In this way, the parents' guilt was compounded, indeed often professionally reinforced. The parents desperately sought ways to cope with the situation, so that they could follow their more natural inclinations to rear and to relate to their child, but they seemed to be trapped in a web of "professional" points of view as to how they should feel about or ought to relate to their "abnormal" child.

Perhaps behind this onslaught of false advice lies the popular cultural myth perpetuated in first- or second-grade primers or in certain "ladies" magazines that somewhere there is an ideal family. The existence of an ideal family model is questionable. Families are comprised of individuals. They change with each addition. Although initially formulated and altered by parental attitudes and beliefs, families, in turn, are influenced and changed in accord with the differences of each member. Parents who understand their children's temperaments, capabilities, interests, and levels of activity, consider these factors when formulating aspirations and plans for the child. In simple, common-sense terms, plans can be made for a child's limitations when he is a functional member of a family. Parents map hope to see a child surpass them in social standing or even replace themselves in the world of the future. These issues are important considerations in any healthy, parent-child relationship. However, they are forces that enter a field of interacting variables. They should not, as they often were, be regarded as excuses to emotionally abandon a child with imperfections of a physical or mental nature.

THE MYTH THAT LIKES MUST BE CLUSTERED

Contrary to the popular "birds-of-a-feather" belief, recognition must be given to the human desire for diversity and novelty. In all humans, a narrowing of horizons or a restriction of interest can only lead to lack of motivation or diminished interest. Age grading, both in its implications for the banishment of the elderly and the regimentation of peer groups, exaggerates and distorts developmental stages of life. Sexual and racial segregation buttress and reinforce poorly founded stereotypes, while they limit opportunities for a greater understanding of or empathic response to the designated opposites. The myth that likes must be clustered together stems from the defensive conceptualization that human beings lack the ability to tolerate social differences or deviancy. It may take years to dispel this myth, but an urgently needed step in that direction is to develop an appreciation for the plights of groups at the extremes of social banishment. For previously stated reasons, the mentally retarded will probably continue to remain close to the point of ostracism. However, it cannot be denied that considerable tolerance and understanding must immediately be developed. The ethical dilemma of presenting banishment as a social good, because the banished are difficult to understand and therefore can understand and support one another, must be seen as a logical non sequitur.

Schools similarly may perpetuate an idealized myth that the standard curriculum in some magical manner brings *every* child to an acceptable place in adult society. Progress in the field of education is dispelling this myth. Preschool education has advanced to a point where number concepts and reading are consistently being introduced to younger children. The results of these procedures and the effects of mass-media investments in preschool stimulation to date are astonishing. The child does not have to wait until mental age 6 to become "educable." Similarly, in the school years, allowances for individual rates of advancement as well as for the pursuance of singular interests and individualized study have created a new understanding of academic expectations. In addition, the court requirement that public instruction be made available to all handicapped persons will undoubtedly enhance the appreciation of what school can do for "normals." All students will eventually be allocated strategies and plans designed more on the basis of individualized advancement than on preformulated concepts as to what and how groups of similar-aged students should learn.

THE SELF-CONTAINED CLASSROOM

The decision in special education to segregate into self-contained classrooms was a blatant attempt to isolate the child who learns at a slower rate. In three ways, this segregation defeated its intended purpose: to assist in avoiding feelings of failure that result from peer competition for grades in a regular classroom.

First, it emphasizes the viewpoint that something is so drastically wrong that the segregated child cannot be educated in any way with normal children in the standard manner. For many educable children, the unfairness and injustice in such a viewpoint are obvious. Many times, exclusion from the standard curriculum is the result of an exaggerated reaction on the part of a teacher. At other times, the exclusion is a subtle excuse to cover up a less tolerable rejection on the basis of a racial or social difference or perhaps an even more minor difference of orientation or personal attitude. Segregation often appears more acceptable when the child is trainable. The conceptualization of "trainable" is that the child can never master basic academic skills. More often than not this viewpoint results in the conclusion "Why bother?" As a result, many children who are trainable are deprived of a basic orientation to academic skills that is desperately needed to understand travel directions, to use public facilities including rest rooms, to achieve a social understanding that would help in both orientation to adult living and in access to working and recreational activities, and the like. All growing children are interested in learning about what adults do. Even if the degree of retarded development is severe enough to necessitate a more unique system of academic orientation, basic reading and mathematical skills can never be totally ignored. Yet this is exactly what happened in many so-called "trainable" classrooms.

The second reason segregation is self-defeating is that it effects detrimental reactions toward the children it is intended to help. Segregation creates an artificial social situation. Segregated children are actually much more alike than they are different from other children. Mental retardation is an artificial classification. Deficient intelligence is in no way a uniform trait. It is very difficult to apply generalizations to the heterogenous collection that comprises a mentally retarded group or class. The artificial segregation of trainable students creates artificial social judgments, such as: "They are all like Mongols." "They are all fat." "They're all funny looking." Of course, these generalizations are basically unsupportable, but they exist because of the artificial coincidences and associations precipitated by segregated groupings.

Segregation can cause detrimental effects regarding the teacher's situation as well. The monetary increments (incentives) used to entice teachers into special-education fields are viewed with mistrust by other teachers: "Well, she's getting paid more to work with that kind of kid." "You couldn't make me do it for love or money." The impression has been fostered that incentive is necessary to get people to do this demeaning type of work. Special-education teachers may also be considered different and may not be permitted to interact in normal social exchange with other teachers.

Finally, segregation in itself is always self-defeating because it can never be "separate but equal." One side always seems to be more "equal" than the other side. The retarded, who rarely speak up for their own interest or rights, are most often shortchanged; they may have inferior classrooms, basement assignments, noisy, poorly lighted, and unventilated quarters, inadequate teaching materials, slighted budgets for special programs, and the least access to ancillary or extracurricular activities from which they could receive the greatest socialization benefits. These inequalities appear in any segregated system. Their cumulative nature only pushes the deprived toward the revolutionary point, which produces the cyclic demand that the system be reordered.

PRIOR PRACTICES OF EXCLUSION

Ethical issues in the educational field have shifted dramatically since court decisions such as *PARC v. the Commonwealth of Pennsylvania.* With the recognition that all citizens have the right to educational opportunity, the emphasis became one of safeguarding rights. Previously, the main question had been the degree to which a school system could exclude children from the standard curriculum. Authorities were preoccupied by what grounds justified exclusion and in what ways the criteria for exclusion could be altered, avoided, or circumvented in subtle and often socially undesirable maneuvers.

Previous practices of absolute exclusion from the standard curriculum could only verge on the point of social viciousness. The ethical violations were legion. Little allowance was made for individual difference. If a teacher felt intellectually, behaviorally, or socially at odds with a child, the child was considered a disruptive influence in the classroom, and grounds were actively sought for the child's exclusion. In the so-called educable retarded groupings, this meant that many more lower- than middle-class children were eligible for exclusion. Some school systems even pressed for the second standard deviation below the age mean (Wechsler IQs 70–84) to be labeled "borderline retarded." This meant that theoretically 16% of the normal population were eligible for exclusion on the basis of a potential diagnosis of mental retardation. Taking into account the IQ–socioeconomic status correlation, a much greater proportion of lower-class children were thus destined for exclusion by comparison with their middle-class counterparts. Court cases have diminished the chance of this injustice, but we must examine some more subtle violations of the failure to recognize cultural economic differences and ultimate variations in individual preferences. We must also consider the even more subtle but equally vicious educational practices such as "tracking" or clustering, which are merely devices of blocking mobility and maintaining the status quo.

Individual educational programming is the only answer to this problem. For years, special educators have been developing methods to achieve such programs for children who have special needs. Unfortunately, the missing element is the goal of returning as many of these children as possible to the educational mainstream. That goal, of course, can be seen to be in direct conflict with the exclusion-intent of previous special educational practices. Once the "establishment" had segregated the problem, every effort was made to avoid future confrontations. The most expedient and finalized solution, seemed to be to keep special children within a segregated setting until they grew too old to be problems in the educational system. Thus education became an integral part of the "social-sanitation" process so aptly described by Braginsky and Braginsky (1971). No threat of reassimilation was allowed to stress the educational system. The system had merely discarded its refuse. "The job of society, then, is (was) to keep its house in order by identifying its deviants and excluding them forever from the mainstream" (Braginsky and Braginsky, 1971, p. 168).

Mainstreaming is consequently seen as the essential missing element in early special-education programs. With the absence of "due process" protection, this then became a legal issue. If the loss of educational opportunity implied potential civil-rights violations, then broader protection was necessary to assure educational opportunities. A type of hearing process or review became mandatory in such instances. Participants in this review became alert to and aware of specific requirements, such as (1) the zero-reject concept (the fact that no child is to be considered beyond or below the responsibility of the educational system); (2) the need to assure the availability of appropriate teaching methods and techniques; (3) individualized programming; and (4) periodic supervision and scheduled follow-up board review. These more extreme precautions must also be taken to assure educational opportunities in the mainstream.

ETHICAL PRINCIPLES

Some ethical dilemmas reviewed in this chapter are in part ghosts of the past. Court decisions, current and planned legislation, and demands for equal educational opportunity have altered the human-service systems (including education) in a way that will have an indelible effect. It seems assured that we cannot and will not turn back to the previous, primitive and immoral treatment imposed on the mentally retarded. However, some precautions must be taken to avoid future mistakes in developing needed programs and social policies or establishing guidelines to care for the substantially mentally impaired.

First, it must be recognized that every human can be assisted to more fully appreciate or improve the enjoyment of the state of his or her basic experience. This is a principle that is self-obvious among children. The freshness and joy with which the child can approach each new day is something that should be cherished educationally and professionally and recognized as the source of natural motivation that it is. Conversely, nothing is as sad as the presumed and self-prophesized dullness of the unmotivated child's response. Retarded children do *not* have to respond this way. There are numerous nurseries and day-care centers where severely and profoundly retarded children find much genuine enjoyment in their daily activities and learning experiences. The methods of constructively promoting this joy-giving activity must be studied and further developed. All persons can be "turned on."

In a similar vein, the dullness in the eyes of children who have been "turned off" by instruction or schooling is tragic. One of the most disheartening effects for a teacher to face is the listless response of a child who has been conditioned to think of school as an unpleasant place to be. Compound this with the burdened, unmotivated, and hardened continence of the poor, and we are once again faced with the bitter and vicious consequences of socioeconomic deprivation.

These examples demonstrate that the retarded are considered dull and listless and that a self-fulfilling prophesy of this nature is present in other situations such as in poverty. It should be obvious that every child has the capacity to enjoy at least some of the pleasures inherent in existence. The same principle can and should be applied in adulthood as well as in old age, even though the mode of enjoyment may be affected by the circumstances of a different developmental stage. If the capacity to enjoy has not been developed at any time in the life cycle, the professional should be challenged to discover the means of carrying out this task.

The second ethical premise is that all humans can reciprocate in caring and loving relationships. This is an extensive, far-reaching principle. It is amazing how surprised some parents are when they discover that their very impaired and limited child can reciprocate. It is rewarding to help parents overcome their self-defeating expectations and discover that the creature they previously considered subhuman can respond to their parental investment with human kindness and self-giving qualities. Even the sickest child can respond to nurturing and care. How often in acute illnesses this type of investment plays a major role in the child's recovery or in the actual extent of it.

Parents of retarded children are often "professionally" reinforced into self-pitying states of gloom. They are told that they should go through stages of mourning. They are pitied, and in return they feel only more bewildered and sorry for themselves. This is not how individuals or families should be helped to overcome or compensate for a handicap. Persons seeking help need to understand the naturalness of the feelings that surround them. They need to *own* their feelings, to realize that it is acceptable for them to experience these reactions. If they learn to recognize their feelings for what they are and can maintain them in the appropriate perspective, they will not be hindered in their actual pursuits of more important life goals. The rewards of these pursuits include a mutually positive relationship among family members and the opportunity to work toward satisfying and fulfilling life roles.

The third premise is the basic ingredient of human experience: All human beings can learn. All persons seek or want to be provided with conditions that draw them closer to a point of mastery or knowledge. Each person, no matter how immature or regressed, can be rewarded by the sense of mastering a task or understanding a problem that had previously been unsolvable. The opportunity to help a child learn, to witness the self-generated enthusiasm that comes from a sense of gaining competence, is a great privilege that any true teacher cherishes. Perhaps it is the sense that only the child can accomplish this step of mastery that is important. Perhaps it is the humble appreciation that the teacher only provides the climate and the conditions, but the child learns. To the teacher, the appreciation that a student has accomplished a learning task is sufficient in itself. The teacher is amply rewarded in the awareness of being responsible and yet sharing a sense of accomplishment with the more dependent person who has mastered the learning objective. Here, again, this principle may be applied for adults and the elderly as well. All humans can learn. All humans want to learn. To avoid disillusionment, the process of learning and the renewal and regeneration inherent in that process must continue until life ends.

The more positive aspects of living, experiencing, and learning must be emphasized in helping relationships. When these viewpoints are maintained in positive perspective, the ethical dilemmas that condemn helpless individuals can be resolved, and professionals and the persons whom they are attempting to help will be enabled to face even the most negative circumstances.

REFERENCES

Bakan, D. *Slaughter of the innocents.* San Francisco: Jossey-Bass, 1971.

Bettleheim, B. Segregation: New style. *Sch. Rev.* **66** (1958), 251–72.

Blatt, B. *Souls in extremis: An anthology on victims and victimizers.* Boston: Allyn & Bacon, 1973.

Blatt, B, and Kaplan, F. *Christmas in purgatory: A photographic essay on mental retardation.* Boston: Allyn & Bacon, 1966.

Braginsky, D. D., and Braginsky, B. M. *Hansels and Gretels.* New York: Holt, Rinehart & Winston, 1971.

Crocker, A. C., and Cushna, B. Pediatric decisions in children with serious mental retardation. *Pediatr. Clin. North Am.* **19** (1972), 413–21.

Cruickshank, W. M., Paul, J., and Junkala, J. *Misfits in the public schools.* Syracuse: Syracuse University Press, 1969.

Cushna, B., and Crocker, A. C. Three years is still too late. In H. Ohberg (ed.), *Focus on exceptionality.* New York: Simon & Schuster, 1973.

Deno, E. (ed.), *Instructional alternatives for exceptional children.* Arlington, Va.: Council for Exceptional Children, 1973.

Dewey, J. *Experience and education.* New York: Macmillan, 1959.

Edgerton, R. B. *The cloak of competence.* Berkeley: University of California Press, 1972.

Greene, M. A., and Cushna, B. Mental retardation and social class in an out-patient clinic population. *Am. J. Ment. Defic.* **70** (1965), 114–19.

Jones, J., and The Task Force on Children Out of School. *The way we go to school: The exclusion of children in Boston.* Boston: Beacon, 1970.

Lipman, L., and Goldberg, I. *Right to education.* New York: Teachers College Press, 1973.

Mercer, J. R. *Labeling the mentally retarded.* Berkeley: University of California Press, 1973.

Meyerowitz, J. H. Self derogations in young retardates and special class placement. *Child Dev.* **33** (1962), 443–51.

Ryan, W. *Blaming the victim.* New York: Random House, 1971.

Solomons, G., Cushna, B., Opitz, E., and Greene, M. A. Social status differences among educable and trainable children. *Am. J. Ment. Defic.* **31** (1966), 207–12.

Wolfensberger, W. *Normalization: The principle of normalization in human services.* Toronto: National Institute on Mental Retardation, 1972.

So You Want to See Our Files on You?

JONATHAN BRANT,
GAIL GARINGER, and
RENE TANKENOFF BRANT

Any person who seeks mental-health services can expect the professional to whom he or she turns for assistance to compile a record concerning that treatment. This record is commonly maintained as a case file. The primary justification for maintaining such files is simple: professionals record their perceptions and findings so that they can recall particular developments and so that they can relay information to other professionals who may be involved in the case.

Desite the seeming simplicity of the argument for the tradition of maintaining records, the existence of such records and the nature of their contents raise many serious and difficult issues. The basic reason that such questions arise is that information is power; moreover, personal information has a value attached to it. That value has been dramatically demonstrated by the burglary of a psychiatrist's office by agents of the Nixon Administration to obtain Daniel Ellsberg's psychiatric profile and by the nearly secret existence of an organization called the Medical Information Bureau which houses, in coded computerized form, the medical histories of some ten million Americans who have applied for life insurance.

These dramatic examples of the value of transmitted personal information are, however, only the tip of the iceberg when the usual degree of availability of most medical and psychiatric records is considered. Such records are available to all professional personnel in a given hospital or clinic, all of whom are expected to handle the records in a confidential manner and not to disseminate information in them to other parties who have no right to see such records. In addition, the routine dissemination of hospital records now includes insurance companies, state or federal agencies responsible for hospital payments, and selected hospital staff and government personnel who perform quality reviews. The new Professional Standards Review Organizations are the latest developments in an accelerating trend toward the creation of quality or fiscal audits that may have access to medical records under certain circumstances.

PSYCHIATRIST-PATIENT PRIVILEGE

Few specific provisions in the law prescribe standards for the dissemination of personal data. Although most lay people do not realize it, the physician–patient privilege does not act as a general proscription against the disclosure of medical information by physicians. Privileges are legal concepts, created by statute, that are concerned with limiting testimony in a court of law. The existence of a physician–patient privilege means that the physician may not testify in a court of law concerning the treatment of a particular patient unless that patient consents or—and this is the loophole that generally opens the door to testimony—unless the medical treatment is related to the subject of the lawsuit. Thus, for example, if a plaintiff alleges that he or she suffered mental distress and had to see a psychiatrist as a result of an automobile accident, the patient cannot prevent the psychiatrist from testifying about conversations in therapy that are relevant to a determination of the injuries the patient suffered.

The key point to remember here is that a privilege is not a general prohibition against the dissemination of patient information by a physician. The major prohibitions against such general dissemination are not derived from statutes but from principles of medical ethics expressed in such documents as the Hippocratic Oath, the Code of Medical Ethics of the American Medical Association, and from tort law created through the precedent-setting decisions of appellate court judges.

CONTENT OF MEDICAL RECORDS

Thus far in this discussion of the dissemination of medical and psychiatric records we have ignored the content of these records. The issue of such content is a particularly difficult one. Traditionally, medical and psychiatric records are regarded as the property of the mental-health professionals who compile them, and these professionals are encouraged to place all potentially relevant information into the record. This principle is particularly true in teaching settings, where entries in the medical record are made by medical students and other health professionals in training status. For didactic reasons, such students are encouraged to include all thoughts, findings, or speculations concerning patients in the medical record. However inaccurate, incomplete, or irrelevant these statements may prove to be, they remain in the record for posterity and are available to any person who validly or invalidly obtains access to that record. In an earlier day when the relative confidentiality of medical records could be assured, perhaps the maintenance of records containing too much information was not of serious concern. Two trends, however, have combined to make the issue of what kind of information is collected in medical (and particularly psychiatric) records one of major interest.

The first trend is the growing number of lawsuits that arise concerning medical treatment. These include not only malpractice cases in which the patient sues the physician for allegedly improper care, but also litigation such as child-custody cases in which the treatment given a child or a parent is crucial to the outcome of the case. The increasing likelihood that material placed into a patient file may be made public through the medium of a trial casts serious doubts on the current method of medical record keeping in which all thoughts and speculations, including comments by students, are placed into the patient's record. The realization that the speculations of a health–professional student could play a crucial role in the decision in a child-custody case is a sobering thought indeed.

In response to the necessities of a litigious age, medical professionals should formalize their record-keeping practices by making the medical record more a precise official record than a catchall for miscellaneous comments. Here, health professionals can learn from their legal colleagues. For years, lawyers have organized their records into a specific document that can be labeled a "formal record" that is subject to court subpoena and a "working paper" (in legalese, a "work product") that belongs to the professional and cannot be reached subpoenaed by the court. In the case of medical and psychiatric records, the formal record would be the recording of diagnoses and treatment made by a staff person. All other information currently entered in the medical record (most particularly the notes of student trainees, but also the more speculative, day-to-day notations made in the normal course of a treatment routine) would be maintained by the student or by the health professional as his or her own professional working notes. Entries in the formal medical record would only be made by or under the direction of a supervisory person specifically designated for the task, making medical and psychiatric records not only shorter and more tightly organized documents, but also still-useful tools for the provision of high-quality medical care. The working notes would be made available to the professional making entries in the formal medical record, but would remain with the person who had developed them for his or her own use. We expect that reconsideration of the process of collecting and maintaining medical and psychiatric records may well lead to fundamental changes in the process of medical record keeping, but the value of these changes in terms of the advantages to be gained in terms of patient privacy are enormous given the large number of persons who now have routine access to a medical record.

The second major trend illustrating the need to rethink the manner in which medical and psychiatric records are kept is the developing notion that the patient should have the right of access to his or her own medical or psychiatric data. As we noted earlier, the traditional concept is that medical records belong to the professional and that, by implication, patients have no right of access to their records. However, the increasing amount of attention focused on the vast amounts of personal data collected by government and private sources, including but not limited to medical information, has led to a demand that individuals be permitted to see what information is collected about them and to challenge inaccurate or incomplete information. In his seminal work *Privacy and Freedom*, Professor Alan F. Westin (1967), has written that the essence of a right of privacy is the ability of an individual to control the flow of information concerning himself or herself. The important report of the Secretary of Health, Education and Welfare's Advisory Committee on Automated Personal Data Systems (1973) argues for the citizens' general right of access to personal records concerning themselves. The members of the task force, which included many leading experts in the area of data privacy, were not impressed by arguments for exceptions to the general principle of access to medical or psychiatric records. These studies, as well as legislative developments concerning credit, criminal, and educational records, have created a trend toward individual access that is probably inexorable.

The concept of patient access to medical records is developing similarly, albeit more slowly. By statute in Massachusetts and a few other states patients are given access to hospital records concerning themselves. The trend toward accepting the patient's right of access is likely to accelerate. Efforts to provide a right of access for hospital patients are proceeding in a number of legislatures where such a right does not presently exist. In addition, efforts directed toward the enactment of general legislation covering data privacy, which guarantees a subject access to his or her own data (including most medical and psychiatric information), have been successful in Minnesota and are proceeding in other states as well as at the federal level.

IMPLICATIONS OF PATIENT ACCESS

The potential implications for medical record keeping in terms of patient access are enormous. Like the trend toward increased numbers of lawsuits, the trend toward patient access argues for more formal and precise record keeping in which extraneous material is not recorded in the formal medical record. We wish to emphasize that we are not advocating a parallel record-keeping system that contains sensitive information not shown in the formal record that can be subpoenaed or seen by the patient. Rather, we are seeking to make the medical record a clearer and a more consistent document. Sensitive or derogatory material should be recorded where relevant, and all professionals should be willing to explain the basis for such comments to patients or to a court. We recognize that this is not easy. No one likes to have his or her judgment questioned, and few people like to confront those about whom they have written negative comments, even if those comments are accurate. However, evaluations may well affect the data subject's future, and professionals will have to modify their practices and to accept the fact that they cannot operate behind a smokescreen of professionalism to deny the patient the right of access to medical records. Instead, medical professionals must learn to be responsible for their decisions. That is the essence of protecting the rights of all citizens in a free society.

Thus far in our argument, we have made no distinction between medical and psychiatric records. However, in regard to patient access, we acknowledge that there are circumstances when professionals may validly claim that granting a patient access to his or her record may be harmful. However, professionals must be careful not to utilize the rationale of the ostensible "best interests" of the patient to deny a patient access to treatment records.

It is difficult to develop a specific standard for circumstances when access should be denied. A possible formulation, although one that still leaves considerable room for professional discretion, is that access may be denied if in cases where the professional believes that permitting a patient to view personal medical records could cause the patient to become violent and harm him (her) self or others (including the professional) or in cases where the patient could become severely depressed or suicidal. Whenever a request for access is denied a patient, we recommend that the patient be entitled to designate another person to be granted access in his stead. Professionals could encourage patients to designate either a physician or an attorney to receive their medical record, but because many poor persons lack either a regular physician or an attorney, a specific requirement that such a professional be designated to receive information should not be made.

RECORDS OF MINORS

While the general paradigm for a system of psychiatric record keeping is not difficult to develop, this is not the case in regard to the psychiatric records of minors. The major problem in this area results from the fact that necessary medical practice has moved beyond existing legal principles in most jurisdictions. Traditionally, minors have few if any legal rights. The ancient English legal doctrine that children were the chattel property of their families may have been somewhat softened in recent years, but the principle of the basic powerlessness of minority status remains. The legal dilemma created by this powerlessness is felt most acutely by medical and psychiatric professionals who must debate whether minors can consent to treatment. Few of these professionals have yet to be confronted with the question of whether or not to care for an adolescent who seeks medical treatment for venereal disease or an unwanted pregnancy or psychiatric treatment for a drug-induced psychotic reaction and who is adamant that his or her parents not be informed of the request. In many jurisdictions, the law does not recognize the right of a minor to seek medical or psychiatric treatment without parental consent, and physicians who provide such treatment risk lawsuits and even criminal sanctions for their efforts. Some jurisdictions, however, make exceptions to the general rule by permitting minors to consent to emergency treatment or to treatment for certain conditions such as venereal disease.

Moreover, in some circumstances, self-supporting, "emancipated" minors may be able to seek medical or psychiatric treatment without parental consent. A few jurisdictions utilize a subjective test for a "mature minor," who because of an adjudged level of maturity is accorded the right to consent to his or her own medical treatment. The policies of a particular hospital or clinic, of course, must be based on the current law of the particular jurisdiction in which these institutions are located. It is fair to say, however, that the vast majority of states still recognize few if any instances when minors can be treated for medical or psychiatric conditions without parental consent. Because the law is so contrary to existing medical and psychiatric practices, it is obvious that mental-health professionals must join their legal colleagues in seeking to have such laws changed.

The differing degree of independence accorded minors by law in the pursuit of necessary medical and psychiatric care illustrates the most difficult issue that arises concerning records of such treatment (the potential conflicting interests of the parent and the child in regard to records of such treatment). Parents may often seek access to the psychiatric files that record the treatment history of their child. Such requests may be made for a number of disparate reasons, from wishing to ensure that the child is receiving proper treatment to a desire to learn what the child may have been saying about them. In the latter case, it is likely that the interests of parent and child are not coexistensive, and their relationship may indeed be faulty. The child may well have confided in the therapist on the condition that the divulged information not be made available to the parents. The conflicting interests of the parents and the child, then, are often the basic reason that the child is in treatment. In addition, a minor's comment about a parent or a parent's comment about a child, given the apparent confidentiality of the therapeutic relationship, may not be appropriate for dissemination to the other party. Further, it is very common in a psychiatric setting for both the child and the parents to be in treatment simultaneously, and it is not uncommon for the records of an entire family to be maintained together.

Accepting a patient's right to see personal records will require, in the child-psychiatry setting, a reconsideration of the respective rights of both child and parents. To the extent that their rights differ, each party must be respected.

SUMMARY

In regard to access to the psychiatric record, parents should not have the right of absolute access whenever their interests and those of the child conflict. Important in the determination of right of access should be how the child feels about the parents seeing the record. If the child objects, the parents should be denied access to information concerning the child's statements, particularly any assessments of the parents made by the child. This right to deny access to the parents should belong to any child who is old enough to comprehend the decision. Similarly, children above the age of 14 should, subject to the limitations described earlier, have access to their own records, if they so request. Such access would include the right to view all official records having to do with the treatment of the child, but would not include comments by the parents about the child, unless the professional involved in the case deemed such access unlikely to be deleterious to the minor or to infringe on any expectations of confidentiality that the parents may have. Finally, with regard to the records of younger children, the professional should apply the standard of whether access is likely to create a dangerous situation for the child before determining whether or not to grant access to the parents. Obviously, access to a record for a very young child or for an older child who is severely retarded is a meaningless concept, and we do not advocate access in situations other than those where it is potentially meaningful to the data subject.

The paradigm proposed here for access to the psychiatric records of children gives children more rights than they are presently granted by law in most states. Nonetheless, the standard is justifiable, because the laws in most jurisdictions have failed to keep pace with changing social mores.

The standard is based on the realization that the interests of parents and their children may differ, and that children (and their psychiatric records) cannot be treated as appendages of their parents. Rather, the differing interests of parents and children must be recognized and considered within the general context of a system of maintaining careful records that are, with few exceptions, made available to the patients to whom they pertain on request.

Therefore, we propose a system in which the interests of parents and children are balanced; each party is recognized and each merits consideration. To the extent that the rights of the parents and the child differ, the rights of the actual patient should be paramount. This standard is necessary if the rights of privacy for children are to be respected. If adopted, no finer change in professional habits could be made.

REFERENCES

U.S. Department of Health, Education and Welfare. Secretary's Advisory Committee on Automated Personal Data Systems. *Records: Computers and the rights of citizens.* Washington, D.C.: U.S. Government Printing Office, 1973.

Westin, A. *Privacy and freedom.* New York: Atheneum, 1967.

The Question of Due Process in Mental-Health Services to Children and Their Families

The right of citizens to interact with the legal system according to prescribed rules and principles is a cornerstone of democratic society. We must be mindful, however, that children are not entitled to the full rights of citizenship in our society. Thus the "due process of law" that protects adults may simultaneously oppress children. Certain key areas of concern to mental-health professionals are confounded by the current rules and principles for dealing with children and families under the law, especially when parents and children are at odds with each other. Part Three focuses on some of these issues.

Henry A. Beyer and John P. Wilson are both attorneys; they graduated from Harvard Law School a decade apart. Henry Beyer was a successful logic design engineer for a computer company when he reversed career directions to attend law school. He is now Staff Attorney and Research Coordinator at Boston University School of Law's Center for Law and Health Sciences. John Wilson studied international affairs at Princeton University and The Fletcher School of Law and Diplomacy before becoming an Assistant Dean at Harvard Law School. Since 1968, he has been Associate Dean and Director of the Legal Studies Institute at Boston University School of Law. Beyer and Wilson thoroughly probe the nature of the "voluntary commitment" of children to mental-health treatment facilities. The rights of the parents, the rights of the children, and an up-to-date analysis of recent court decisions on the "right to treatment" issue are thoughtfully discussed in this chapter.

The following two chapters deal generally with the subject of child abuse. The first of these chapters is coauthored by Drs. Norma and Seymour Feshbach, both of the University of California at Los Angeles. Norma Deitch Feshbach is now Professor of Education and Head of the Program in Early Childhood Development at UCLA. She has published extensively since completing her doctorate at the University of Pennsylvania; she has taught previously at Stanford, Berkeley, and the University of Colorado. Since completing his doctorate at Yale, Seymour Feshbach has published over 70 scholarly manuscripts. He was formerly Director of The Fernald School at UCLA, where he is still Professor of Psychology. Both Norma and Seymour Feshbach have intensively studied aggression in children and adults, as well as the learning of empathy and aggression by modeling. Their chapter examines the punishment practices of parents and the implications of these practices for child development. The issue of "rites" versus "rights" is extended to the concept of due process for children at home.

Garinger, Brant, and Brant, who coauthored the chapter on access to medical and psychiatric records in Part Two, again combine their legal and psychiatric expertise to raise the question of due process and human rights in child-abuse cases, but in a different context from Feshbach and Feshbach. Attorneys Gail Garinger and Jonathan Brant and psychiatrist Rene Tankenoff Brant consider the problems inherent in current "due process" for child-abuse cases. They discuss the need to regard such cases as whole-family problems, and suggest some new rules and principles worth consideration.

The final chapter in Part Three examines the injustices of the juvenile justice system, a set of rules and principles that makes children liable for punishment on the basis of acts that are tolerated, if committed by adults. Stephen R. Bing is a Harvard Law School graduate and an attorney with an extensive background in public advocacy law, especially with regard to juvenile offenders. He is now Deputy Director of the Massachusetts Advocacy Center in Boston. J. Larry Brown is Executive Director of the Massachusetts Advocacy Center; he holds a Ph.D. in social welfare from Brandeis University and an M.A. and an M.S.W. from UCLA and Brandeis University, respectively. Brown's special fields of interest are urban problems, educational policy, and the special difficulties of the juvenile in court.

Each of the chapters in Part Three contains examples of ways in which the usual and customary rules that assure the rights of adult citizens simply do not apply to children. Special needs are documented, and specific steps are suggested to ensure the best in mental-health services while respecting the rights of all parties involved.

The Reluctant Volunteer:
A Child's Right
to Resist Commitment

HENRY A. BEYER and
JOHN P. WILSON

> ... I have you fast in my fortress,
> And will not let you depart...."
> "The Children's Hour"
> Henry Wadsworth Longfellow

Americans pride themselves on the care they provide their children. That care encompasses children's spiritual, intellectual, and physical needs; it is demonstrated by superb schooling and medical attention for many, and it extends to psychological benefits. As evidence of this concern, some might point to the number of children in mental hospitals. The statistics are incomplete and sometimes in conflict, but they indicate that the number of institutionalized adults has declined in recent years while the number of children in mental hospitals has apparently continued to grow (Ginsberg, 1973; NIMH, 1974A, 1974B).

However, closer examination reveals that it is unclear whether in all cases such growth necessarily indicates concern for the well-being of children. A review of hospital records in one state shows that children are sometimes confined to institutions for the mentally ill or mentally retarded not for their own good, but for the benefit of their parents or other family members. One child's "hyperactivity interfered with the routine of household and disturbed family members" (Ferleger, 1973, p. 4). Another child posed "no serious behavior problem; admitted due to parents inability to

---

Research supported by NIMH research grant number 1 RO1 MH 24934-01 from the National Institute of Mental Health.

provide a satisfactory home environment." Yet another child was admitted because of "emotional instability of mother" (Ferleger, 1973, p. 6). This last case appears to fall within the ambit of a Philadelphia prehospitalization study indicating that in 25% of complaints of alleged mental illness, it was the complainant, rather than the prospective patient, who evidenced signs of mental illness (Ellis, 1974, p. 860; citing Scheff, 1966, p. 171).

THE ADMISSION STAGE

A growing awareness of the way in which the mental-health care system has been used to abuse the rights of children has prompted a recent reexamination of the system. Such abuses may occur on admission, during treatment, or on release. In this chapter, we discuss that stage of the process in which children enter mental institutions; we raise serious questions regarding existing law and practice, and we conclude with several suggestions for improvement.

Of all stages of mental-health treatment, the decision to admit or not to admit a person to a mental institution is probably the most critical and the stage best suited for legal intervention. The stigma that our society unfortunately, but undeniably, attaches to mental illness adheres most strongly to those persons who are admitted to institutions. Further, admission presages a significant change in lifestyle. The curtailment of liberty is massive, particularly for an adult or an older child who is accustomed to great freedom and mobility. Beyond that, admission is the threshold leading to a vast array of treatment situations. These successive events, occurring in a secluded setting behind hospital walls and often involving complex and intertwining medical, psychological, and rehabilitative judgments concerning the appropriateness of specific treatment modalities, are not easily (or perhaps appropriately) amenable to control by the legal process. The admission stage, on the other hand, is a stage that is, or can be made to be, open to public scrutiny and regulation. Moreover, the growing recognition that psychiatric diagnoses are greatly influenced by the contexts in which they are made and are stoutly defended thereafter strongly suggests that the appropriate point at which to challenge and test such diagnoses is before, rather than after, the patient enters the institution.

THE PRESENT SITUATION

Under the present laws of most states, children and adults enter mental institutions by one of two routes, generally termed "involuntary commitment" or "voluntary admission." While state statutes vary substantially, usually the state involuntarily commits, under police power, not only those persons it considers mentally impaired and dangerous, but also, under the theory of parens patriae, those mentally ill or retarded persons who are incapable of caring for themselves (*Harvard Law Review*, 1974). In both situations, because the state is supposedly caring for and not punishing such persons, the civil-commitment process traditionally includes few of the procedural safeguards required in criminal trials.

Recently, however, a small but growing number of lower federal courts have begun to rule on constitutional grounds that those being involuntarily committed must be accorded such rights of due process as notice, a hearing, assistance of counsel, the privilege against self-incrimination, and in a few cases a requirement of proof beyond a reasonable doubt (*In re Ballay*, 1973; *Bell v. Wayne County General Hospital*, 1974; *Lessard v. Schmidt*, 1972; *Dixon v. Attorney General of Pennsylvania*, 1971; *Hawks v. Lazaro*, 1974). To date, the U.S. Supreme Court has not ruled directly on either the standards or the procedures constitutionally required for commitment, but such a decision is likely to be made before long. Depending on the facts of the case and the issues raised on appeal, it is probable that the court ruling will grant both adults and children greater procedural protections than they have heretofore enjoyed.

In cases involving involuntary commitments of children, there has already been an expansion of procedural protections similar to the new protections increasingly afforded adults. For example, in 1968, a federal appeals court upheld a minor's right to counsel at every step of an involuntary commitment proceeding (*Heryford v. Parker*, 1968; *In re Johnnie Barnard*, 1971). The California Supreme Court recently held that juvenile-court wards may not be involuntarily committed without compliance with all procedural safeguards in the state's adult mental-commitment act (*In re Michael E.*, 1975).

The growing recognition of children's rights in the involuntary-commitment process will have very limited import, however, as long as the rules remain unchanged with regard to the more common way in which children enter mental institutions by so-called "voluntary" admission. In almost all states, a parent or guardian can apply to have a child (or ward) admitted to a mental hospital, and if the institution agrees to accept the child, he or she is "voluntarily" admitted.[1] In most cases, the minor may be truly ill or retarded, and the parents' motives may be entirely benign. Indeed, if such parents failed to admit their child, they could be legally charged with neglect for failing to provide necessary medical assistance in the form of mental-health treatment.[2] The motives of the parents, however, and even the legal compulsion placed on them, should not disguise the fact that the child and the parents may perceive the child's interests differently. Indeed, they may disagree vigorously, especially in cases where parental intent is not benign or where factors other than the child's best interests motivate the parents' decision.

Nevertheless, if the admitting authority finds some manifestation of behavioral or psychic abnormality, admission usually occurs regardless of the child's views; this admission is classified as "voluntary." There is no judicial, administrative, or any other review of this parental/institutional decision. Furthermore, in most states, the child has absolutely no recourse, no legal means of appealing to any outside authority for a review of his or her admission. Unlike a voluntary adult patient, who can demand to be released at any time, or an involuntarily committed patient, who has the benefit of periodic review, the time and manner of the release of a "voluntary" child patient is entirely at the discretion of others.

How did this situation arise, and why is it permitted to continue? It is the result of an extensive body of law regulating family life and the reciprocal relationships between family members (Kleinfeld, 1970). Thus, as previously stated, parents in this society are obligated to support and care for their minor children. Moreover, so that children do not, in their immaturity, become involved in disadvantageous arrangements, the law has long denied minors the legal capacity to make contractual arrangements themselves, except in special circumstances.[3] Only parents may enter into agreements for their children. This rule not only protects the children, but also, and perhaps more importantly, protects the parents who might otherwise be held liable for their offspring's imprudent agreements. By preventing minors from contracting with others, the law also assures parents that they will not suffer the loss of their children's services, a matter of considerable importance in early rural, small-farm societies.

By analogy, in medical matters, the doctrine of complete parental control prevents children from contracting for or consenting to their own treatment. Conversely, it gives parents the power to contract for and consent to treatment for their children. This rule, which survives to date with certain narrow exceptions,[4] constitutes the basis of the parents' right to "volunteer" their children for mental commitment. It also grants parents the right to deny their children's requests for release from mental institutions.

PROBLEMS WITH THE PRESENT SYSTEM

It can be argued that the present system of voluntary admission provides the best possible protection for children in general. After all, who can be better entrusted with the responsibility for acting in a child's best interest than the child's own parents? Undoubtedly, such confidence is well placed in most but not all cases. Inappropriate admission may be the result of parental ignorance, both of the nature of their child's problem and of the availability of less restrictive outpatient treatment. Financial considerations or the interests of siblings may supersede the interests of the mentally ill or retarded child. Or parents may simply be irresponsible or vindictive. The examples cited at the beginning of this chapter clearly illustrate that it cannot be assumed that all parents are acting in the best interests of the children whom they "volunteer" for psychiatric hospital commitment.

The scope of the problem is compounded by the fact that not only parents but also guardians may "voluntarily" admit children. Moreover, the child's guardian is frequently not a person but a state agency, usually a division of the welfare department. Such institutional guardians, when unable to find foster homes for their wards, may "voluntarily" admit them to mental hospitals. This practice, which normally involves older, nonwhite children, is prevalent enough to have gained the aptly descriptive label "dumping."

But if parents or guardians sometimes fail their trusts, cannot mental institutions be relied on to refuse to admit those children inappropriately "volunteered" for admission? Again the answer must be not always. Some children who definitely will not profit by confinement in such institutions are nevertheless admitted. There is no agreement as to the number of these children, but it has been estimated that they comprise at least 5–15% of all child inpatients. Hospitals probably fail to reject these improper admissions because inadequate staffing permits only perfunctory admission examinations or because of deference to the desires of the parents, who in many cases are paying for the services of the admitting psychiatrist. Under such circumstances, it is hardly surprising that the psychiatrist sometimes assumes the role of agent of the parents rather than of the child.

MOVEMENT OF THE LAW IN RELATED AREAS

Emerging and dramatic changes in two areas of the law related to voluntary admission suggest that analogous changes may be forthcoming in this aspect of children's mental-health care.

One related area involves the new rights afforded children in the juvenile justice process. In the last decade, the U.S. Supreme Court has granted an elaborate array of procedural protections to juveniles accused of delinquency (*Kent v. U.S.*, 1966; *In re Gault*, 1967; *In re Winship*, 1970). Rejecting the argument that a system with the the ostensible objective of rehabilitation justifies the use of noncriminal procedures in juvenile-delinquency proceedings, the Supreme Court focused on the fact of incarceration as the potential and frequent result of a juvenile court trial. In light of the overwhelming significance of this result, the court reasoned that most of the safeguards afforded adults in criminal proceedings should apply (*In re Gault*, 1967; but see *McKeiver v. Pennsylvania*, 1971).

The other related area involves the civil commitment of adults or children to mental institutions. A few lower federal courts, previously cited, have reasoned that an intention to "treat" (not "punish") and commitment through a noncriminal proceeding do not justify lax procedural protections. In the view of these courts, loss of liberty and the fact of confinement require protections similar to those afforded in criminal trials.

With these changes in the juvenile justice system and in mental-health, civil-commitment procedures, can states continue to support the present unmonitored systems for the voluntary admission of children? Or can it be said that such support deprives children of their right to equal protection under law, as stated in the Fourteenth Amendment to the U.S. Constitution?

The doctrine of equal protection used by courts to test the constitutionality of state action is complex (*Harvard Law Review*, 1969). It should be sufficient here to state that the Supreme Court has adopted a two-tiered approach (*San Antonio Independent School District v. Rodriguez*, 1973). If a suspect classification (such as race or national origin) or a fundamental right is not involved, then the court will uphold a state's dissimilar treatment of similar classes of people, as long as the minimum rationality can be established ". . . that a distinction made have some relevance to the purpose for which the classification is made" (*Baxtrom v. Herold*, 1966). If, on the other hand, a suspect classification or a fundamental right is involved, a state must demonstrate a compelling interest for treating similar classes of people in dissimilar ways.

Assuming for the moment that emotionally disturbed or retarded children are not a suspect classification and that their fundamental rights are not involved, is a state justified in granting these children almost no procedural protection during "voluntary" admissions when it requires such protection in civil-commitment or juvenile-delinquency proceedings? Can this distinction be rationally related to a legitimate government objective, so that a court can find at least some minimum justification for it?

It can be argued that the present system of parental or guardian authority and responsibility for child rearing with all its inadequacies, efficiently and successfully provides for the broad range of a growing child's needs. A necessary corollary to this authority is a substantial degree of discretion, including the discretion to provide mental-health care in any circumstances that the parents or guardian deem appropriate.

There are, then, two possibly significant distinctions between children who are "voluntarily" admitted and persons who are involved in civil-commitment or juvenile-delinquency proceedings. In "voluntary" admission, it is assumed that the child lacks the maturity to exercise independent, informed judgment and that the child's best interests can be properly weighed by others. In civil commitment, however, a person may be detained by the state in an institution only if his or her condition meets certain standards that must be proved to exist before an appropriate tribunal. In theory, these standards should be rigorous. Delinquency proceedings can be distinguished by the argument that such proceedings are quasi-criminal in nature, whereas "voluntary" admissions seek mental-health treatment.

Weighed against these distinctions is the fact that there may be as much duress and the confinement may be just as involuntary in all cases. If the result is the same, it is illogical to require the state to adhere to strict procedures in juvenile-delinquency or civil-commitment adjudications and not to require at least a modicum of procedural protection for "voluntary" admissions. The procedures need not be identical in all cases and, in deference to parental discretion, should probably be less stringent in the "voluntary" admission of children. But in all cases, the child's interests are in liberty and normal development, and surely the child whose admission, commitment, or sentence is based on inappropriate grounds suffers a great and similar loss. The state's interest in the proper development of one of its citizens does not differ appreciably from the interest of the child. It is a trivial burden to require parents or guardians to scrutinize their reasons for admission, whereas the deleterious effect of inappropriate admission can be enormous, both in terms of the child's loss of present liberty and in the warping of his or her future development.

Moreover, distinctions among classes of children become even less justifiable when assignment to one class or another often appears to be largely fortuitous. For example, the reasons given for the "voluntary" admission of children in many cases are identical to the reasons that require other children to appear in juvenile court. "Runaway, incorrigible"; "firesetting, stealing"; "theft, violence in school"; and "runaway, truancy, delinquent behavior" were the reasons given for the "voluntary" admission of four Pennsylvania children (Ferleger, 1973, pp. 3–4). For such behaviors, the parents could have brought their offspring to juvenile court, where, after sufficient notice, the children would have received a hearing before an impartial arbiter. There, aided by counsel, they would have had the opportunity to present evidence, to challenge adverse testimony, and to require that their delinquency be proved beyond a reasonable doubt. An appeal to a higher court would have been possible. Instead, these children were brought to a mental institution, where an employee of the institution, acting without outside review, admitted them at the request of their parents.

Nor can the great disparity in procedural protections be justified by the varying purposes of the mental-health and juvenile justice systems. Both systems are intended to provide care and treatment, although many facilities in each system have fallen painfully short of this goal. Actually, they are warehouses, often understaffed and occasionally brutalizing in their conditions. They do not adequately treat or rehabilitate, and a plethora of court suits demonstrates the violations of rights involved (*Wyatt v. Aderholt*, 1974; *Donaldson v. O'Connor*, 1974; *Welsch v. Likins*, 1974; *Nelson v. Heyne*, 1974; *Inmates of Boys Training School v. Affleck*, 1972). Because of a lack of appropriate treatment or rehabilitation, the courts considering juvenile-delinquency and involuntary mental-health commitments have concluded that commitment procedures in both the mental-health and juvenile justice systems should be radically changed to more closely resemble the protections afforded in criminal proceedings. Because "voluntarily" admitted children are placed in such institutions, these children should also receive greater procedural protection.

While the preceding arguments indicate that there may not be even a minimally rational basis for the significant distinctions in commitment procedure that exist, some Supreme Court decisions (*McGowan v. Maryland*, 1961; *Williamson v. Lee Optical*, 1955; see note, *Yale Law Journal*, 1973) suggest that almost any justification will satisfy the court's minimum rationality standard. However, in the "voluntary" admission of mentally ill or retarded children to state institutions, and arguably to private institutions as well, the state should be required to demonstrate a *compelling* interest for these procedural differences. While it may be novel to consider children who are labeled mentally ill or retarded as a suspect classification, their condition meets several of the definitive indexes required by the Supreme Court. A suspect classification, meriting strict judicial scrutiny, has been defined as a group ". . . saddled with such disabilities, or subjected to such a history of purposeful unequal treatment, or relegated to such a position of political powerlessness as to command extraordinary protection from the majoritarian political process" (*San Antonio Independent School District v. Rodriguez*, 1973). Traditionally, mentally ill and retarded adults and children have been subjected to discrimination and opprobrium. They can point to a long history of purposeful unequal treatment compared to the physically ill, and this treatment has often been shockingly cruel (*Wyatt v. Stickney*, 1972; *Wheeler v. Glass*, 1973; *N.Y. State Association for Retarded Children v. Rockefeller*, 1973). They have frequently been denied the right to vote, a right denied to children in any event. Thus the mentally ill and retarded may merit special protection as a politically powerless minority, unable to defend themselves in the majoritarian political process.

The fact of greatest import and clearest certitude, however, is that fundamental rights are involved in the admission of children to mental hospitals and state schools for the retarded. Stated simply and generally, a fundamental right is explicitly protected by the Constitution or, within carefully construed limits, falls within the ambit of rights that are so protected. Thus the evolving right to privacy has been held to be a fundamental right applied to the states by the Fourteenth Amendment (*Griswold v. Connecticut*, 1965). Rights protected within the penumbra of the Constitution by the Supreme Court—to travel, to associate freely, to privacy— are clearly involved in each institutional admission. Moreover, the child's very freedom is at stake, a right that undergirds all others (Chambers, 1972).

Of course, these rights have greater validity for adults than for children. In the exercise of discretionary authority, a parent or guardian may, for example, confine a child to his or her room for a reasonable period, may inspect the room, may place restrictions on the other children with whom the child may play. Indeed, parental authority is vast; parents may move across an entire continent, and the child is obliged to accompany them.

But the discretionary authority of a parent or guardian is not boundless. Under its parens patriae power, a state may remove a child from the control of an abusing or neglectful parent or guardian. Parental authority is limited in that it must be exercised in the best interests of the child. At the very least, if children do not have a fundamental right to travel, they have a right not to be placed in unreasonable confinement; if children do not have an unfettered right to free association, they have a right to be protected in most instances from the sick or depraved. Minors' rights are limited aspects of adults' rights, but they are nonetheless real.

Therefore, when a child is "voluntarily" placed in a mental institution, possibly for an indeterminate period, we argue that such placement may substantially violate the limited exercise of that child's fundamental rights. This fact, combined with the child's vulnerable status and the possible harm that confinement may cause, requires at least some procedure to verify admission. At the present time, states can offer no justification, compelling or otherwise, for the vast disparity that exists between the procedures to test the confinement of children in other circumstances and the lack of procedure to test "voluntary" admissions.

Even when the "voluntary" admission process for children is not contrasted on equal-protection grounds with civil commitments or with juvenile justice proceedings, its lack of due process safeguards is abundantly apparent. If children can be admitted against their will to an institution where they may be deprived of liberty for years, it should be of no constitutional consequence that the facility for confinement is called a mental hospital. As stated in *In re Gault* (1967), the case that radically changed juvenile justice procedures.

...however euphemistic the title, a "receiving home" or an "industrial school" for juveniles is an institution of confinement in which the child is incarcerated for a greater or lesser time. His world becomes "a building with whitewashed walls, regimented routine, and institutional hours. . . ." Instead of mother and father and sisters and brothers and friends and classmates, his world is peopled by guards, custodians, [and] state employees. . . . (p. 27)

The mentally ill or retarded child's world is also peopled with other patients, who may be confined for any reason from schizophrenia to waywardness. As *Gault* concludes, "In view of this, it would be extraordinary if our Constitution did not require the procedural regularity and the exercise of care implied in the phrase 'due process' " (pp. 27–28).

As a final point, several federal courts have also held that even when justified in abridging fundamental individual rights, states must do so by the narrowest or least drastic means possible. In the mental-health area, this doctrine requires a state, in giving unsolicited care, to employ the least restrictive alternative, providing outpatient treatment at a local facility, for example, rather than inpatient treatment at a large and remote institution (Chambers, 1972; *Covington v. Harris*, 1969; *Lake v. Cameron*, 1966). The present system provides no assurance that less restrictive alternatives are known or considered in decisions to "voluntarily" admit a child.

SIGNS OF CHANGE IN CHILDREN'S "VOLUNTARY" ADMISSIONS

Although the general rule permitting parents and guardians to "volunteer" children for mental hospital commitment is still law in most states, there are indications in scattered jurisdictions that changes may be forthcoming. Some of these changes relate only to older minors. Michigan's new Mental Health Code, for example, permits persons 13 years of age or older to object to their own "voluntary" admissions (*Michigan Statutes Annotated*, 1975). Also a 1952 NIMH model statute provides that a person may apply for voluntary admission to a mental hospital without parental consent at age 16 (Brakel and Rock, 1971, Appendix A). In Connecticut, one of several states that have adopted this or a similar provision in their mental-health codes, a state superior court decided that a boy who had been "voluntarily" admitted to the Yale Psychiatric Institute by his parents at age 15 had the power, at age 17, to demand he be released on his own authority, although his parents objected (*Melville v. Sabbatino*, 1973). The court reasoned that the right to admit oneself voluntarily at age 16 implied a corresponding right to demand release at the same age. It is instructive to note that this 17-year-old boy, after his release, returned to the hospital regularly to continue therapy with the same doctor who had treated him in the institution.[5]

Even before the Connecticut decision, a few other states had granted to those minors old enough to voluntarily admit themselves under the state's statutes all of the rights accorded to voluntarily admitted adult patients, including the right to demand release.[6] This approach, however, is taken in only a small minority of jurisdictions, and it remains to be seen how widely the Connecticut court's reasoning will be adopted.

For younger children, too, there are a few indications that the issue of "voluntary" admission may be changing. One of the most significant inroads into the concept of unmonitored, forced "volunteering" has been made in Tennessee. In 1974, the Nashville federal district court ordered, on due process grounds, the creation of a three-member admissions board at the Clover Bottom Developmental Center (*Saville v. Treadway*, 1974). The board's function is to conduct hearings on the appropriateness of the proposed admissions of all children under age 16 (and those over age 16 who lack the requisite understanding) to this institution for the mentally retarded. The board is composed of persons knowledgeable in the area of retardation but not affiliated with the institution. At each hearing, the proposed resident is assured the assistance of counsel and is afforded the right to be heard, to question witnesses, and to request further professional evaluations.

A different, more limited approach was taken by the Circuit Court of Cook County, Illinois, when it ruled that all children between the ages of 13 and 17 who had been admitted as "voluntary" patients to Illinois mental-health facilities by parents or guardians had the right to request their own discharge (*In the interest of Lee and Wesley*, 1972). Within five days, the institutions were required either to release these children or to request court hearings for involuntary commitment. At such a hearing, the minor was entitled to counsel, a jury, and other due process protections. The court's order was both retrospective and prospective in nature.

It is noteworthy that although the Tennessee and Illinois decisions both provide children with the means to resist "voluntary" admission, the procedural methods prescribed in these cases are quite different. In Illinois, the child (or a child advocate) must initiate a request for release, and this request must be granted unless the institution seeks the child's involuntary commitment through a judicial proceeding. However, the child's ignorance or fear may inhibit such a request, and the hearing, if one occurs, takes place *after* admission. In other words, the damage must be done before it can be rectified. The Illinois court apparently has assumed that the loss of liberty involved while a child contests an erroneous admission is not a substantial interest to be protected. In Tennessee, on the other hand, the proposed minor patient is accorded an automatic hearing *before* admission. However, the hearing is conducted by an administrative agency, and any subsequent appeal to the courts requires the initiative of the patient or an attorney.

These three major differences—(1) precommitment versus postcommitment review; (2) court versus administrative-agency review; and (3) review initiated automatically versus review only on the patient's request—represent basically different legal models for ensuring a child the right to refuse an improper admission. In July 1975, versions of these models were implemented in two states. The Tennessee legislature followed the Illinois court's approach by granting voluntary patients of any age the right to request release after admission (*Tennessee Code Annotated*, 1975). A federal court in Pennsylvania, on the other hand, adopted some features of each model (and added several of its own) in holding that minors have a due process right to commitment hearings (*Bartley v. Kremens*, 1975). The Pennsylvania court ruled that a preliminary hearing must be held within 72 hours of a child's admission and that another postcommitment hearing must be held within two weeks. The court noted that these hearings could be conducted by the state's court system until the legislature could establish "an unbiased tribunal" to hear them.

On March 22, 1976, as this book goes to press, the U.S. Supreme Court has agreed to review the *Bartley* decision. The high court's opinion, when it is rendered, should go far toward resolving many of the issues discussed here.

Presumably, still other approaches will be proposed by courts, legislatures, or others (Ellis, 1974, p. 910). Taken together over time, these models should provide a good basis for evaluating different procedures to protect children while striking an appropriate balance between the interests of parents and child.

The Tennessee, Illinois, and Pennsylvania courts all assured children the assistance of counsel during admission hearings. The Cook County court went a step further when it appointed the Legal Assistance Foundation of Chicago as child advocate for all state wards hospitalized in mental-health facilities. The court directed the Foundation's attorneys to examine the records of hospitalized minors and, if necessary, to interview them to determine if a request for release or any other action should be taken on their behalf. With the aid of these advocates, dozens of children have applied for and have obtained release.

TOWARD A NEW SOLUTION

In the hope that our views will assist and further the development of an admission procedure that protects the rights of children while preserving the legitimate prerogatives of parents or guardians, we propose the following guidelines. Our proposals are tentative pending the results of further research, which we are conducting.

First, an admission procedure should specify the age at which a child may act autonomously with the same capacity as an adult to consent to or to refuse admission and to demand release. The age most commonly suggested for such autonomy is 16 (by the NIMH model statute, several state statutes, and the Tennessee judicial opinion). The choice of 16 is arbitrary, as would be any specified age threshold. In the absence of a better rationale for the choice of another age, however, 16 probably best reflects society's opinion of the age at which most children can make adult choices in this complex area.

Prospective patients younger than 16 should be assured an impartial review of the parental/institutional admission decision. The review should take place, except in emergency situations, *before* the child's admission. To ensure administrative efficiency, that review should be conducted by an advocacy office that is independent of the institution, rather than by an admissions committee. A member of the office should be assigned to advise and, if necessary, to argue on behalf of the child. Providing the child with an independent, professional advocate is the necessary precursor to every other right the child may claim. Only with the aid of such a person will the child be fully advised concerning the availability of all his or her procedural rights. Only with the aid of such a person will other "children's rights" be legally established (Forer, 1969).

The advocate would represent the child, not the parent or the guardian. The advocate's functions would be to investigate the facts supporting the proposed admission, to inform the child of his or her rights, to advise the child of the course of action the advocate believes would be in the child's best interest, and to represent the child's professed desires to the best of his or her abilities.

Undoubtedly, most admissions should proceed without interruption; in particular, the very presence of an advocate should inhibit third-party "volunteering" on frivolous or improper grounds. However, if the child wishes to resist admission, or if the advocate believes the child should resist admission, the advocate would convene a hearing before an independent authority with power to approve or deny admission. In our view, an administrative board composed of persons of varied occupational backgrounds who are unaffiliated with the institution but who have a knowledge of mental illness or retardation, institutional conditions, patients' rights, and available, alternative treatment modalities is probably the most suitable body for this task. Before this board, the advocate could challenge the motives or reasons of the parent or guardian, the accuracy of the diagnosis of the child, and the adequacy and effectiveness of the proposed institutional treatment. Perhaps more importantly, the advocate could suggest and investigate the availability of less restrictive treatment alternatives and recommend them to the parents, the guardian, or the administrative board.

Judicial appeal of the board's decisions would be permitted but probably would not be requested frequently. Admissions should be of limited duration. After an appropriate period (perhaps, three months), the institution, to continue the admission, would be required to demonstrate to the review board that the child is still in need of treatment and is either progressing or is benefiting from custodial care. Any subsequent continuances of the admission would be permitted only through conformance with a similar procedure.

It is past time to review the rule of law that gives parents or guardians the unmonitored power to "voluntarily" admit their offspring to mental institutions. As Oliver Wendell Holmes once said:

It is revolting to have no better reason for a rule of law than that so it was laid down in the time of Henry IV. It is still more revolting if the grounds upon which it was laid down have vanished long since, and the rule simply persists from blind imitation of the past.

An act involving another's liberty that will not bear public scrutiny should not be performed. The right of parents to control their offspring need not, and should not, extend to the point of precluding an impartial review of their actions in a matter of such serious consequence to the child.

NOTES

1. For example, see: *Cal. Welf. and Inst. Code,* Sec. 6000; *Ohio Rev. Stat.,* Secs. 5122.02 and 5125.311; *Pa. Stat. Ann.* 50-4402. *See also Ellis,* 1974, pp. 840–41.

2. The District of Columbia Code, for example, includes in its definition of "neglected child" one "... (B) who is without proper parental care ... necessary for his physical, mental or emotional health. ...." *D.C. Code Ann.,* Sec. 16-2301 (9).

3. The major exception to the general rule is that minors may contract for "necessaries." Medical care has been held to be a "necessary" where the parent fails to provide such care. For example, see: *McAllister v. Saginaw Timber Co.,* 171 Wash. 448, 18 P.2d 41 (1933).

4. For example, Massachusetts permits minors to consent to treatment for venereal disease (M.G.L., Ch. 111, Sec. 117) and, if 12 years of age or older, for drug dependency (M.G.L., Ch. 112, Sec. 12E).
5. Letter from W. Wagoner, New Haven Legal Assistance Association (July 1, 1974), on file at Center for Law and Health Sciences.
6. For example, see: *Mass. Dept. of Mental Health Reg.* MH 15.2, Sec. 4.

REFERENCES

Bartley v. Kremens, —— F. Supp. ——, Civil Action No. 72-2272 (U.S.D.C., E.D. Pa., July 24, 1975).

Baxtrom v. Herold, 383 U.S. 107, 111 (1966).

Bell v. Wayne County General Hospital, **384** F. Supp. **1085** (E.D. Mich., 1974).

Brakel, S. J. and Rock, R. S. (eds.). *The mentally disabled and the law.* Chicago: University of Chicago Press. American Bar Foundation, 1971.

Chambers, D. Alternatives to civil commitment of the mentally ill: Practical guides and constitutional imperatives. *Mich. Law Rev.* **70** (1972), 1107, 1155–68.

Covington v. Harris, 419 F.2d 617, 623 (D.C. Cir., 1969).

Dixon v. Attorney General of Pennsylvania, 325 F.Supp. 966 (M.D. Pa., 1971).

Donaldson v. O'Connor, 493 F.2d 507 (5th Cir., 1974), Vacated (on other grounds) sub nom *O'Connor v. Donaldson,* —— (U.S. —— 1975).

Ellis, J. Volunteering children. *Calif. Law Rev.* **62** (1974), 840–916.

Ferleger, D. Incarcerated juveniles—why? An analysis of partial data submitted by defendants in response to interrogatories by plaintiffs. In *Bartley v. Kremens,* Civil Action No. 72-2272 (U.S.D.C., E.D. Pa., September 17, 1973).

Forer, L. Rights of children: The legal vacuum. *Am. Bar Assoc. J.* **55** (1969), 1151–52.

Ginsberg, A. An examination of the civil rights of mentally ill children. *Child Welfare* **52** (1973), 14–15.

Griswold v. Connecticut, 381 U.S. 479 (1965).

Harvard Law Review. Note: Developments in the law—equal protection. *Harv. Law Rev.* **82** (1969), 1065.

Harvard Law Review. Note: Civil commitment of the mentally ill. *Harv. Law Rev.* **87** (1974), 1190, 1201 Et Seq.

Hawks v. Lazaro, 202 S.E.2d 109 (W. Va., 1974).

Heryford v. Parker, 396 F.2d 393 (10th Cir., 1968).

Inmates of Boys Training School v. Affleck, 346 F.Supp. 1354 (D.R.I., 1972).

In re Ballay, 482 F.2d 648 (D.C. Cir., 1973).

In re Gault, 387 U.S. 1 (1967).

In re Johnnie Barnard, 455 F.2d 1370 (D.C. Cir., 1971).

In re Michael E., Supp., 123 Rptr. 103 (1975).

In re Winship, 397 U.S. 357 (1970).

In the interest of Lee and Wesley, Nos. 68J(D) 1362, 66J(d) 6383, and 68J 15805, Cir. Ct. of Cook County, Cnty. Dept., Juv. Div., Ill. (February 29, and August 24, 1972).

Kent v. U.S., 383 U.S. 541 (1966).

Kleinfeld, A. J. The balance of power among infants, their parents, and the state. *Fam. Law Q.* 4 (1970), 409.

Lake v. Cameron, 364 F.2d 657 (D.C. Cir., 1966).

Lessard v. Schmidt, 349 F.Supp. 1078 (E.D. Wis., 1972), vacated (but with no opinion on substantive issue) 94 S.Ct. 713 (1974).

McAllister v. Saginaw Timber Co., 171 Wash. 448, 18, P.2d 41 (1933).

McGowan v. Maryland, 366 U.S. 420 (1961).

McKeiver v. Pennsylvania, 403 U.S. 528 (1971).

Melville v. Sabbatino, 30 Conn.Sup. 320, 313 A.2d 886 (1973).

Michigan Statutes Annotated, Ch. 127, Sec. 14.800, 417 (1975).

Nelson v. Heyne, 491 F.2d 352 (7th Cir., 1974).

NIMH *Hospital inpatient treatment units for emotionally disturbed children: United States, 1971–1972*. Department of Health, Education and Welfare Pub. No. (ADM) (1974A), 74–82.

NIMH *Residential psychiatric facilities for children and adolescents: United States, 1971–1972*. Department of Health, Education and Welfare Pub. No. (ADM) (1974B), 74–78.

N.Y. State Association for Retarded Children and Patricia Parise et al v. Rockefeller, 357 F.Supp. 752 (1973).

San Antonio Independent School District v. Rodriguez, 411 U.S. 1, 18 (1973) et seq.

Saville v. Treadway, Civil Action No. 6969 (U.S.D.C., M.D. Tenn., opinion of March 8 and order of April 18, 1974).

Scheff, T. *Being mentally ill: A sociological theory*. Chicago: Aldine, 1966.

Tennessee Code Annotated, Sec. 33-601 amended (1975).

Welsch v. Likins, 373 F.Supp. 487 (D. Minn., 1974).

Wheeler v. Glass, 473 F.2d 983 (7th Cir., 1973).

Williamson v. Lee Optical, 348 U.S. 483 (1955).

Wyatt v. Adeholt, 503 F.2d 1305 (5th Cir., 1974).

Wyatt v. Stickney, 344 F.Supp. 373 and 387 (M.D. Ala., 1972) affirmed sub nom *Wyatt v. Aderholt*, 503 F.2d 1305 (5th Cir., 1974).

Yale Law Journal. Note: Legislative purpose, rationality, and equal protection. *Yale Law J.* 82 (1973), 129.

Punishment:
Parent Rites
versus Children's Rights

NORMA DEITCH FESHBACH and
SEYMOUR FESHBACH

This chapter examines the question of children's rights in the context of parent practices, values, and prerogatives. The issues of children's rights can be approached from many different perspectives inasmuch as they relate to many aspects of our social structure and values.

In the past some attention has been given to children's rights in regard to the industrial exploitation of child labor (Berger, 1971), gross neglect, sexual abuse (Helfer and Kempe, 1972; Kempe and Helfer, 1972), and physical harm (Gil, 1970; Light, 1974). More recently, the scope of issues has been broadened to include a new set of considerations generated by changes in society. Thus there is now concern with children's rights in regard to therapy (Robinson, 1974), diagnostic labeling (Mercer, 1974), incarceration (Ohlin, Coates, and Miller, 1974), foster care and adoption practices (Berger, 1971; Jenkins and Norman, 1972; Mnookin, 1974), the effects of educational practices (Falk, 1941; Finkelstein, 1975), and even privacy and other legal privileges (Rodham, 1974).

However, with the exception of the extreme violation of children's physical integrity, relatively little attention has been given to issues bearing on children's rights within the family structure. A number of reasons may account for this state of affairs. Most paramount is the view of the family as a sacrosanct unit, invulnerable and impervious to outside inspection

We would like to express our appreciation to Professors Sol Cohen and Ruby Takanishi for their thoughtful comments and suggestions and to Patricia Jordan for her assistance in assembling the bibliography.

149

and influence. Only when a family system or its subsystem parts manifests open deviation from prescriptive behaviors is license extended for intervention into the internal workings of the family.

It appears to us that an adequate understanding of the ramifications of the concept of children's rights requires an invasion of the family sanctum. An appropriate vehicle on which to focus this analysis is the question of parental punishment practices. In so addressing ourselves, it is recognized that we may encroach on the traditional domain of parent rights, an issue which we examine later. Further, the complexity of evaluating children's and parents' rights in regard to punishment practices is also acknowledged. Social values regarding types of punishment vary markedly as a function of cultural settings, age and sex of the child, "legitimacy" of the provocation, historical period, and presumed function of the punishment. Moreover, psychologists are not unanimous in their views and advocacies regarding the desirabilities and effects of different forms of punishment. These difficulties notwithstanding, it is our plan to evaluate the degree to which various categories of punishment infringe on children's rights in relation to psychological effects.

One category of punishment is not a contemporary issue: the use of extreme physical punishment that results in visible physical injury to the child. Such injuries may include single or multiple cuts, fractures, burns—in brief, those signs or symptoms that are encompassed by the "battered-child syndrome," the designation that currently signifies the problem of child abuse by caretakers (Kempe et al., 1962).

This social problem has become an important and salient public and professional issue. In the fields of public and mental health, a variety of preventive and interventive programs is being developed and implemented to reduce the incidence of child abuse. These programs include therapeutic and counseling help for the child abusers and, more importantly perhaps, the development of diagnostic procedures for the prediction of high-risk parents (Kempe and Helfer, 1972; National Center for Prevention and Treatment of Child Abuse and Neglect, 1973; Parents Anonymous, Inc., 1972; Paulson and Blake, 1969). It is instructive to note that this major social problem has only recently achieved visibility. When we consider the number of families involved, with estimates ranging from 500,400 to 2,000,000 in the United States alone (Gil, 1970; Light, 1974; Parke, and Collmer, 1975), and the few helping services available, the degree of resistance to intervention in family practices becomes evident.

The fact that we are witnessing a dramatic change in interest in the problem of child abuse and in the expansion of funding efforts and programs in this area does not necessarily represent a significant change in fundamental child-rearing values by either the family or society at large.

For some time now, there have been legal sanctions (Paulsen, 1966; Rodham, 1974), community-group efforts (McFerran, 1958; Parke and Collmer, 1975), periodic expressions of professional concern (Gil, 1974; Kaufman, 1962; Kempe, 1973), and broad social disapproval regarding the physical abuse of children. These various forces have now coalesced into a more integrated and potent movement aimed at reducing the incidences and effects of child abuse, especially in the United States.

Not so long ago, many of the child training practices that are now considered brutal and abusive were regarded as acceptable procedures for socializing the child. These practices were not merely reluctant expressions of "last-resort" actions, but were recommended, advocated, and endowed with virtue and even biblical support (Radbill, 1968). This history of child training, from antiquity to the present, especially as reflected in the writings of deMause (1974B), among others, portrays what appears to us to be a panorama of horrors. In classical Greece, children were subjected to such devices and practices as shackles for the feet, handcuffs, gags, and bloody Spartan flagellation contests that resulted in youths being whipped to death (deMause, 1974A). Beating instruments included whips of all kinds, shovels, canes, iron rods, bundles of sticks, special whips made of small chains, and a special instrument used by school masters called a flapper, which was designed to raise blisters. Even royalty was not spared the prescribed dosage of corporal punishment; Louis XIII, for example, was whipped every morning from the age of 25 months.

By the late medieval period, the extraordinary excesses of "acceptable" child abuse began to be tempered. Thus a thirteenth-century law stated that if a child were beaten until (s)he bled, it was good for the child's memory; however, it was illegal to beat a child to death (deMause, 1974B). The severity and frequency of child beating, while undergoing a civilized decline from the Renaissance to the nineteenth century, still persisted in many contexts and communities. Thus a German schoolmaster could reckon that he had given 911,527 strokes with the stick, 124,000 lashes with the whip, 136,715 slaps with the hand, and 1,115,800 boxes on the ears. The administration of corporal punishment was not reserved for the child's parents, but extended to all of the child's caretakers and socializing agents.

While not all historians concur in this consistently dismal image of the history of child training (Aries, 1962; Calhoun, 1974), even a modified interpretation leaves us with a more than sobering impression of the ways in which children were disciplined—all socially, legally, and morally acceptable, if not normative. During this all too long period, parents, teachers, and society at large concurred in the use of disciplinary methods that today would lead to legal sanction as well as severe social disapproval.

In terms of contemporary values and psychological orientation and insights, practices that were once socially approved are now considered part of the battered-child syndrome, requiring therapeutic intervention for both the victim and the abuser. Because practices that were once considered appropriate are now viewed as reprehensible, the disquieting possibility arises that practices considered acceptable today may be judged barbaric by future generations. In other words, the question raised is whether there are extant parental punishment practices that we consider legitimate methods of child training and discipline that in a few decades will be perceived as examples of child abuse.

The extrapolation that can be made from this historical perspective strongly suggests that society's attitudes toward punishment practices will undergo continuous and significant modifications with the passage of time that will produce increased insight into the effects of various disciplinary experiences on children's development. Given the past course of historical changes in child-rearing methods (Bronfenbrenner, 1958; Stendler, 1950; Vincent, 1951; Wolfenstein, 1953), it seems reasonable to infer that the path of future change will be in the direction of more compassionate caring for children and will be in part reflected in a decline of corporal punishment and its psychological equivalents. The possibility of accelerating this process and creating, in the present, the more effective and harmonious child-rearing behaviors that we anticipate in the future is appealing. Our consciousness of this historical development and of the psychological variables involved may make this possibility a reality.

Our conjecture regarding the future pattern of disciplinary practices is not based solely on inferences drawn from historical modes. We believe that an analysis of the psychological effects of various modes of punishment and discipline provides a rationale for and leads to a similar conclusion. Moreover, when we view the issue of punishment practices in the context of children's rights, the concept of child abuse and what constitutes the infringement of children's rights can be extended to include a broad range of physical and psychological punishments.

We begin our analysis of the issue of punishment practices with the basic assumption that a child has a right not to be subjected to cruel and unusual punishment. Further, we wish to go beyond current definitions of child abuse and child battering to include all forms of punishment that have negative consequences for the growth and well-being of the child. Moreover, we wish to question not only the prerogatives of teachers and caretakers in regard to disciplinary practices, but also the disciplinary prerogatives of the parents themselves.

In broadening the domain of children's rights within the family, the responsibilities of children and the rights and responsibilities of parents are clearly acknowledged. Children's rights cannot be articulated without delineating the province and role of the parent. Unlike the relationship of the child to most institutions in our society (as examples, the child in school, the child in a children's center), there are no written documents that explicate, define and enumerate the rights and responsibilities of parents and children. While some religious maxims and social traditions are related to discipline and laws pertain primarily to exceptional situations, the rules and regulations guiding family interactions remain vague and implicit. Even less clear is the rationale and justification for many routine parental actions that often become endowed with authority through the process of ritualization. A behavior that may have had some functional value in some special circumstances can become exaggerated, transformed, and perpetuated into a parental practice or "rite" that may no longer be "right" for the child. Thus, in historical periods when survival depended on raw if not brutal modes of social interaction, there may have been some justification for parents and society to provide aggressive models and to employ corporal punishment. Similarly, in a time when children were highly vulnerable to sexual assault and exploitation, the repression of masturbation and related erotic behaviors in young children may have been protective and functional. Further vestigial practices can be cited in regard to sex-role differentiation and discrimination in occupational choice and opportunity.

The fact that a behavior is ritualized or traditional does not imply that it is, ipso facto, nonfunctional, inappropriate, or psychologically harmful. Behaviors serve many different values and obviously have different functions in different cultures. As psychologists, we need to examine the psychological consequences of particular modes of discipline in different cultures and to provide social agents with alternatives from which they may choose, acting both on the basis of their particular values and as advocates of children's rights. Before embarking on this task it is useful to review and summarize current patterns of parental punishment practices.

PATTERNS OF PARENTAL PUNISHMENT PRACTICES

Complete data on normative and comparative child-rearing practices, especially modal techniques that are descriptive and typical of different segments of our society, simply do not exist. In fact, with passing time, information as to how parents actually socialize their children is becoming increasingly scarce. Interest in conducting studies on the effects of different child-rearing practices on the development of children (Sears, Maccoby, and Levin, 1957) has waned; this interest has been partially supplanted by more controlled but narrower studies on the dyadic mother–child interaction (Feshbach, 1973; Hess and Shipman, 1967). Further, the once raging controversy regarding the relative permissiveness of the middle class and the greater punitiveness of the lower class in overall child training behaviors (Havighurst and Davis, 1955) is no longer an issue of great concern. This decreased concern is partially a result of the inconsistent conclusions and/or varying methodologies of the different studies and partially a consequence of the overlapping practices of all classes in our society and the increased attention to variability within class (Bronfenbrenner, 1958; Erlanger, 1974; Robinson et al., 1973).

Thus it is impossible to present specific descriptions of particular punishment techniques employed by parents of different social classes and ethnic backgrounds. However, extant studies enable us to make nonspecific statements regarding general categories of disciplinary techniques that include a variety of parental punishment practices. Punishment is frequently dichotomized into two broad categories: physical punishment, and psychological or love-oriented punishment (Bronfenbrenner, 1958; Hoffman, 1970). The term "love-oriented" does not imply, nor is it used synonymously with, positive training and control procedures, because it includes guilt-inducing and isolation techniques that are not considered favorable strategies to promote mental health.

Physical punishment seems to be the more frequent child-rearing practice in the family's repertoire of training strategies. In a series of papers addressing the use of physical punishment, Steinmetz and Straus conclude that corporal punishment is almost a universal practice in England and the United States, with 84–97% of parents resorting to physical punishment at some period in their children's lives (Steinmetz and Straus, 1973, 1974). Rather surprising, is the data concerning the use and threat of physical punishment by parents of high-school seniors, an age at which we might expect more verbal, nonviolent, and egalitarian parent–child interactions to occur (Straus, 1973). The specific behaviors included here (as elsewhere) under the rubric of physical punishment are beating, slapping, kicking, and throwing things at the child.

In a broad, longitudinal study conducted in England (Newson, 1968), it was found that 60–70% of mothers of 4-year-olds "smacked" their children between once a day and once a week. It should be pointed out that most of the published data on punishment practices, historically or concurrently, focuses on maternal practices. Inspection of the data does not reveal whether this one-sided parental picture is a reflection of procedures used (Cook-Gumprez, 1973) or whether discipline at home is a maternal-linked role behavior (Sunley, 1955).

Parents and citizens who interpreted the early student revolts at Berkeley and elsewhere during the 1960s as indicative of the more permissive, non-punitive child-rearing practices of the 1940s would be surprised to learn that in a study conducted by Heinstein (1965) on 809 mothers, 50% reported using some form of physical punishment when questioned about their usual method of punishment. In that study, as in others (Cook-Gumprez, 1973), the mother's use of physical punishment was found to be related to the extent of her education.

Clifford (1959), interviewing mothers of children in three age groups (3-, 6-, and 9-year-olds), found that the younger the child, the more frequent the instances of discipline; that mothers were largely responsible for discipline; and that the type of discipline shifted with age from a "manual," physical technique to a verbal approach. Clifford's study indicated that the ten most frequent disciplinary methods used at home were reasoning, scolding, coaxing, spanking, diverting, threatening, ignoring, forceable removal, isolation, and withholding privileges. Two general conclusions may be suggested by this data. First, our knowledge of how parents rear children is very limited. Second, what is known about child-rearing practices indicates that parents make frequent use of physical as well as psychological punishment in raising their children, probably without fully realizing the effects of the punishments they employ.

EFFECTS OF PHYSICAL AND PSYCHOLOGICAL PUNISHMENT PRACTICES

The avowed purpose of punishment is to reduce or to eliminate the behavior that is being punished. Thus in evaluating the effects of different modes of punishment and related disciplinary practices, an important criterion is the change that occurs in behavior following punishment. However, the effects of parental reactions are not limited to an isolated, prohibited response. Parents function as models, as sources of emotional security, as socializers and protectors. Because of the intimate relationship between child and parent, the effect of a parental reaction to a particular deviant behavior extends to nondeviant behaviors, to the child's self-system, and may therefore foster unintended and undesired side effects. Consequently, in assessing certain practices such as punishment and discipline, it is necessary to go beyond the intended response change and assess other areas of the child's personality that may have been differentially affected by the use of a particular mode of punishment. A parent who hits a child for being late to dinner serves as an aggressive model. In addition to becoming motivated by fear to be prompt for dinner, the child is also learning that aggression is appropriate under certain circumstances;

that is, when one is disappointed or frustrated by others. Admittedly, the situation is complex, with many parameters influencing the child's response to the punishment administered for the infraction. However, the essential point is that the effects of a specific mode of punishment or discipline must be evaluated within the context of a larger, interpersonal response system.

Most research bearing on the effects of variation in modes of punishment is carried out within a larger fabric of unassessed parental and social influences. Further, it is difficult to isolate the effects of a unitary mode of discipline. Despite these restrictions and qualifications, research on punishment practices does yield meaningful results that provide an empirical framework for determining children's rights in regard to parental disciplinary behaviors. In summarizing a representative sampling of studies on the effects of different punishment practices, we first consider physical punishment and then turn to the effects of such psychological punishments as the use of ridicule, shame, and guilt. It should be noted that in a number of the studies reviewed here, the mode of punishment is unclear or is comprised of a mixture of disciplinary measures.

The Effects of Physical Punishment

The first systematic data on the effects of punishment emerged in the course of experimental studies of animal learning in which a form of physical punishment (electric shock) was contingent on a particular response by the animals (Estes, 1944; Skinner, 1938). In these early studies, punishment seemed temporarily to suppress a response rather than to extinguish it, leading Skinner to conclude that punishment was a relatively ineffective technique for eliminating undesirable behaviors. Skinner consequently focused on positive reinforcement as the critical element in his theory and methods of behavior shaping and modification.

The idea of the positive reinforcement of behavior prevailed for several decades, until challenged by Solomon (1964) and his associates and subsequently by other investigators (Boe and Church, 1966; Parke, 1970). In recent years, additional research on punishment effects has been conducted with children, but for obvious ethical reasons, reproof and deprivation rather than physical pain have been used as the principal modes of punishment. After an extensive series of studies with 6- to 8-year-old children, Parke (1970) concluded:

It is unlikely that a socialization program based solely on punishment would be very effective; the child needs to be taught new appropriate responses in addition to learning to suppress unacceptable forms of behavior (p. 281).

These studies not only indicate that punishment fails to communicate to the child what the appropriate response is, but also question the ineffectiveness of punishment in suppressing the undesirable behavior. To suppress a behavior through punishment requires the right combination of a number of parameters, including timing, intensity, consistency, and the affectional relationship between the child and the punitive agent. Although physical punishment was not employed in these later studies, its effectiveness should be dependent on the same parameters as other modes of punishment.

The data most relevant to the effects of parental use of physical punishment are those from studies of child-rearing practices primarily conducted under naturalistic circumstances. The data reflect methodological limitations, including bias and error inherent in retrospective reports: the use of physical punishment confounded with variations in affection toward the child and the degree of family stress, as well as clustering different types, degrees, and frequencies of physical punishment into one category. However, there is a surprising degree of consistency in the overall pattern of findings in spite of the diversity of procedures, measures, and populations employed by the various investigators.

Studies of child-rearing practices that assess the effects of parental punishment, especially physical punishment, reflect a consistent outcome. In general, the degree of parental punitiveness has been found to be positively correlated with various forms of psychopathology, especially delinquency and aggressive acting-out behavior (Feshbach and Feshbach, 1971; McCord, McCord, and Howard, 1961). The positive relationship found in a large number of studies between parental use of physical punishment and aggressive, antisocial behavior in the child is especially revealing. The suppressive potential of physical punishment that undoubtedly exists appears to be substantially outweighed by the instigating and modeling properties of parental resort to physical punishment. It is difficult to find any empirical justification for the old adage, "Spare the rod and spoil the child."

We concur with the methodological reservations raised by Yarrow, Campbell, and Burton (1968) in recognizing the difficulty of establishing casual relations between specific child-rearing practices and specific behaviors in the child. Parental behaviors, such as severe punishment or maternal rejection, do not operate in isolation, but rather occur in conjunction with other aspects of the home environment. In addition, the child's behavior may well affect the parents' reactions to the child, so that it is sometimes difficult to determine whether a particular parental method of handling a child is the cause or the result of that child's action (Bell, 1968). Finally, a variety of methods, all subject to varying sources of distortions and error, has been used to assess the attitudes of both parent and child.

It is reasonable to infer from the empirical data that the use of physical punishment tends to be counterproductive. It often fails to suppress the response it is intended to inhibit, and in the case of aggression, may even exacerbate the behavior. There is also evidence that children who are subjected to physical punishment are less likely to have internalized moral standards than children who are subjected to other modes of discipline; such children often display less guilt and acceptance of responsibility for deviant behaviors (Hoffman, 1970) and a weakened ability to resist temptations (Feshbach, 1975B).

Obviously, an occasional spanking is not going to traumatize a child, destroy the spirit, or produce anxiety and hostility. However, the use of corporal punishment by schools and by parents as a prescribed mode of discipline for certain infractions is objectionable. It sets a poor example for the child. It teaches the child that physical punishment is the appropriate response to use in conflict situations. The use of corporal punishment by the state, the school, or the parent is simply a poor method of socializing children.

In addition to rejecting the use of physical punishment on empirical grounds, we can also question its use on humanistic grounds, because being subjected to physical punishment can be seen as a violation of children's rights. Physical punishment is unfair; there is a basic inequity in an adult physically striking a child—the match is not equal. Physical punishment is also an undifferentiated response. Given the unique importance of language for the human species, the use of nonverbal, physical, and perhaps even violent methods in the training of our young possesses the qualities of an atavistic response. Also, physical punishment cannot be escaped; there is no apparent way to avoid the distress of physical pain. Subjecting other children or adults, to deliberate physical pain is the prototype of inhumane behavior. It is human to be angry; it is also human to lose control over aggressive behavior. But to engage in the institutionalized, normative infliction of physical pain as a mode of punishment is unnecessary and, in our judgment, uncivilized.

Psychological Punishment

The empirical evidence on the effects of psychological punishments such as ridicule, shame, rejection, and guilt induction is not nearly as substantial or as consistent as evidence relating to physical punishment. Punishment practices grossly categorized as love-withdrawal techniques and their effects are more complex and subtle and less easily assessed than the effects of physical punishment. We believe that psychological punishment is also a destructive socializing technique.

A major difficulty in evaluating the empirical literature on the use of various modes of psychological punishment is the fact that most studies do not distinguish among the different types of psychological punishment. The parent who punishes a child by refusing to speak to the youngster or acting in a cold manner is engaging in a form of rejection. This category of love-withdrawal may well produce different effects than the use of shame and guilt. Certainly, there is abundant evidence that as a generalized attitude toward the child, rejection by the parent has particularly destructive effects (Glueck and Glueck, 1950; Goldfarb, 1945; Lowrey, 1940; McCord, McCord, and Howard, 1961). Studies on the effects of specific love-withdrawal techniques in the context of a less negative, familial atmosphere suggest that when the parents use guilt, shame, and emotional coldness, excessive anxiety and inhibition (Hoffman, 1963; Hoffman and Saltzstein, 1967; Sears, 1961) and more extreme psychopathological disturbances result (Anthony, 1958; Bromberg, 1961; Rodnick and Garmezy, 1957). Thus Colby (1974) considers shame avoidance the key dynamic in his computer-simulation model of paranoid behavior. The use of shame and related love-withdrawal techniques have been most extensively studied in relationship to moral development (Hoffman, 1970). While the evidence here is not consistent, overall the data indicates that love-withdrawal techniques do not facilitate the internalization of moral, prosocial attitudes and standards and, like physical punishment, may sometimes result in a lack of generosity and resistance to temptation and increased cheating and aggressive behaviors (Feshbach, 1973). Hoffman (1970) maintains that when love-withdrawal contributes to effective moral development, it is accompanied by explanation, reasoning, and related cognitive induction procedures. After reviewing pertinent experimental and child-rearing data, Hoffman states ". . . love-withdrawal does make the child more susceptible to adult influence, but this has no necessary bearing on moral development" (Hoffman, 1970, p. 302). He concludes that the disciplinary practices most conducive to moral development are other-oriented induction procedures.

Another area of research that questions the efficacy of either physical or psychological punishment that is dependant on anxiety-provoking mechanisms, concerns the behavioral accompaniments of aggression anxiety. The results of a number of studies indicate that under permissive conditions, subjects with a high degree of aggression anxiety actually respond more aggressively than subjects with a low degree of aggression anxiety (Eron, Walder, Toigo, and Lefkowitz, 1963; Feshbach and Jaffe, 1969). Rather dramatic evidence on the violence potential of aggression-inhibited individuals is provided in studies of extremely assaultive, homicidal individuals. Within this group, Megargee (cited in Bromberg, 1961) has isolated a personality pattern labeled "chronic overcontrol," in which the offender outwardly appears to be highly repressed but inwardly is alienated and potentially capable of extremely violent acts.

Case histories of individuals who have committed homicides (Bromberg, 1961) seem to indicate that Megargee's chronic overcontrollers are subjected to physical as well as to psychological punishment. Although the data on psychological punishment is not as substantial as the data on physical punishment, there appears to be a reasonable basis for concluding that neither fear of physical pain nor fear of psychological pain is conducive to optimal psychological development and functioning. The question then arises, if we reject both physical and psychological punishments as infringements on children's rights and as empirically ineffective, what methods can the parent use to enhance child training and socialization?

ALTERNATIVES TO PHYSICAL AND PSYCHOLOGICAL PUNISHMENT

Alternatives to punishment can be grouped into two broad categories: (1) training behaviors that are incompatible with disapproved responses, and (2) parental action contingent on the child's commission of a deviant act.

Training approaches have been discussed extensively elsewhere and are only briefly treated here (Feshbach, 1970; Feshbach and Feshbach, 1972). They include the positive reinforcement of prosocial behaviors and the arrangement of the child's environment to facilitate the evocation of these desired behaviors. There is abundant evidence to support the proposition that the facilitation through reinforcement or modeling of responses that are incompatible with socially disapproved behaviors is an important element in the effective socialization of the child. If a child is raised in a household in which the parents display and reinforce cooperative behaviors and reasoned, nonaggressive solutions to conflict, then the child is more likely to manifest these same behaviors and less likely to engage in deviant behaviors requiring some form of disciplinary response. This observation, although simple, is important. This implies that a substantial component of the effective discipline of a child is the modeling and reinforcing of responses that reduce the frequency of disapproved behaviors that occasion disciplinary actions. Another direct method for accomplishing the same objective is to arrange the child's environment in such a way as to minimize the motivation and opportunities for infractions. Parents utilize this procedure when they remove fragile objects from the reach of toddlers. A similar principle is involved when a child therapist helps a parent to modify the style in which communications are transmitted to a child; the parent presents a modified stimulus pattern which, in turn, elicits a modified response from the child (Patterson, Cobb, and Ray, 1972).

In addition to these direct methods for enhancing the probability of desired behaviors, a number of processes and behavior patterns have a more indirect but nevertheless significant influence on the occurrence of socially undesirable behaviors. One such process is empathy (Feshbach, 1975A). The child who is empathic is more able to perceive events from the perspective of others and to share affective experiences. Because of these capabilities—the ability to experience another's pain as well as pleasure and the capacity to understand a situation in terms of another's frame of reference—an empathic child is less likely to apply aggressive solutions to conflict situations and more likely to engage in prosocial behaviors than a child who is not empathic (Feshbach and Feshbach, 1969; Hoffman, 1975). There is some evidence linking empathic behavior in the child, particularly in girls, to parental use of reasoning, explanation, and related cognitive strategies in interactions with the child (Feshbach, 1975A; Hoffman, 1975). These cognitive strategies, more generally characterized as induction techniques, also constitute an important alternative available to the parent following the child's commission of a deviant act.

Yet in spite of exemplary parent-training behaviors, children still exhibit deviant behaviors. A substantial frequency of parent–child interactions pertains to the regulation of and the response to infractions by the child. These infractions vary widely with respect to type, severity, and antecedents of provocation. Most parents are somewhat cognizant of this variability in the nature of the child's misbehavior and employ a variety of disciplinary procedures accordingly. At the same time, the extent to which parents still rely on physical and psychological punishment is a reflection of the degree to which principles of effective discipline are inadequately understood and practiced.

This is not to imply that alternative formulas can be readily prescribed. Psychologists have not yet developed guidelines or manuals of discipline for parents to employ in socializing the child. Individual differences among children and the almost infinite variety of circumstances with which parents must deal render a programmed approach inappropriate. However, it is possible to designate some useful principles that can be employed as guidelines when responding to infractions by the child. These principles, which are designed to provide alternatives to physical and psychological punishment practices, presuppose that the function of discipline is not to penalize the child but "to correct, mold, or perfect the [child's] mental facilities or moral character" (Webster, 1968). Also, while these alternatives are intended to enhance children's rights, they are not intended to diminish children's responsibilities. By children's "responsibilities" are meant those age-appropriate behaviors characterized by independence, self-regulation, and serving familial or social needs. Expectations of the child's responsibilities must take into account the child's developmental level and his or her other needs. Nevertheless, given these restrictions, the assumption of responsibilities is important for the child's development, and the proposed alternatives are compatible with this requirement.

The critical dimension that the parent must consider in disciplining a child for an infraction is the cause of the child's misbehavior, rather than the negative consequences of the misbehavior. The Piagetian hierarchy of moral development in which moral judgments made in terms of the causes of an infraction (accidental versus intentional) are at a higher level of cognitive development than judgments made in terms of the consequences of an action (a valuable broken vase versus an inexpensive broken vase) applies with special cogency to the disciplinary actions of a parent. It would be unrealistic to expect the parent to function as a psychologist when attempting to account for the child's misbehavior. However, by being attuned to particular categories of "causes" or antecedents of misbehaviors, the parent is able to take a more differentiated, articulated, and therefore a more appropriate, disciplinary action.

CAUSES OF MISBEHAVIOR

We can distinguish at least four major categories of determinants of infractions (Feshbach and Feshbach, 1973): (1) inadequate ego controls; (2) misappraisals; (3) objectionable habits; and (4) cognitively mediated objectionable behaviors.

Inadequate Ego Controls

In particular, the young child performs actions on impulse and commits infractions because (s)he lacks self-control mechanisms. Verbal admonitions with age-appropriate explanations are useful here. The parent who says "No, don't play with the radio; it may break, and then you won't be able to listen to it," provides a verbal structure that the child can repeat and can use to help regulate his or her behavior. Changing the environment and removing objects that evoke undesirable behaviors is also a useful approach, but it may not always be a feasible one. In general, the parent's goals are to prevent the impulsive action from occurring and to provide the child with verbal explanations and other responses that facilitate the development of self-control.

Misappraisals

Children frequently fail to carry out a designated task or commit some other infraction when they receive ambiguous communications regarding what is expected of them and the consequences of their failure to conform to expectations. "Ignorance of the law" may be an inadequate excuse in the courtroom, but it is very germane in the home. Parents must clarify the behaviors that are approved, those that are disapproved, and the nature of the contingent punishment. In considering possible "punishments," Piaget's (1948) and Kohlberg's (1963; 1969) distinction between retributive and distributive justice is very useful. Retributively based punishments are retaliatory in nature and bear little relationship to the infraction. Distributively based punishments are restorative in nature and are intrinsically related to the infraction. Swatting a child who has been aggressive to a peer is an example of retributive punishment. Requiring the aggressive child to aid or make an adjustment to the injured child is an example of distributive punishment. Loss of a privilege that is contingent on positive social behavior is another example of distributive punishment. Distributive punishments generally entail not only a loss of some privilege of the expenditure of time and effort but also participation in an approved behavior.

Objectionable Habits

If a child's misbehavior is persistent, specific, and habitual, then the parents' best strategy is to ignore the behavior and to elicit and reinforce a desirable response in the presence of the stimuli that evoke the disapproved response. Rather than punishing a child for eating with his or her fingers, the parent should provide the child with a utensil and focus on the reinforcement of appropriate eating responses. Sometimes, a habitual misbehavior may be so disruptive that the parent must exercise immediate control through punishment. At such times, the principle of distributive punishment should apply.

Cognitively Mediated Objectionable Behaviors

These are misbehaviors that are not due to lack of control, poor habit, or misinformation, but are carried out by children with forethought, challenge, and awareness of the consequences of their actions. In such situations, it is best to apply the principle of distributive punishment. If the behavior persists, increasing the level of punishment is not likely to be effective and may actually be counterproductive. Under these circumstances, the parents are advised to seek outside guidance and help.

This presentation of alternatives is intended to be illustrative rather than complete, and the propositions offered here require further empirical study, validation, and refinement. However, we believe that such alternatives are more productive than approaches that focus on obedience derived from rigid role definitions and enforced by the use of physical punishment (Baumrind, 1974).

IMPLICATIONS AND IMPLEMENTATION

Having arrived at a constellation of disciplinary practices that promise to serve the functions of socialization while furthering the cause of children's rights, the implementation of effective child training practices becomes the crucial task. How is this to be achieved?

A major barrier in the education of and communication to parents of effective and psychologically sound socialization practices is the guarded attitude that many parents have concerning their disciplinary techniques. Parents may be uneasy and embarrassed about disclosing their attitudes and behaviors in the realm of child training, especially in regard to their use of discipline, and it is difficult to obtain child-training information about the kinds of responses these parents employ when their children fail to meet their demands or otherwise misbehave.

A counterpart to this difficulty is the lack of freely available, accessible sources of information, advice, and facilities for parents. A prevalent attitude in our society is that parenting is a private responsibility. Yet the plethora of books providing parental advice and the mushrooming of parent training programs reflect parental anxiety and curiosity and a need for guidance and support in child-rearing efforts and roles.

What is needed to serve the interests and the rights of both the child and the parents is *an invasion of parent privacy* in the area of child rearing. As long-standing members of groups concerned with the maintenance of civil liberties, including the right to privacy, we recognize that our suggestion deviates from an important social principle. However, in our hierarchy of values, protecting the child is a more important principle than protecting parental privacy.

We believe that the way in which parents rear their child should be open to discussion, help, and inquiry. The very change in the communication status of child-rearing practices from a private to a public domain, in itself, could produce profound, constructive effects. It would heighten the parents' awareness of the character and consequences of their practices; it would help reduce the anxieties and uncertainties so often connected with child rearing; and it would facilitate shared communication, mutual support, and understanding between the parents and the child. We would like to emphasize that the most effective route to the invasion of parental privacy is through education and the provision of concrete support mechanisms for the assistance of individuals in their critical social roles as parents.

Thus reciprocity is a vital element in our proposal to remove the nonconstructive shield of privacy currently surrounding parental socialization practices—parent rites. Parents have a right to expect help and to receive assistance from their community in the forms of information, guidance, and child-care resources. Children's rights will then be served in two fundamental ways: the community will function as a resource to the parents, and it will serve as both protector and advocate for the children.

REFERENCES

Anthony, E. J. An experimental approach to the psychopathology of childhood: Autism. *Br. J. Med. Psychol.* **31** (3, 4) (1958), 211–25.

Aries, P. *Centuries of childhood: A social history of family life.* New York: Knopf, 1962.

Baumrind, D. Coleman II: Utopian fantasy and sound social innovation. *Sch. Rev.* **83** (1) (November 1974), 69–91.

Becker, W. C. Consequences of different kinds of parental discipline. In M. L. Hoffman and L. W. Hoffman (eds.), *Review of child development research.* New York: Russell Sage, 1964.

Bell, R. Q. A reinterpretation of the direction of effects in studies of socialization. *Psychol. Rev.* **75** (1968), 81–95.

Berger, N. The child, the law, and the state. In P. Adams et al. (eds.), *Children's rights.* New York: Praeger, 1971.

Boe, E. E., and Church, R. M. The permanent effect of punishment during extinction. Paper presented at the meeting of the Eastern Psychological Association, New York, April 1966.

Bromberg, W. *The mold of murder; A psychiatric study of homicide.* New York: Grune & Stratton, 1961.

Bronfenbrenner, U. Socialization and social class through time and space. In E. E. Maccoby, T. M. Newcombe, and E. L. Hartley (eds.), *Readings in social psychology.* New York: Holt, Rinehart & Winston, 1958.

Calhoun, D. On the psychohistory of childhood. Review of L. deMause (ed.), *The history of childhood. Hist. Educ. Q.* **14** (3) (fall 1974), 371–77.

Clifford, E. Discipline in the home: A controlled observational study of parental practices. *J. Genet. Psychol.* **95** (1959), 45–82.

Colby, K. M. *Ten criticisms of Parry.* Stanford Artificial Intelligence Laboratory. Computer Science Department #STAN-CS-74-457, 1974.

Cook-Gumprez, J. *Social control and socialization: A study of class differences in the language of maternal control.* London: Routledge & Kegan Paul, 1973.

deMause, L. The evolution of childhood. *Hist. Child. Q.* **1** (4) (1974A).

deMause, L. (ed.) *The history of childhood.* New York: The Psychohistory Press, 1974B.

Erlanger, H. S. Social class differences in parents' use of physical punishment. In S. K. Steinmetz and M. A. Straus (eds.), *Violence in the family.* New York: Dodd Mead, 1974.

Eron, L. D., Walder, L. O., Toigo, R., and Lefkowitz, M. M. Social class parental punishment for aggression and child aggression. *Child Dev.* **34** (4) (1963), 849–67.

Estes, W. K. An experimental study of punishment. *Psychol. Monogr.* **57** (Whole No. 263) 1944.

Falk, H. *Corporal punishment: A social interpretation of its theory and practice in the schools of the United States.* New York: Teachers College Press, 1941.

Feshbach, N. D. The effects of violence in childhood. *J. Clin. Psychol.* **11** (3) (1973), 28–31.

Feshbach, N. D. Empathy in children: Some theoretical and empirical considerations. *Couns. Psychol.* (1975A), **5** (2), 25–30.

Feshbach, N. D. The Relationship of Child-rearing Factors in Children's Aggression, Empathy, and Related Positive and Negative Social Behaviors. Paper read as part of a NATO conference on Determinants and Origins of Aggressive Behavior, Monaco, July 1973. On J. DeWit and W. W. Hartup (eds.), *Determinants and origins of aggressive behavior.* The Hague, Netherlands: Mouton Publishers, 1975B.

Feshbach, N. D., and Feshbach, S. The relationship between empathy and aggression in two age groups. *Dev. Psychol.* **1** (2) (1969), 102–07.

Feshbach, N. D., and Feshbach, S. Children's aggression. *Young Child.* **26** (6) (1971), 364–77. Reprinted in W. W. Hartup (ed.), *The young child,* Vol. 2. Washington, D.C.: NAEYC, 1972.

Feshbach, N. D., and Feshbach, S. Cognitive Processes in the Self-Regulation of Children's Aggression: Fantasy and Empathy. Invited paper presented at the Conference on Developmental Aspects of Self-Regulation, La Jolla, Calif., February 1972.

Feshbach, S. Aggression. In P. H. Mussen (ed.), *Carmichael's manual of child psychology* (3rd ed.). New York: John Wiley & Sons, Inc., 1970.

Feshbach, S., and Feshbach, N. D. Alternatives to corporal punishment: Implications for training and controls. *J. Clin. Child Psychol.* 11(3) (1973), 46–48.

Feshbach, S., and Jaffe, Y. The effects of group versus individual decisions on aggressive behavior. Unpublished study, University of California at Los Angeles, 1969.

Finkelstein, B. Pedagogy as intrusion: Teaching values in popular primary schools in nineteenth-century America. *J. Psychohist.* 2(3) (winter 1975).

Gil, D. G. *Violence against children: Physical child abuse in the United States.* Cambridge: Harvard University Press, 1970.

Gil, D. G. Paper presented at a conference on Child Abuse and Neglect at the National Institute of Child Health and Human Development, Bethesda, Maryland, June 1974.

Glueck, S., and Glueck, E. *Unraveling juvenile delinquency.* Cambridge: Harvard University Press, 1950.

Goldfarb, W. Psychological privation in infancy and subsequent adjustment. *Am. J. Orthopsychiatry.* 15 (1945), 247–55.

Havighurst, R. J., and Davis, A. A comparison of the Chicago and Harvard studies of social class differences in child rearing. *Am. Sociol. Rev.* 20 (1955), 438.

Heinstein, M. *Child rearing in California: A study of mothers with young children.* Bureau of Maternal and Child Health, State of California, Sacramento, California. Department of Public Health, 1965.

Helfer, R. E., and Kempe, C. H. (eds.). *The battered child and his family.* Philadelphia: Lippincott, 1972.

Hess, R. D., and Shipman, V. C. Cognitive elements in maternal behavior. In J. P. Hill (ed.), *The Minnesota symposia on child psychology,* Vol. 1, Minneapolis: University of Minnesota Press, 1967.

Hoffman, M. L. Child-rearing practices and moral development: Generalizations from empirical research. *Child Dev.* 34 (1963), 295–318.

Hoffman, M. L. Moral development. In P. H. Mussen (ed.), *Carmichael's manual of child psychology* (3rd ed.). New York: John Wiley & Sons, Inc., 1970.

Hoffman, M. L. Moral internalization, parental power, and the nature of parent–child interaction. *Dev. Psychol.* 11(2) (1975), 228–39.

Hoffman, M. L., and Saltzstein, H. D. Parent discipline and the child's moral development. *J. Pers. Soc. Psychol.* 5 (1967), 45–57.

Holt, J. *Escape from childhood: The needs and rights of children.* New York: Dutton, 1972.

Jenkins, S., and Norman, E. *Filial deprivation and foster care.* New York: Columbia University Press, 1972.

Kaufman, I. Discussion of Physical Abuse of Children. Presented at National Conference on Social Welfare sponsored by Children's Division, American Humane Association, New York City, June 1, 1962.

Kempe, C. H. A practical approach to the protection of the abused child and rehabilitation of the abusing parent. *Symp. Child Abuse Pediatr.* **51** (1973), Part 3.

Kempe, C. H., and Helfer, R. E. *Helping the battered child and his family.* Philadelphia: Lippincott, 1972.

Kempe, C. H., Silverman, F. N., Steele, B. B., Droegemueller, W., and Silver, H. K. The battered-child syndrome. *J. Am. Med. Assoc.* **181** (1962), 17–24.

Kohlberg, L. Moral development and identification. In H. Stevenson (ed.), *Child psychology: 62nd Yearbook of the National Society for the Study of Education.* Chicago: University of Chicago Press, 1963.

Kohlberg, L. Stage and sequence: The cognitive-developmental approach to socialization. In D. A. Goslin (ed.), *Handbook of socialization theory and research.* Chicago: Rand-McNally, 1969.

Light, R. Abused and neglected children in America: A study of alternative policies. In *The rights of children. Harv. Educ. Rev.* (1974), Series 9, 198–240.

Lowrey, L. G. Personality distortion and early institutional care. *Am. J. Orthopsychiatry.* **10** (1940), 576–86.

McCord, W., McCord, J., and Howard, A. Familial correlates of aggression in nondelinquent male children. *J. Abnorm. Soc. Psychol.* **62** (1961), 72–93.

McFerran, J. Parents' groups in protective services. *Child.* **5** (1958), 223–28.

Mercer, J. R. A policy statement on assessment procedures and the rights of children. In *The rights of children. Harv. Educ. Rev.* (1974), Series 9, 328–44.

Mnookin, R. H. Foster care: In whose best interest? In *The rights of children. Harv. Educ. Rev.* (1974), Series 9, 158–96.

National Center for Prevention and Treatment of Child Abuse and Neglect. *Natl. Child Prot. Newsl.* **1**(2) (1973), 1–3.

Newson, J. E. *Four-year-olds in an urban community.* Chicago: Aldine, 1968.

Ohlin, L. E., Coates, R. B., and Miller, A. D. Radical correctional reform: A case study of the Massachusetts Youth Correctional System. In *The rights of children. Harv. Educ. Rev.* (1974), Series 9, 120–57.

Parents Anonymous, Inc. *Procedures and concepts manual.* Redondo Beach, Calif.: National Parent Chapter, 1972.

Parke, R. D. The role of punishment in the socialization process. In R. A. Hoppe, G. A. Milton, and E. C. Simmel (eds.), *Early experiences and the processes of socialization.* New York: Academic Press, 1970.

Parke, R. D., and Collmer, W. Child abuse: An interdisciplinary review. To be published in M. Hetherington (ed.), *Rev. Res.* **5** (1975).

Patterson, G. R., Cobb, J. A., and Ray, R. S. A social engineering technology for retraining families of aggressive boys. In H. E. Adams and I. P. Unikel (eds.), *Issues and trends in behavior therapy*. Springfield, Ill.: Thomas, 1972.

Paulsen, M. G. Legal protections against child abuse. *Child*. 13 (1966), 42–48.

Paulson, M., and Blake, P. The physically abused child: A focus on prevention. *Child Welfare* 48 (1969), 86–95.

Piaget, J. *The moral judgment of the child*. New York: Harcourt Brace Jovanovich, Inc., 1932; (republished) Glencoe, Illinois: Free Press, 1948.

Radbill, S. X. A history of child abuse and infanticide. In R. E. Helfer and C. H. Kempe (eds.), *The battered child*. Chicago: University of Chicago Press, 1968.

Robinson, D. Harm, offense, and nuisance: Some first steps in the establishment of an ethics of treatment. *Am. Psychol.* 29(4) (1974), 233–38.

Robinson, H. B., Robinson, N. M., Wolins, M., Bronfenbrenner, U., and Richmond, J. B. *Early child care in the United States of America*. New York: Gordon & Breach, 1973.

Rodham, H. Children under the law. In *The rights of children. Harv. Educ-Rev.* (1974), Series 9, 1–28.

Rodnick, E. H., and Garmezy, N. An experimental approach to the study of motivation in schizophrenia. In M. R. Jones (ed.), *Nebraska symposium on motivation*. Lincoln: University of Nebraska Press, 1957.

Sears, R. R. Relation of early socialization experiences to aggression in middle childhood. *J. Abnorm. Soc. Psychol.* 63 (1961), 466–92.

Sears, R. R., Maccoby, E. E., and Levin, H. *Patterns of child rearing*. Evanston, Ill.: Row, Peterson, 1957.

Skinner, B. F. *The behavior of organisms*. New York: Appleton-Century-Crofts, 1938.

Solomon, R. L. Punishment. *Am. Psychol.* 19 (1964), 239–53.

Steinmetz, S. K., and Straus, M. A. The family as a cradle of violence. *Soc.* 10 (September-October 1973), 50–56.

Steinmetz, S. K., and Straus, M. A. (eds.). *Violence in the family*. New York: Dodd, Mead, 1974.

Stendler, C. B. Sixty years of child-training practices. *J. Pediatr.* 36 (1950), 122–34.

Straus, M. A. Some social antecedents of physical punishment: A linkage theory interpretation. *J. Marriage and the Fam.* 2 (November 1973), 658–63.

Sunley, R. Early 19th-century American literature on child rearing. In M. Mead and M. Wolfenstein (eds.), *Childhood in contemporary cultures*. Chicago: University of Chicago Press, 1955.

Vincent, C. E. Trends in infant-care ideas. *Child Dev.* 22 (1951), 50–58.

Webster's Third New International Dictionary of the English Language, Unabridged; Springfield: G&C Merriam, 1968.

Wolfenstein, M. Trends in infant care. *Am. J. Orthopsychiatr.* **23** (1953), 120–30.

Yarrow, M. R., Campbell, J. D., and Burton, R. V. *Child rearing: An inquiry into research and methods.* San Francisco: Jossey-Bass, 1968.

Protecting Children and Families From Abuse

GAIL GARINGER,
RENE TANKENOFF BRANT, AND
JONATHAN BRANT

Recognition of child abuse as a social problem is a relatively recent historical development. In previous times and cultures, children were viewed as chattels of their parents who, with few exceptions, were entitled to do with them as they pleased, even to the point of openly murdering them [see the historical overview of infanticide documented by Bakan (1971)]. As the status of children has changed, attitudes toward children have become more ambivalent. Such ambivalence manifests itself in loving and caring feelings toward children as well as hateful feelings that may be vented in child abuse or neglect. Ambivalence toward children is not characteristic of parents alone; it permeates governments, institutions, and professions, and it therefore follows that child abuse may arise at any of these levels.

There is danger in the paradigm that sees the child as the innocent victim, the parent as the malevolent assailant, and the state as the loving rescuer of children. In fact, child abuse arises from a complicated interaction of child, parent, and environment. Because the state can exercise great discretion in deciding what will happen to a family once intervention in the family's life is deemed "appropriate," children and families may suffer abuse at the hands of the state. Institutional and governmental abuse is all the more pernicious, because a cloak of official sanction serves to protect and perpetuate it. Few safeguards exist to protect children and families from such abuse.

The State as a Source of Abuse

In thinking about abuse by parents and the "benevolent" intrusion into family matters by the state, we must consider a very delicate system of

171

balances. On one hand, the strong societal conviction exists that parents should be free to decide how to raise their own children and that families are entitled to privacy and freedom from unwarranted intrusion. On the other hand, the doctrine of parens patriae has been invoked to justify state intervention to protect children from harm, to limit parental prerogatives, and to remove children from the home when necessary.

It is important to recognize that when the state chooses to intervene in a family's life because of confirmed or suspected child abuse, three parties are involved: the child, the parents, and the state. It is significant that the parents and the state have traditionally been treated as the primary parties in such cases. The child's interests have often been ignored; either it has been assumed that the state will act in the best interests of the child (thereby making the child's interests synonymous with the state's), or the "family's" interests have been considered as a whole (thereby merging the child's interests with those of the parents).

Much of the present abuse of children and families by the state occurs because of the failure to clearly recognize the child's interests and the failure to provide safeguards for all parties involved.

We propose that the child be elevated to primary-party status in all child-abuse cases and that the child be assured of an advocate to advance his or her interests. In addition, we propose that substantive and procedural safeguards be established to protect all parties. The examination of the process of child-abuse management that follows underscores the need for adopting these principles.

Reporting Statutes.   As previously mentioned, our society values familial privacy; we advocate the view that families should be free from intrusion by the state, unless parental actions or inactions place a child in jeopardy. Child-abuse reporting statutes are an attempt to delineate circumstances where some form of state intervention in a family's life is warranted. Since the diagnosis of the "battered-child syndrome" (Kempe et al., 1962), every state in the United States has enacted a statute requiring certain groups of persons to report cases of child abuse. [A comparison of state laws in this regard can be found in DeFrancis and Lucht (1974).] Whereas most states previously adopted a fairly narrow definition of what was reportable,[1] at present many states have expanded their definition of child abuse to include sexual abuse, emotional abuse, and/or neglect. As the definition of abuse has expanded, so too has the category of professionals mandated (obligated) to report cases of abuse. In addition to medical professionals, many states now require other professionals (teachers, social workers, visiting nurses, school administrators, law enforcement officials, psychologists, and the like) to report cases of abuse to some specified state agency. All state statutes grant immunity from civil and criminal liability to persons who report abuse cases, and more than half the state statutes impose a penalty for willful failure to report abuse (DeFrancis and Lucht, 1974).

Broad and often vague definitions of abuse, coupled with equally broad mandates to report abuse, are potentially dangerous for all parties involved. With an expansion of the definition of abuse in some states to include neglect and emotional abuse, standards for determining what is reportable become increasingly subjective. As Gil (1970) points out, our society sanctions the use of physical force in parent–child discipline, and some social classes and ethnic and cultural groups condone a greater use of physical force than other groups. It is important that both statutory definitions and reporters of abuse consider the differing concepts of "acceptable parenting."

Labeling Issues. Bias in identification and reporting of abuse seems unavoidable. Low-income, nonwhite groups are most frequently reported (Gil, 1970). This may be primarily because of their greater use of physical punishment, but research suggests that the overrepresentation of these groups may be caused largely by the reluctance of private physicians and others to report abuses in middle- and upper-income families. Thus a double abuse may be inflicted on low-income families: if child abuse is associated with poverty, we are merely isolating the symptom (child abuse) and ignoring the problem (poverty).

More than 30 states provide statewide central registries that list data about abused children and their families (DeFrancis and Lucht, 1974). Such listings often contain the names of "suspected" as well as confirmed abuse cases; provisions for expunging information about "unfounded" cases frequently do not exist. Given the fact that the information in these registries is often accessible to professionals and to other persons, a child or a family may suffer much embarrassment and harm as a result of a hasty or erroneous listing in a central registry. Many states have made no provisions for expunging the data contained in these registry listings, even after a given number of years have elapsed or after a child reaches maturity; thus the stigmatic label of "abuse" or "abusive" may plague a child or a family indefinitely.

In addition to the general problems that arise from such labeling (Goffman, 1963), abused children and their families must face two other potential problems. Some theorists are presently advancing the view that today's abused children grow up to be tomorrow's criminals (Fontana, 1973). Central registries with no provisions for expungement would facilitate the long-term tracking of children and families. A second area of concern is the recent effort of some groups to establish a nationwide registry of abused children. The potential abuse that could occur if data were shared among state and national government agencies is frightening.

Procedural Problems. All these factors that make abuse by the state possible are compounded by the absence of procedural due process safeguards for children and parents. Many states have no requirement that a family be notified (informed of the fact) that a child-abuse report has been filed. This means that a state agency may be in the process of investigating a family without the family's knowledge of the report or investigation. Even those states that notify families often do not provide any procedure whereby a child or a parent may challenge the report. Vague definitions of abuse and the anonymity afforded reporters in many states make it difficult, if not impossible, to challenge child-abuse reports even in states where such a mechanism is available. Furthermore, counsel for children or parents is almost never provided at this initial stage, even when a procedure for challenging the report does exist.

Once a report has been filed, the intrusion into a family's private life has just begun. In California, for example, reports of child abuse are routinely made to the police. A typical investigation might include the following: the family is listed in a police report log, father's employer is contacted, neighbor is questioned, child is tested by a psychologist, and possibly other professionals. There are usually no limitations on the type of investigation that follows a report; few states provide guidelines for the investigators trying to determine whether there is a basis for the report. What is relevant and appropriate to investigate is most often left to the discretion of the designated investigator (usually a police officer or a state social-service worker). Families usually have no recourse if an overzealous investigator's questions and actions extend beyond the scope of a "reasonable" investigation. Even if the report is later deemed "unfounded," the investigation has injured the child and the family.

If the investigator "substantiates" the report, to what extent are the child and the parents compelled to accept therapeutic treatment or any other form of intervention by the state? In other words, once the state determines that it has grounds to intervene in a family's life, what are the limits of such an intrusion? This question is particularly important given the prevalence of the "in-need-of-services" theory of child abuse (Kempe and Helfer, 1972). This theory is based on the premise that most child abuse cases occur in isolated, multiproblem families who are cut off from needed community resources. The theory then postulates that the way to remedy the situation that produced the abuse is to provide services for the child and the parents. But does a child or a family have the right to disagree with the quality or the quantity of services deemed appropriate by the state?

Massachusetts, for example, attempts to address the problem in the following manner. The Massachusetts Department of Public Welfare Regulations states that when "reasonable cause" for a child-abuse report is found, the person responsible for the investigation and evaluation "shall develop, in cooperation with the parents or other persons responsible for the care of the child, and in cooperation with the child where practical, a Service Plan for the household."[2] The Regulations define the Service Plan in terms of "mutual expectations developed between the Department and the household . . . ," but at no point in the Regulations are provisions made for the child or the parents to disagree with a particular form of intervention offered by the investigator and/or to suggest alternative modes of intervention. The Regulations then clarify the primary goals of the Service Plan, the purposes of services under the Plan, and the like, and then specifically address the issue of removing the child from the home, based in part on the family's nonparticipation in the Service Plan:

If a family declines or is unable to accept or participate in the offered services, and the person responsible for the investigation and evaluation has reasonable cause to believe the child is suffering from serious physical or emotional injuries, said person, with the prior approval of his supervisor, may file a petition in the proper Juvenile or District Court. . . .[3]

In the absence of a mechanism whereby a child or a family can challenge the "appropriateness" of the services offered, a family's "cooperativeness" or "ability/inability to accept or participate in offered services" is left to the assessment of an individual social-service worker. All too frequently, the parents' refusal to accept the particular services offered results in the threat of and the actual removal of the child from the home. Substantial abuses of children and families can result from the absence of substantive and procedural guidelines for determining the degree of allowable state intrusion in a family's life following a report of child abuse.

Benefits of State Intervention

Thus far, we have been speaking primarily of the embarrassment or harm to children or families that can result from state intervention. But what about the potential benefits of state intervention to children and families? Most often, state intrusion in child-abuse cases is predicated on the protection of the child. Thus the primary goal of intervention is seen as the alleviation of risk to the child. Does the state have an affirmative obligation to provide services? Is the state obligated to provide a child with a better living situation if it seeks to remove the child from his or her own home environment? What recourse does a child or a family have if the state promises services and is then lax in providing them?

Unfortunately, all too often the state demands action from a family but makes no equivalent promise to act itself. In states where intervention is based solely on protecting children from "risk" and where there is no specific commitment to provide state services, it seems difficult to construct a legal theory that grants recourse to the family to force the state to assume responsibility. However, in states where there is a specific statutory duty to provide services to abused children and their families, families can argue that the state by virtue of its commitment must provide adequate services. The family can argue that failure of the state to provide adequate services violates the family's "right to services." Such a legal right would be analogous to the "right to treatment" that has been argued successfully by some involuntarily confined mental patients and by retarded children housed in state institutions. These patients argued that the state, in accepting the responsibility for housing them, also accepted the responsibility for seriously attempting to improve their condition. In cases where the state had failed to provide adequate services, judges in Alabama and New York ordered additional expenditures to improve the qualities of the institutional services (*N.Y. State Association for Retarded Children v. Rockefeller*, 1973; *Wyatt v. Stickney*, 1971). If this principle were applied to child-abuse cases, families not offered services would have the right to receive the services promised by the state or to be free from state intervention. Such a legal principle, if established, would force states to bolster the social services that they offer to children and families in need.

After the report has been made and the investigation has been conducted, some cases of alleged child abuse are taken to court. The exact percentage of child-abuse cases referred for court action varies; however, as previously noted, a low percentage is not necessarily desirable. Perhaps the child and the parents should have recourse to the court if they do not feel that the state is treating them fairly. All too frequently the state may petition the court, but the child and the parents can only have their case considered by a judge when the state brings them to court.

The rationale for court involvement differs from state to state and from case to case. Most frequently, court action is taken when removal of the child from the home for a period of time is deemed necessary or desirable. Another basis for using the court is to give added authority to the social-service worker who deals with the family. The worker may feel that the court and the judge can coerce the family to "cooperate" with a particular service plan.

The standards for court intervention also vary considerably. A fairly typical statute for those courts utilizing a neglect or "without proper care" standard is:

> . . . that said child is without necessary and proper physical, educational or moral care and discipline, or is growing up under conditions or circumstances damaging to a child's sound character development, or who lacks proper attention of parent, guardian with care and custody, or custodian, and whose parents or guardian are unwilling, incompetent, or unavailable to provide such care. . . .[4]

The same degree of potential abuse for child and parents results from vague and overbroad definitions at the court stage as it does at the reporting stage of the process. The child and the parents often do not know exactly why they are being brought before the court.

The forum and procedure for resolving child-abuse cases are not adequate. The forum may be the district court (the lowest general court), or the juvenile court, as in Massachusetts, or even a specialized family court, as in New York. Whatever the court, judges all too frequently have no particular background or expertise in dealing with child-abuse cases. The proceeding may be criminal or civil in nature. Procedural safeguards, if they do exist, are inadequate. There may be no requirement that the parents or the child be notified at the initial (and often crucial) stage in the court process. Most states do not require the appointment of counsel for child or parents. Rules of evidence are often lax; much of the evidence introduced to prove a case may be nothing but hearsay (Thomas, 1972).

Compounding these potential abuses is the critical problems of the length of time a case may remain in the courts. Often no provisions are made for periodic reviews of the case or for dismissal after a given period of time. A frequent practice is to draw the case out over a lengthy period of time while continuing efforts are made to engage the family in the treatment process; such continuances can extend over several years. In certain situations, continuing court involvement may be desirable; however, as a general rule, the absence of provisions for periodic review and dismissal can keep a child and family in "limbo" for a number of years. All parties (the child, parent, and the state) should have the right to a final disposition of the case before an extended period of time elapses. The disastrous effects on children who remain in limbo for a long period of time is eloquently addressed by Freud, Goldstein, and Solnit (1973), who stress the importance of a constant, "psychological-parent" figure for such a child and advocate a placement system in which the child's interests are paramount. We support this view (Brant and Brant, 1974).

Suggested Guidelines

Given the potentials for the abuse of children and families by the state that presently exist at all stages of child-abuse management, it seems imperative that basic guidelines for state intervention in the lives of abused children and their families be developed. We would propose the following general guidelines:

1. *Reporting:* It should be acknowledged that any definition of abuse is arbitrary and such a definition implies an action/inaction approach that is unacceptable because it places a child "at risk." Differing subcultural standards of acceptable child rearing should be considered when arriving at the definition of abuse to be included in a reporting statute and when evaluating the reports received.

2. *Notice:* If the state intervenes in a family's life because of a report of child abuse, the child and the parents should have the right to notice (a) that a report has been made; (b) who made the report; (c) the action or inaction of the family that caused the child to be reported "at risk"; and (d) their right to challenge the report and their right to counsel.

3. *Challenge:* The child or child advocate and the parents should have the right to challenge the child-abuse report. Anonymous reporting should not be permitted, but immunity should be granted for reports made "in good faith." A child (or child advocate) or a parent who feels that a report has not been made "in good faith" should have the right to sue the reporter. A procedural mechanism for challenging the report should be provided. All parties should have the right to counsel, and the court should provide counsel for indigent parties.

4. *Expungement:* If a report is found to be "unsubstantiated," provisions should be made for the immediate expungement of all information pertaining to the family.

5. *Plan:* If a report is found to be "substantiated," all parties should work toward alleviating the conditions that resulted in the child being reported "at risk." Each party should have the right and opportunity to suggest alternative plans for alleviating the "at risk" situation.

6. *Contract:* If the parties agree to a plan for alleviating the "at risk" situation, they should draw up a contract specifying the rights and responsibilities of each party. If the state has promised to provide services to abused children and their families, the "right to services" theory could be invoked by the child or the parents to guarantee that adequate services are provided. Provisions should be made for periodic review and modification of this contract.

7. *Court:* If the parties do not agree to a plan for alleviating the "at risk" situation or if one party believes that another party is not complying with the terms of the contract, any party should have the right to appeal to the court to resolve the issue. All parties should have the right to counsel, and the court should provide counsel for indigent parties. The judges hearing cases should have special training and experience relevant to child-abuse cases.

NOTES

1. . . . "reasonable cause to believe that a child is suffering serious injury or abuse inflicted by a parent or other person responsible for the care of such child. . . ." *Massachusetts General Laws Annotated,* Ch. 119, Sec. 39A, repealed by Acts of 1973, Ch. 1076, Sec. 6.
2. Massachusetts Department of Public Welfare Regulations, 1974, Sec. 258.36.
3. Regulation s, Sec. 258.60.
4. *Massachusetts General Laws Annotated,* Ch. 119, Sec. 24.

REFERENCES

Bakan, D. *Slaughter of the innocents.* San Francisco: Jossey-Bass, 1971.

Brant, J., and Brant, R. Book review of *Beyond the best interests of the child. Trial* 10 (1974), 35.

DeFrancis, V., and Lucht, C. L. *Child abuse legislation in the 1970s.* Denver: The American Humane Association, Children's Division, 1974.

Fontana, V. J. *Somewhere a child is crying.* New York: Macmillan, 1973.

Freud, A., Goldstein, J., and Solnit, A. *Beyond the best interests of the child.* New York: Free Press, 1973.

Gil, D. *Violence against children: Physical child abuse in the United States.* Cambridge: Harvard University Press, 1970.

Goffman, E. *Stigma: Notes on the management of spoiled identity.* Englewood Cliffs, N.J.: Prentice-Hall, 1963.

Kempe, C. H., and Helfer, R. E. *Helping the battered child and his family.* Philadelphia: Lippincott, 1972.

Kempe, C. H., et al. The battered-child syndrome. *J. Am. Med. Assoc.* 181 (1962), 17–24.

N.Y. *State Association for Retarded Children and Patricia Parise et al. v. Nelson Rockefeller,* 357 F. Suppl. 752 (1973).

Thomas, M. P. Child abuse and neglect; Part I: Historical overview, legal matrix, and social perspectives. *N.C. Law Rev.* 50 (1972), 293–449.

Wyatt v. Stickney, 325 F. Suppl. 781 (M.D. Ala., 1971).

The Juvenile Court:
Ideology of Pathology

STEPHEN R. BING and
J. LARRY BROWN

> "A child may be arrested for committing the behavi
> of a child in need of services."
>
> Chapter 1073 of the *General Law*
> *of Massachusetts;*[1] enacted 1973.

This excerpt from recent legislation adopted in Massachusetts sums up, albeit unwittingly, how far the reform of the criminal justice system has come in its treatment of children. It represents the final step in the victimization of young people who engage in activity deemed unacceptable by the prevailing class and culture that both define deviant behavior and construct the social, political, and economic institutions that impinge on the lives of young people in America (Ryan, 1971).

This chapter discusses the history of attempts by society to deal with troubled and troubling young people and examines how that history led to the adoption of such a bizarre statutory authorization for arrest as the one quoted above. We suggest that the history itself shows that a radical reorientation of the juvenile justice system and its attendant support services is long overdue. Unless such a reorientation occurs, the excesses of the juvenile justice system will continue unabated and hundreds of thousands of children annually will be harmed by those who believe they are helping.

The writers wish to thank I. Ira Goldenberg, Ph.D., and Peter Edleman, Esq., who provided instructive criticism and insight in the preparation of this chapter.

181

IDEOLOGY OF REFORM

Reformers in the early part of the twentieth century were completely successful in amending the form and substance of the way juveniles were treated by the criminal justice system (Barrows, 1904; Mack, 1909). They argued that the harsh and sometimes brutal demands of criminal law should be tamed and mitigated when the defendant before the court was a child. What was needed, these reformers asserted, was a more rational, more humane approach that focused on the actor rather than on the act. Periodic or episodic deviance was simply evidence of the child's underlying problems. Successful discovery and treatment of such underlying, individual problems would permit these children to conform to the prevailing social ethic.

Thus juvenile courts began to appear, the first in Illinois (Hurley, 1927). These courts were dressed by their architects in a cloak of benign concern for children's welfare, a concern soon raised to an ideology termed, variously and seriatim, "parens patriae," "the best interests of the child," and the search for "individualized treatment." Forever banned from the lexicon of juvenile-court personnel would be such terms as "punishment" and "retribution." From this treatment and rehabilitative ideology sprang the assertion that the state legitimately could institutionalize children who "habitually associate with immoral and vicious persons" or "habituate railway yards or bucket shops," as some early statutes phrased it. Clearly, to these early thinkers, such conduct indicated a propensity to commit crime if it remained untreated, particularly because the affluent, educated, and troubled youth they knew did not do such things (or, it might be suggested, were not apprehended doing such things).

The early statutes that created the juvenile courts empowered them to rule on every conceivable form of conduct by the young, ranging from the truancy and rebelliousness of the stubborn child to acts that would be crimes if committed by adults. Thus, the reform gave birth to a monster that still rages among us today, as evidenced by a piece of legislation adopted by perhaps the most progressive legislature in the nation on juvenile corrections, that a child may be arrested for "committing behavior" (Rutherford, 1973).

PROCEDURAL REDRESS TO THE EXCESSES OF REFORM

It is true that the juvenile court and its disposition of children have come under substantial attack in recent years, but this attack has been basically procedural and legalistic. Until 1967, juvenile courts asserted that because the state acted in the best interests of the child, the accepted principles of due process of law defined in the Constitution of the United States and in judicial interpretations were unnecessary.[2] Accordingly, juveniles were not entitled to the right to confront their accusers, the right to remain silent, the right to a lawyer, or the right to be free from unreasonable search and seizure. This practice prevailed despite the widespread recognition that young people appearing before the court could be incarcerated in settings that never met the high rehabilitative standards promised in the early years of reform. Indeed, many juvenile institutions were far worse than adult prisons (Rutherford, 1973). Advocates of the juvenile court system staunchly adhered to the belief that because the state was acting in a benevolent fashion, complicated adversarial ritual was at best irrelevant and at worst an impediment to helping the child adopt and accept an adult approach to life (Driscoll, 1964).

THE CONTINUING CONSPIRACY

Most of the questionable procedures used to determine whether a child was a delinquent were eliminated in 1967 by the *Gault* decision. Juvenile courts are now required to follow minimal standards of due process of law, at least in theory, and other procedural reforms have been instituted. What has not changed, and shows little evidence of changing, is the organizing principle that these criminal tribunals are designed to act in the best interests of the child and, in fact, do act in the best interests of the child. When the obvious failings of the juvenile justice system are pointed out, defenders frequently argue that insufficient resources exist to realize the full potential for treatment and rehabilitation embodied in the process. This rationalization then provokes a long debate on the questions of who should be given resources and for what reasons.

It is not our purpose here to engage in that debate. The argument is diversionary and deflects necessary critical analysis from the structure and purpose of the juvenile justice system to discussions on how to make the current system work better. Instead, we wish to examine the political and therapeutic premise of the system and to explore whether any criminal court can substantiate its arrogance that it is able to discover the "best interests of the child" and provide the individualized treatment to satisfy that interest.

Juvenile courts are established to deal with the delinquent child. This self-evident assertion raises all the questions surrounding the juvenile justice system. What is delinquency? Who or what institution should define it? How does it happen? Should society do anything about it? If so, what?

The reform movement answered all of these questions. It incorporated and codified the universal "medical model" of criminality and boldly stated: delinquency is a pathology; individualized treatment can deal with pathology; the child can thus be cured (that is, made nondelinquent).

For example, if a child appears before a juvenile court on a complaint that he is stubborn or incorrigible, the child's failure to conform behaviorally to social norms, perhaps because he does not agree with those norms, is viewed by the court as an operational, psychiatric sign of pathology. This pathology presumably demands treatment to develop the juvenile's capacity to conform to the requirements of the law. Thus the court turns the matter over to the therapists, the treaters from the mental-health community. Here the court's initial perception that the judge was correct in determining that incorrigibility is a sign of pathology will be confirmed.

The concept of delinquency is viewed by a large segment of the mental-health community as a symptom of underlying psychiatric disease, complicated in many instances by intellectual handicaps, mental retardation, perceptual disorders, or learning disabilities (Offerd, 1967; Peeples, 1970; Ames et al, 1974). Therefore, the court and the therapists determine what treatment is needed and then provide it.

In such a situation, the concept of the therapeutic state is realized (Kittrie, 1971). This concept is governed by and is dependent for survival on the mental-health professional. Treatment or rehabilitation based on the medical model of criminality inevitably becomes a process of emphasizing personality or psychological functioning and involves altering the juvenile's perception of reality, attitude toward reality, and ability to cope with or adjust to reality.

The fundamental failing of this process is that it leaves the reality untouched. Any effort to change the reality rather than the child's reaction to it is dismissed as nontherapeutic and dangerously political. We can characterize the therapist, the court, and persons who can conceive of arresting children for "committing behavior" as involved in a mutually reinforcing and deeply conservative conspiracy, however inadvertent, to victimize the child and to bar social change.

Court intervention simply results in labeling the child delinquent and allows society to avoid labeling itself delinquent by not radically transforming the social, economic, and political conditions that contribute to the child's anger and supposed deviancy. Treatment under more or less coercive settings is provided. The children are referred to probation officers for phantom services that are based all too frequently on faulty clinical investigations—investigations demanded by the treatment approach. Yet the child's family is still broken or breaking, the home is still crowded or dilapidated, and time is spent on the streets or in poor schools.

The anger of the child, who has every reason in the world to be angry, is typically translated by the mumbo-jumbo of many mental-health professionals into a need for a "structured environment to deal with tendencies to act out." One of us vividly remembers representing a youngster in New Jersey who was found not delinquent because another juvenile subsequently admitted involvement in the delinquent act (a theft). The blameless child had been detained pending his trial in a youth facility where a series of diagnostic tests were performed. On the basis of the report of the psychiatric social worker, the child was provided treatment in a coercive setting, because he did not "accept his stay in detention." Why a black child should accept imprisonment by a white judge for something he did not do was never made clear.

In this regard, a notable characteristic of the therapeutic state is that while it is governed by mental-health professionals with the participation of legal authority, its population is only one class of children—the poor. These children are excluded from school (Task Force on Children Out of School, 1970; Children's Defense Fund, 1974), denied adequate nutrition (Food Research and Action Center, 1972), housed in lethal environments (Massachusetts Advocacy Center, 1974), and brought to juvenile court if they fail to adjust to these conditions.

A "CURE"—LET'S TREAT THE REFORM

Obviously, a conscious, purposeful conspiracy to accomplish such "therapeutic" results does not exist. But functionally it prevails, and it will continue to prevail until a fundamental reorientation of the system is accomplished. Children who break the law frequently do so because the law itself proscribes perfectly predictable and anticipated juvenile behavior as criminal, because they may have good reasons for their actions, or because the law itself is broadly expansive and based on the faulty premise that professional people are able to predict future criminal conduct by analyzing early characteristics of juvenile conduct. The juvenile court and its accessories, so long imbued with an overzealous sense of righteousness and benevolence, have violated the constitutional rights of the young for nearly half a century. We cannot expect, anticipate, or even hope, that this legal institution will reexamine its own assumptions.

Accordingly, the mental-health professionals on whom the juvenile justice system depends must consider whether their continued participation in such a system is right and proper. For example, can the medical model of criminality be sensibly applied to behavior such as truancy, incorrigibility, running away, idly roaming the streets at night—all the so-called status offenses, some form of which are committed in every jurisdiction in the nation? Even if this model can be sensibly applied, do the necessary skills, knowledge, and resources exist to deal with such actions? If the answer is yes, is it at all sensible to apply these resources to the individual child, rather than to the conditions that surround the child?

Very well, one might say, the therapeutic approach to status offenses should be terminated (Ichur, 1973). It is too costly and too threatening to civil liberties and civil rights, and it gains little in the end. But what about the juveniles who commit real crimes, acts that would be deemed criminal if committed by adults? What about the dangerous juvenile offender?

We submit that these questions and ones like them are simply new attempts to reinvigorate a discredited juvenile justice system with a new form of "mental healthism." Once the debate is defined by the need to deal with "dangerousness," then the proclivity of the system, spawned by the medical model of criminality to research ways to predict it and to treat it, acquires new life. This process has been called the codifying and institutionalizing of a metaphor (Schucter, 1974). The term "dangerousness" is simply a revision of the medical model to make it more palatable to those who realize the substantial hazard of this approach to juvenile behavior. Clearly, the history of the juvenile court, the evidence of misdiagnoses, mistreatments, and abuses to which children have been subjected, tells us that rethinking the problem in terms of dangerousness does not solve anything. Simply put, "dangerousness" is a new emphasis of an old theme.

We submit that a better way to proceed is to place serious restrictions on the juvenile justice system, which, at present, is implicitly organized on assumptions of force and coercion. Now we must ask only one thing of the court: the protection of the public. This would mean the elimination of much of the juvenile court's jurisdiction. The court could then, by meticulous and fair process, determine whether a juvenile has actually committed an act—not a behavior—to which society should respond. Any response should consider the youth of the convicted offender to ensure that the barbaric sentencing practices of the adult criminal are not inflicted on children. However, the response should not be a request for treatment. Counseling, diagnosis, therapy, or similar treatment should be provided at the juvenile's option. Under no circumstance should participation in any kind of treatment be a condition of the sentence.

We do not suggest or argue that all services presently delivered to children through the mechanism of the juvenile justice system be eliminated. Rather, the range of human services should be organized and founded on a basis of voluntary participation. Then children and their families can seek the kind of help they want, when they want it, for the problems they deem important. In this way, we can secure the limitation of the court's jurisdiction without jeopardizing the humane proposition that people who need help are entitled to receive it. What should be eliminated is the unwarranted assumption that the state, functioning as a law-enforcement agency can legitimately determine who needs help and what kind of help is needed.

Lawyers across the nation are beginning to develop theory and litigation strategies for so-called "right-to-treatment" lawsuits, but lawyers and other professionals must pay equal attention to the child's right *not* to be treated. Providing concrete and definite sentencing patterns in the juvenile justice system and creating truly voluntary social-assistance programs will finally divest the juvenile court system of its medical model and the abuses that that model generates.

If the right *not* to be treated is recognized by the courts and by the mental-health community, we can hope to tame the excesses of those who would commit and abandon young people to a juvenile justice system that ignores the social, political, and economic conditions that lacerate them on a daily basis and simultaneously teaches them that reacting in pain to those lacerations is sick.

NOTES

1. "[A] child in need of services [is] a child below the age of 17 who persistently runs away from the home of his parent or legal guardian, or persistently refuses to obey the lawful and reasonable commands of his parents or legal guardian, thereby resulting in said parents' or guardian's inability to adequately care for and protect said child, or a child between the ages of 6 and 16 who persistently and willfully fails to attend school or persistently violates the lawful and reasonable regulations of his school." §3. Ch. 1073, General Laws of Massachusetts, 1973.

2. *In re Gault,* 387 U.S. (1967). A curious aspect of this case is its anachronistic title. *In re* is legal terminology for a state proceeding against a *thing,* such as a bout or a hazardous nuisance. In addition, when the case was argued, the Ohio Council of Juvenile Court judges argued against procedural protections, stating that a juvenile has the right not to liberty but to custody.

REFERENCES

Ames et al. *Stop school failure.* New York: Harper & Row, 1974.

Barrows, S. (ed.). *Children's courts in the United States.* Washington, D.C.: U.S. Government Printing Office, 1904.

Children's Defense Fund. *Children out of school in America.* Cambridge, Mass.: Children's Defense Fund, 1974.

Driscoll, P. The privilege against self-incrimination in juvenile court proceedings. *Juvenile Court Judges J.* **15**, 17 (1964).

Food Research and Action Center. *If we had ham, we could have ham and eggs, if we had eggs: A study of the national school breakfast program.* New York: New Republic, 1972.

Hurley, T. Origin of the Illinois Juvenile Court Law. In Jane Addams (ed.). *The child client and the court.* New York: The New Republic, Inc., 1927.

Ichur, E. *Radical nonintervention: Rethinking the delinquency problem.* Englewood Cliffs, N.J.: Prentice-Hall, 1973.

Kittrie, N. *The right to be different: Deviance and enforced therapy.* Baltimore: Johns Hopkins Press, 1971.

Mack, J. The juvenile court. *Harv. Law Rev.* **23**, 104 (1909).

Massachusetts Advocacy Center. *State of danger: Childhood lead-paint poisoning in Massachusetts.* Boston: Massachusetts Advocacy Center, 1974.

Offerd, D. R. Youth and rebellion. *Correct. Psychiatr. J. Soc. Ther.* **15**(2) (1967), 6–17.

Peeples, W. J. Local diagnostic and advisory service for handicapped children. *Md. State Med. J.* **19**(4) (1970), 89–90.

Rutherford, A. *The dissolution of training schools in Massachusetts.* Columbus, Ohio: Academy for Contemporary Problems, 1973.

Ryan, W. *Blaming the victim.* New York: Random House, 1971.

Schucter, Arnold. The policitcs of treatment. Unpublished paper for the Juvenile Justice Standard Project, 1974.

Sullivan, C., Grant, J. D., and Grant, M. Q. The development of interpersonal maturity: Application to delinquency. *Psychiatr.,* **20** (1956), 373–85.

Task Force on Children Out of School. *The way we go to school: Exclusion of children in Boston.* Boston: Beacon, 1970.

Warren, M. Q. Classification of offenders as an aid to efficient management and effective treatment. *J. Crim. Law, Criminol., Police Sci.* **62** (1971), 239–58.

Professional Responsibility in Public-Policy Problem Areas

In Part Four, the contributors are united by a common concern about the public-policy problem areas that originate in mental-health service areas. Each chapter in Part Four examines how a concept originated by mental-health professionals has achieved significance in the public arena. The problem inherent in this process is that mental-health professionals no longer seem to be in control of the "monsters" they have created. The need for professionals in the field to reassert themselves constructively in the public-policy arena and to assume leadership roles in the fight for children's rights is clearly stated in each chapter.

In the first chapter, professional responsibility for the potential long-term effects of labeling and classifying children is discussed. Dr. Donald P. Bartlett, who earned his Ph.D. from George Peabody College, is uniquely qualified to address these issues. Before assuming his present position on the Psychology Faculty at the State University of New York at Buffalo, Bartlett was Research Associate to the Project on the Classification and Labeling of Exceptional Children at Vanderbilt University. His coauthor, Stephen E. Schlesinger, is a graduate student at SUNY at Buffalo. He was formerly a Special Education Consultant at the University of Michigan and has worked as a registered social worker in Michigan.

In the following chapter, Drs. Robert L. Williams and L. Wendell Rivers discuss the language biases of some standardized psychological tests. The right of a child to be evaluated in the context of his or her own language system and cultural values is amply demonstrated here. Dr. Williams is a past National Chairman of the Association of Black Psychologists and has published *The BITCH Test,* a counterbalanced intelligence test weighted in favor of urban blacks. Williams received his Ph.D. from Washington University, St. Louis, Missouri, where he is now Professor of Psychology and Director of the Black Studies Program. Dr. Rivers earned his Ph.D. at St. Louis University, concentrating in developmental and clinical child psychology. He is currently Assistant Research Professor and Director of the Mental Health Specialists Program at the University of Missouri, St. Louis,

The last three chapters in Part Four focus on the use of psychoactive drugs to treat children. Although differing viewpoints are presented, all the authors recommend a careful review of this issue and changes in treatment programs to ensure the rights of the children to whom these drugs are administered. J. Larry Brown and Stephen R. Bing, both of the Massachusetts Advocacy Center, who coauthored the chapter on juvenile justice in Part Three, bring the viewpoints of educator, social planner, and attorney to bear on the question of whether psychotropic drugs ought to be used at all. Dr. Mark A. Stewart, a child psychiatrist who has published major reviews on the use of such drugs, then discusses current problems in the routine use of psychotropic drugs that lead to violations of the child's basic rights. Stewart is the Ida P. Haller Professor of Child Psychiatry at the University of Iowa Medical School. Finally, Rodman McCoy and Dr. Gerald P. Koocher attempt to integrate the key issues of the problem of using psychotropic drugs and to establish the elements of a basic policy for using these drugs to treat children. Dr. Koocher is the general editor of this volume, as well as the author of the chapter on children's rights as psychotherapy patients that appears in Part One. Mr. McCoy, who worked with Koocher in the latter's seminar on Child Development and Public Policy at Boston University, originated the concept of drafting a pediatric drug-policy statement. Their joint chapter is intended to show the evolution of the ideas presented by Brown, Bing, and Stewart.

While there are certainly other areas in which mental-health professionals have spawned concepts, tests, drugs, or devices that have broad implications in terms of public policy, the areas examined in the following chapters are among the most broadly applicable and most topically sensitive in the mental-health field. It is hoped that presenting these issues for discussion may lead to a reassumption of responsibility by the professionals who originated them and who seem to have lost sight of their impact on the rights of children.

Toward an Enlightened Consumer: Professional Accountability in Behavioral Assessment

DONALD P. BARTLETT and
STEPHEN E. SCHLESINGER

Much consideration has recently been given to the legal rights of children. The number of litigations on this matter adjudicated in courts throughout the country demonstrates a renewed concern on behalf of children with a variety of problems. The focus on the rights of children has clearly been on legal reform to adjust the gaps and inequities in the mental-health system that deprive children of their right to fair and equal treatment. The struggle for legal reform is certainly a *necessary* part of the advocacy on behalf of our nation's children, but it is not a *sufficient* effort. While we support and encourage those who seek remedy through the courts, we wish to examine the issue from another vantage point. Professionals should not be seduced into thinking that the basis for reform rests solely on legal issues and matters of due process. It is the professionals who must ultimately operationalize decisions rendered by the courts; the crucial part of legal reform depends on the professionals' responsibility and attention to parents' and children's rights to know about and be a part of the services that are directed toward them. Although it has been demonstrated that courts frequently render decisions without adequate regard to the availability of such resources as funding, personnel, and the space and time to implement these legal mandates (Kirp, 1974), it is important that professionals do not lose sight of their responsibilities as personnel crucial to the formulation and implementation of change.

The alphabetical listing of the authors indicates equal contribution to the chapter.

First, there is a need to debunk the myth of assessment and treatment. Primarily because these processes have been underexposed to the public eye, assessment and treatment methods have acquired a false aura of accuracy and universal applicability. Such a myth may preserve a sense of professional identity, but it does not serve the interests of the consumers of these professional services, the parents and children who have been unwittingly caught up in and have thereby helped perpetuate the myth by failing to insist on professional accountability in the delivery of services. Parents, as the ultimate advocates for their children and as the consumers of services, must now be enfranchised in the system of service delivery; this will create a constructive tension in the system that will allow parents to obtain more adequate services and to have more accurate expectations of service.

There are two basic ways to approach the need to enfranchise parents in the professional systems of assessment and treatment services. First, professionals should "give away" their expertise, enabling consumers to ask more intelligent and pertinent questions of the providers. Second, informal and formal mechanisms can be created to monitor the relationships between professionals and parents. Before detailing what we believe to be reasonable actions for professionals, it is important to ground ourselves in definitions of "label," "diagnosis," and "assessment" and to describe briefly the types of problems parents and professionals alike face in managing assessment and service delivery for individual children.

We focus attention here on diagnoses rather than on labels. This distinction is an important one. *Labels*, once a shorthand for behavioral descriptions, have become powerful, stigmatic forces that remain tenaciously affixed. The process of labeling compresses a large quantity of data into a relatively few key words that contain none of the qualifiers that characterized the original evaluation. Labels purport to describe the present status of the child, and specify defined parameters within which they are to be applied. Nor do labels provide a sufficient basis of fact on which to plan useful remediation.

Diagnosis, as we use the term here, refers to an end product of the process of assessment. A diagnosis includes data to support the conclusions drawn from the assessment and leads to the discussion of strategies for intervention and remediation. By *assessment*, we mean any process to which the child and the parents are subjected to determine the cause(s) of the alleged difficulties encumbering the child. The problems may be emotional or physical, at home or at school, large or small. The assessments may be carried out by a medical doctor, if they are neurological or physiological in nature, or by a psychiatrist or a psychologist, if they are nonphysical assessments of behavior. Difficulties experienced by children are, in our view, best understood by means of a multibased asssessment. Such an assessment recognizes that a problem tends to be multicausal and does not necessarily have a single "key" solution. Most professionals agree that the best present-day assessment approaches are interdisciplinary in nature. Such assessments may involve physicians, psychiatrists, psychologists, social workers, nutritionists, dentists, and other professionals. They may consist of psychological interviews and tests, as well as blood and urine tests, such procedures as eye and ear examinations and electroencephelograph (brain-wave) tests, and recording comprehensive medical histories.

THE PROBLEMS PARENTS FACE

Parents may reach the point of considering assessment for their child in one of two basic ways: either they notice that there is something "wrong" with the way their child is behaving, or someone else does. That someone else may be a friend, a relative, or a neighbor, or a counselor or teacher at the child's school who may suggest some "testing" for the child. The experience of seeking assessment for a child can be painful. It is not uncommon for parents to feel somewhat lost at this point: "What is it all about?" "Where do I have to have this done?" "How much will it cost?" "What good will it do?" are questions that frequently arise. Parents who have had little or no contact with the system of professionals who deal with children's emotional or physical problems often foresee a bewildering maze of professional procedures about which they know very little, if anything. They may feel they are facing a unique problem that may somewhat frighten or embarrass them. But if parents and child are not to feel like mere "objects whose inner determinants are being x-rayed," they must take an active part in the assessment (Fisher, 1973). What at first may appear to be a jungle ideally begins to resemble a tree farm—the same product arranged in an orderly manner. The key to this change in outlook is the parents' feelings of involvement in the whole assessment process that they and their child are experiencing. Many assessors or assessment clinics provide a comfortable atmosphere within which the parents and the child can feel sure that they know what will happen. Assessors explain the process, answer any questions, and may include a tour of the facility and an explanation of the equipment to be used. If this information is not volunteered, parents should ask to spend time with the tester or physician and ask about the procedures to be used. If parents and children know what is going to happen during an assessment, it makes the procedure itself more comfortable.

After the assessment procedure is over and "the results are in," parents often find that information is either withheld or incomprehensible. Parents should determine whether they have been given a label or a diagnosis. If the outcome of assessment is merely a label, an important question to ask is, "Is this helpful? Does it add anything to my or to the professional's knowledge of how to help my child?" A label usually does not. The parents should then ask for a more detailed diagnosis. Once given the diagnosis (or if the assessor originally gave a diagnosis), the parents should ask themselves whether they received an explanation that was understandable and that satisfied them. We like to think of it in terms of whether the results, as explained, are "comprehensive and comprehensible."

Unfortunately even a satisfactory and detailed diagnosis can be an end in itself, unrelated to a plan for intervention. Often the test results imply "Johnny's problem is . . . ," and that's that. Parents should press for detailed explanations and plans for treatment. If they cannot obtain this information, then one could justifiably ask what the point of the whole process was.

Once the diagnosis has been explained and possible interventions have been detailed, it is important to identify the resources that are available to provide the services needed to deal with the identified problems. Relevant questions might be whether the assessor can suggest alternatives, taking into account practical constraints such as travel and family budget. Parents who have come this far are part of the whole assessment process and are in a good position not only to seek appropriate services for their children, but also to continue in their roles as active advocates for their children.

In general, then, we have covered a number of issues relevant to parents' involvement in the process of obtaining assessment services for their children. We have asked whether parents feel they are informed partners in the assessment process; whether they feel they are wholly dependent on the system or the assessors and can have no impact on the assessment or intervention(s); whether they feel "defeated" by the system or feel that the system is somehow "mystical"; and whether, if they do feel in these or similar ways (and many parents *do*), they feel that the assessors support them in their efforts to become actively involved, prime advocates for their children.

THE PROBLEMS PROFESSIONALS FACE

The most efficient assessments appear to be those that seek to evaluate problems in their many facets. In practical terms, this means that specialists in various areas (pediatrics, psychology, nutrition, opthomology, audiology, and the like) form an interdisciplinary assessment team to attempt to diagnose a child's difficulties. The results of that evaluation should be furnished and fully explained to the parents and/or the person who referred the child for assessment. Managing the case from this point can be a frustrating experience for the responsible professional.

Interdisciplinary approaches are not only the most efficient assessment technique, but they are also the most beneficial to communities in delivering services to the children who need them. Often the availability of such interdisciplinary services is restricted or nonexistent. The problem for the professional may be twofold. First, the required range of readily accessible services may not be available at reasonable cost in a given area. Thus the chance for an interdisciplinary approach to remediation may not be promising, because the component services may not exist. Second, the services may exist in the community but may not be linked in such a way as to make a coordinated, team approach to intervention possible. A fragmentation of *support services* (the services needed to solve the problems highlighted by the diagnosis) means that the professional must usually work with each diagnostic case to assemble, if possible, a team of professionals in the community who will work together to help the child.

An associated problem concurrent with the problem of the fragmentation of support services in a community, and one that may contribute to the problem of fragmentation, is that professionals in a community may view their roles as entirely within the boundaries of one position of the assessment-treatment process; that is, some professionals may view themselves as assessors, whereas others may view themelves as intervenors. When this is the case, an assessor makes a diagnosis, but the parent must then bridge the gap between these two "camps" to obtain support services. Gorham et al (1974) conclude that "most professional people are singularly uninformed of community resources serving exceptional children, resources that are, in fact, an indispensable complement to their clinical services" (p. 215). Therefore, the system in which the assessor helps seek support services for the child is preferable (Falkenstein, 1972; Schwartz et al., 1969). In this case, assessors aid parents in obtaining optimal services, and they may also consult with those who deliver services and aid in the service coordination efforts within the community. Hansell's (1967) proposal of a "screening, linking, planning" model as the most applicable approach to planning a service-delivery system is especially relevant here. The process, which operates from a center, establishes the capacity of a group of professionals to identify persons at risk (in this case, children) and to "identify the network of persons and agencies that can be linked tó the predicament of this particular person in trouble" (p. 205). Further, the practical adoption of such a model helps promote an understanding of professional capabilities among members of the service-delivery system. The routine planning of service delivery eliminates the fragmentation of services in a community and the need for a practitioner to manage a separate service plan for each new client.

Although the need for pragmatic support for parents in the assessment and treatment processes and the need for coordinated systems of support for the professional who helps to guide the parents cannot be overemphasized, the equally important need for emotional support for parents must not be neglected. On one hand, seeking service for their children is in itself a wrenching experience for parents; on the other hand, they must learn to deal with their own emotions during assessment (perhaps some guilt, anger, embarrassment, and the like). Professionals should be as sensitive to the process the parents are undergoing as they are to the difficulties the child is facing. Some parents view assessment and service delivery as a time of crisis (Perlman, 1960; Menninger Foundation staff, 1969). The crisis may consist of stages similar to those described by Hexter (1969) — shock, denial, guilt, hostility, intellectualization, involvement, and resolution—each producing characteristic parental reactions and readiness to accept certain types of information and responsibility. Miller's (1968) identification of the three stages of parental adjustment—shock, adjustment, and reintegration—also helps professionals to view the dynamics of the crisis from the parents' eyes and to place parental reactions and the need for support in the proper perspective.

TOWARD AN ENLIGHTENED CONSUMER

As we have already stated, parents are the ultimate advocates for their children. In the acquisition of assessment and treatment services, the parents must decide whether the child is to be assessed and/or treated by the professional community. Thus the *parents*, as well as their children, are the consumers of assessment services and, as such, must be concerned with the degree to which they are enlightened in regard to these services. There are three ways in which a consumer can become enlightened. One is to find out all there is to know about the "product" in which they are interested; a second is to learn the right questions to ask the "suppliers"; and a third is to work cooperatively with other "consumers" in an effort to acquire services.

Of course, the "products" here are assessment services, so the first path to enlightenment would appear to be somewhat impractical. Freedman (1974), a psychologist concerned with the methodology of consumer action, believes that the technology of normal goods and services has become so complicated that it is virtually impossible for a consumer to know the finer technical points of every possible selection in a given product area. Moreover, even if a consumer knows a product area well today, that consumer will not necessarily be familiar with the same product area six months from now, because technological and design changes are so rapid. For similar reasons, it is not practical for parents to find out all there is to know about assessment before seeking assessment for their child. First, the instruments of assessment are numerous, intricate in design, and complicated in interpretation; second, different assessors use different combinations of instruments.

Let us now consider the second path to consumer enlightenment, in which parents learn to ask probing questions of the assessor so that they can satisfy themselves as to the quality of service being offered. The parents would be entitled to a pretesting briefing by and a posttesting debriefing of the examiner; they would be able to ask that these sessions be held if they were not forthcoming. In addition, parents would become familiar with the appropriate service groups in their community and with the types of service to expect from the community, the third path to enlightenment.

Some might advise against giving assessment information on to the consumer(s) of assessment services, citing ethical considerations or other concerns about the effect of presenting such information to the recipient. This presents an important concern for the professional, who must somehow weigh the effects of releasing and the effects of withholding information. On one hand, releasing information may only confuse or frighten the recipient, who has no special knowledge in the problem area and who may have inappropriately strong and possibly detrimental reactions to this information. On the other hand, withholding information may lead to a false sense of dependency on the part of the recipient, who may believe the professional can do more than present knowledge allows, or it may convey to the recipient a sense of the professional's distrust, or it may even give rise to an inappropriate interpretation of the decision to withhold (Vane, 1972). In this and in many similar situations, no particular legal or ethical answer is appropriate, and the professional must recognize the implications of each alternative and act according to a responsible interpretation of the best interests of the client.

The following outline presents some orientation material in the form of questions for parents to consider to make themselves better "consumers" in obtaining assessment services for their children. This material would be a suitable supplement to an organized effort to help parents in this area; such an effort could be sponsored by parents' groups and/or professionals working within the community. The outline is presented here with specifics designed to help the reader examine his or her own situation.

Preassessment Phase

1. Who can help decide what assessments are most appropriate? Physician? Teacher? School psychologist?
2. Do you know other parents who have faced similar decisions with whom you could talk?
3. Are there parents' organizations in your community that you could consult and/or join? If you do not know of any, can you find out where the nearest parents' organizations are by contacting the school? Your physician? The local mental-health clinic? The local United Fund (or some other community-service agency)?
4. Are you satisfied with the decision that your child needs to be assessed for the problem described?
5. Are you keeping records of your contacts (phone calls, meetings, conferences, and so on), complete with date, who attended, what was discussed and agreed on, and what you were promised (Gorham et al., 1974)?
6. Have the assessment procedures and their implications for intervention in your child's problems been explained to you in terms that you understand and in sufficient detail to satisfy you? Have the limitations, if any, of making interpretations from these assessments been explained to you?
7. Do you know who will conduct the assessment? When and where it will occur? Is there more than one part to the assessment? Are you satisfied with the role *you* are to play in the assessment? Are the terms of the assessment (time and money, primarily) agreeable to you?
8. Do you feel that the assessment procedure is somewhat confusing or mystifying, even after the explanations given by the assessor? Do you feel at the "mercy" of the assessment technology? Do you feel supported by the assessor? Do you have any questions or thoughts that you could ask or voice that would clear up any uncertainties?
9. Do you feel you can have an impact on the assessment procedure, based on the explanations you have received?

Postassessment Phase

1. Did the assessment result in a *diagnosis* or a simple label?
2. Did the assessor explain the diagnosis to you in terms that you fully understood and in a manner that satisfied you?
3. Is the diagnosis an indication of the child's difficulties? Is intervention implied (that is, is it clear where the revelations of the diagnosis will lead)? Is it clear to you who will do what next and by when?

4. Have the possible sources for service delivery, given the implications of the diagnosis, been explained? Have alternatives been discussed? Are you satisfied that you will be able, on the basis of the explanations given you, to arrange for satisfactory services?
5. Are there any strategies that the examiner can suggest that you and your child can apply to supplement intervention?
6. Do you feel that you have an impact on the type of intervention to be pursued?

Intervention

1. Do you have the name(s), address(es), and phone number(s) of the professionals in your community whom you would like to contact about intervention?
2. Has the professional who will design the treatment (the practitioner) explained to you how the intervention will proceed and what it will entail in terms that you understand and in sufficient detail to satisfy you?
3. Is it clear to you what your part in the treatment will be?
4. Do you have accurate records of the plans that have been made to begin treatment (when, by whom, where, and so on)?
5. Are you satisfied that the treatment arrangements are complete, comprehensive, and comprehensible to you?
6. Are periodic sessions scheduled throughout the treatment period to evaluate progress and possibly to alter the treatment course?

General

1. Have you joined and/or found support from a parent or other lay organization in your community?
2. Have you, either through these organizations or from other contacts, gained a good perspective as to how the entire *system* (of which the assessment and treatment services are a part) works? In other words, are you aware of who controls what services, of how services are usually offered to parents and children, of "political" considerations that have either caused problems for others in the past or helped expedite matters for parents seeking the services you now seek?
3. Has the "state of the art" of the particular service you seek been explained to you? In other words, are there limitations on what certain assessment procedures can determine about your child or on what certain treatments can be expected to do for your child, and are you aware of those limitations? Do some assessment instruments seem to work better than others? If so, which do you want to pursue?

Thus far, we have attempted to give an overview of an important area that is often neglected: the difficulties faced by parents who act as advocates for their children in obtaining assessment and treatment services to remedy the wide range of difficulties that encumber children. We have approached this subject by addressing the problems that both parents and professionals face in this area. We have tried to present a practical outline to orient parents to the issues involved in their role in the assessment and treatment of their children. We feel that this type of approach should be provided for parents in an effort to improve the integrative quality of the services available to parents and children. Such an approach is adaptable to a workshop or workbook format and can be readily molded to the needs of a variety of types of groups either by professionals working with parents or by the parents themselves. By whatever means, it is important that complex procedures of assessment be explained to parents (or to any nonprofessional) and that the involvement of nonprofessionals in these procedures be the result of a maximal sharing of expertise by professionals to improve service delivery to children in need.

THE ORGANIZATION OF COMMUNITY SERVICES

In addition to educational, consumer-oriented concerns, the needs remain for professionals to develop comprehensive systems of service delivery along the lines of Hansell's (1967) "screening-linking-planning" model, to become more involved with self-help groups that supplement services rendered by professionals, and to help bring about legislative changes to complement legal and professional progress in addressing the need for reform. Ideally, the screening-linking-planning model is implemented by some sort of center that coordinates organizational conferences and conducts service-delivery follow-ups. Where such centers exist and where this type of model does not, professionals would perform an enormous service, not only to their clients but also to themselves by initiating or facilitating the development of such a system. It is possible for the professional community to organize such a system through an interagency coordinating committee that would oversee the coordination of community services and their application to individual cases.

Second, professionals can perform an important community service by consulting with self-help groups. Such groups, which are usually organized to deal with the common difficulties of persons with similar afflictions, have much to offer their members in the way of guidance (emotional support) and logistical assistance (practical support). Although some self-help

groups exist in an adversary relationship to professionals, many s\
groups can and do provide important services for their members tha\
plement the services of professionals. Parents and nonprofessionals c   ⌐
effective members of the treatment regimen for children, and a sharing of
expertise between professionals and nonprofessionals is a positive alternative to the traditional and inefficient one-to-one model of service delivery
in the health and health-related disciplines. Perhaps the major advantage
professionals have in most of their work is that they systematically investigate problems and formulate methods to approach these problems through
research. This means that it is the *research methods,* and not necessarily
the "discoveries" stemming from those methods, that para- and nonprofessionals are not experienced or qualified enough to handle. The literature
is consistent in emphasizing that techniques of intervention can be passed
on to parents and paraprofessionals whose work with children is of excellent quality.

Indeed, this is a major point of departure by those who consider improving efficiency in the delivery of mental-health services of prime importance
from those who rely on a one-to-one model of service delivery. Hobbs
(1969) sums it up succinctly when he says:

... the mental-health specialist must be trained in ways to multiply his effectiveness by working through other less extensively and expensively trained
people. The one-to-one model of much current practice does not provide a
sound basis for a public-health, mental-health program (p. 21).

Third, it is clear that reform in any system is not a simple or a single-
faceted event. When change is to take place, people's understanding of the
professions involved and the services they deliver must also change. When
one part of a system of service delivery changes, it produces a "ripple
effect" throughout the entire system. As has been witnessed in recent court
decisions ordering standardization and improvement of services to children, the courts have not coordinated their efforts with the legislatures
that must provide the resources or with the professionals who must implement the court decisions. Professional organizations must become more
active in legislative lobbying at all government levels to assure that those
who must provide the resources for change have an accurate and an up-to-
date understanding of how the service professions function. If legislative
members who cannot keep abreast of the developments in each service
area in which they must make funding decisions are not appraised of
current changes in these fields by the professionals themselves, then funding requests for reforms will be subjected to scrutiny by legislators
applying outdated views and criteria to innovative plans. It is axiomatic

that "the best consumer is the informed consumer," and this holds as true for legislators preparing to "invest" in innovative programming as it does for parents advocating for their children.

REFERENCES

Berkowitz, B. P., and Graziano, A. M. Training parents as behavior therapists: A review. *Behav. Res. Ther.* **10** (1972), 297–17.

Bernal, M. E. Training parents in child management. In R. N. Bradfield (ed.), *Behavioral modification of learning disabilities.* San Rafael, Calif.: Academic Therapy Publications, 1971.

Denham, W., Felsenfeld, N., and Walker, W. *The neighborhood worker, a new resource for community change: A monograph on training and utilization.* Washington, D.C.: Howard University Institute for Youth Studies, 1966.

Falkenstein, D. Learning disabilities in the family. *Woman Physician* **27** (1972), 64–69.

Fisher, C. T. Contextural approaches to assessment. *Community Ment. Health J.* 5 (1973), 38–45.

Fishman, J. Baker's dozen: A program of training young people as mental-health aides. In J. Segal (ed.), *The mental health of the child.* Washington, D.C.: U.S. Government Printing Office, 1971.

Freedman, M. Personal communication, 1974.

Galloway, C., and Galloway, K. C. *Parent groups with a focus on precise behavior management* Vol. III, No. I. Nashville, Tenn.: Institute on Mental Retardation and Intellectual Development (George Peabody College for Teachers), 1970.

Gorham, K., Scheiber, B., Page, R., Pettis, E., and Des Jardins, C. The effects on parents of the labeling of their children. In N. Hobbs (ed.), *Issues in the classification of children.* San Francisco: Jossey-Bass, 1974.

Hansell, H. Patient predicament and clinical service: A system. *Arch. Gen. Psychiatr.* **17** (1967), 204–10.

Hexter, G. Mental retardation. In H. R. Lamb, D. Heath, and J. J. Downing (eds.), *Handbook of community mental-health practice.* San Francisco: Jossey-Bass, 1969.

Hobbs, N. Mental health's third revolution. In G. B. Guerney (ed.), *Psychotherapeutic agents: New roles for nonprofessionals, parents, and teachers.* New York: Holt, Rinehart & Winston, 1969.

Homme, L. E. *How to use contingency contracting in the classroom.* Champaign, Ill.: Research Press, 1969.

Johnson, C. A., and Katz, R. C. Using parents as change agents for their children: A review. *J. Child Psychol. Psychiatr.* **14** (1973), 181–200.

Johnson, S. M., and Brown, R. A. Producing behavior change in parents of disturbed children. *J. Child Psychol. Psychiatr.* **10** (1969), 197–221.

Johnston, R. Some casework aspects of using foster grandparents for emotionally disturbed children. In B. G. Guerney (ed.) *Psychotherapeutic agents: New roles for nonprofessionals, parents, and teachers.* New York: Holt, Rinehart & Winston, 1969.

Katz, L. G. Helping local Head-Start staff and parents plan their own program: An enabler model. *Child. Today* **1** (1972), 20–23.

Kirp, D., Kuriloff, P., and Buss, W. Legal mandates and organizational change. In N. Hobbs (ed.), *Issues in the classification of children.* San Francisco: Jossey-Bass, 1974.

Klein, W., Denham, W., MacLennan, B., and Fishman, J. *Training nonprofessional workers for human service: A manual of organization and process.* Washington, D.C.: Howard University Institute for Youth Studies, 1966.

Menninger Foundation staff. *Disturbed children.* San Francisco: Jossey-Bass, 1969.

Miller, L. G. Toward a greater understanding of the parents of the mentally retarded child. *J. Pediatr.* **73** (1968), 698–705.

Mitchell, L. *Training for community mental-health aides as leaders of child and adolescent therapeutic activity groups.* Washington, D.C.: Howard University Institute for Youth Studies, 1966.

O'Keefe, R. A. Home start: Partnership with parents. *Child. Today* **2** (1973), 12–16.

Perlman, H. H. Intake and some role considerations. *Soc. Casework* **41** (1960), 171–77.

Project on Classification of Exceptional Children. *The futures of children: Categories, labels, and their consequences.* Nashville, Tenn.: Vanderbilt University, 1974.

Schwartz, D. J., Wynn, L., and Lamb, H. R. Services for children. In H. R. Lamb, D. Heath, and J. J. Downing (eds.) *Handbook of community mental-health practice.* San Francisco: Jossey-Bass, 1969.

Valett, R. E. *Effective teaching: A guide to diagnostic prescriptive task analysis.* Belmont, Calif.: Fearon, 1970.

Vane, J. R. Getting information from school and clinical psychologists. *Prof. Psychol.* **3** (1972), 206–208.

Wagner, M. K. Parent therapists: An operant conditioning model. *Ment. Hyg.* **52** (1958), 452–55.

The Effects of Language
on the Test Performances
of Black Children

ROBERT L. WILLIAMS and
L. WENDELL RIVERS

> "How do you know where I'm at
> if you ain't been where I've been?
> Understand where I'm coming from?"
> "Good Times"
> CBS Telecast
> October 22, 1974

Many studies report that white students obtain higher scores on standardized tests than black students do. As a result, it has been assumed that the cognitive development and language acquisition processes of black children are deficient to those developmental processes of white children. Still others report that black children (1) enter school without the skills necessary for coping with kindergarten and first-grade curricula; (2) have poor language development; (3) have underdeveloped auditory and visual discrimination skills; (4) are more likely than white children to drop out of school before completing high school; and (5) have poorly developed self-concepts. We reject the above assertions for the following reasons. The problem with many of the research studies in the areas of language, intellectual, and self-concept development of black children is that the research is conducted (1) by white researchers; (2) with instruments such as the Binet, Wechsler, and Peabody, all of which have been standardized on white children; (3) without relevant ethnic content; and (4) from a deficit or pathology-model point of view.

The purpose of this chapter is to review briefly five conceptual models

205

that are generally provided as explanations for the black child's low test performances and academic achievements. In addition, we provide a conceptual model (discontinuity and mismatch) as an alternative explanation to the problem. The five conceptual models to be discussed are: (1) the deficit model; (2) cultural-difference model; (3) the school-as-failure model; (4) the bicultural model; and (5) the general systems model.

THE DEFICIT MODEL

For the past two or three decades, the leading assumptions of the causes of the black child's failure in school were dominated by a "deficit model" or deficiency hypothesis. The *deficit model* created more heat than light by proposing that black children were deficient in cognitive, linguistic, and intellectual skills due both to genetic and environmental factors (Bernstein, 1961; Bereiter and Engelmann, 1966; Jensen, 1969; Shockley, 1972A and 1972B).

Employing such pejorative labels as "culturally deprived," "disadvantaged," and "deficient," deficit-model theorists maintained that the educational problems of black children were due to a deficient genetic pool, evidenced by scores on ability tests and poor classroom performance, and to their deprived home backgrounds that denied them the cognitive and linguistic input to accumulate information and skills necessary for successful classroom work.

One allegation of the deficit-model theorist is that black children have acquired less language than white children. Special programs have been developed to "compensate" for these alleged deficiencies. A major proponent of the language deficiency school of thought, Basil Bernstein (1961), identifies two forms of communication codes or styles of verbal behavior: restricted and elaborated. *Restricted codes* are classified as stereotyped, limited, condensed, and lacking in specificity needed for precise conceptualization and differentiation. The restricted code uses sentences that are short, simple, and often unfinished. It is alleged to be a language with implicit meaning, easily understood, and commonly shared.

Elaborated codes, on the other hand, are those in which communication is individualized and the message is specific to a particular situation, topic, and person. The elaborated code is reported to be more particular, more differentiated, complex, and precise. It permits the expression of a wider and more complex range of thought with more discrimination among cognitive and affective content.

Bernstein (1961) further proposes that lower-class parents employ different child-rearing techniques than those utilized by middle- and upper-class parents. In his view, middle- and upper-class child-rearing practices rely mostly on verbal exchange, characterized by elaborate and complex subtleties, abstractions, and logical structure. Such a verbal medium, according to Bernstein, prepares the speech and thought of the child for complex intellectual activities and subsequent average-to-superior test performances.

In contrast, Bernstein proposes that lower-income class language is characterized by crude expressions of logical relationships and that it is based mainly on simple, concrete sentences. These sentences have no value within a planning function such as that possessed by more complex language. Bernstein concludes that the absence from lower-income class language of such conjunctions as "if" and "then" as well as the initial subordinate clause "if A . . . then B," renders the language code of the lower-income class person restricted, at best, and deficient in dealing with hypothetical complexities. Accordingly, black children's language system restricts them to a low level of conceptual functioning and thus to a low performance level on tests of intelligence and achievement.

Bereiter and Engelmann (1966) are also deficit theorists. These proponents assume nonstandard English to be inferior to standard English. The underlying notion here is that black children develop speech and thinking patterns that are at variance with what they need to learn. Bereiter and Engelmann (1966) developed special programs to remediate the language deficiency. Other special programs (Deutsch, 1967) have been developed for black children at the preschool level, with the following goals: (1) to arrest the cumulative deficit observed in so-called disadvantaged children; (2) to emphasize language and cognitive development by providing special training to help the children make abstractions and generalizations from their concrete experiences; and (3) to develop programs that facilitate maximum growth and utilization of intellectual potential. It is to be noted that the deficit model has been vigorously discredited by a number of researchers and scholars (Hunt, 1969; Kagan, 1969; Baratz, 1970; Labov, 1970).

THE CULTURAL-DIFFERENCE MODEL

In contradiction to the deficit model, another view of the educational problem of black children is that they have acquired background learning experiences that, although not deficient, differ from those of their middle-class counterparts. This conceptualization, called the *cultural-difference model,* proposes that the black child grows up in a culture that has its own language, traditions, strengths, and weaknesses. For example, although nonstandard English (that is, the informal language characteristics of many black people) may be adaptive in one's community, the middle-class teacher may not appreciate this dialect. What, then, is an asset and adaptive in the peer culture is basically a liability in the classroom. Loban (1963), Baratz and Shuy (1969), Baratz and Baratz (1969), Stewart (1969), Labov (1970), Wolfram (1970), and F. Williams (1970), have been the most vocal proponents of the cultural-difference model, especially as it applies to linguistic features of the black child.

Loban (1963) performed a number of longitudinal studies that provide interesting data on the speech of poor black and white children. One study emphasized the nature and degree of deviation from standard English demonstrated in the speech of lower-class children. Standard English is characterized by Loban as the dialect that receives the most social acceptance in this country. The major finding of that research was that lower-class black children in Loban's sample spoke a dialect that was different from the type of dialect (standard English) utilized by lower- and middle-class white children. This difference was most pronounced in use of verbs and, to a much lesser degree, pronouns and nouns.

Baratz and Baratz (1969) examined the failure of urban education to prove effective for ghetto children. They point out that one major fault of our urban educational system is its failure to understand why teaching an urban black child to read is so difficult. These writers contend that a cultural variable is at work that is basic to the difficulty, suggesting that the reading problems experienced by black children are a function of standard English syntax rather than spelling, pronounciation, or word recognition. They insist that those who have been responsible for designing educational systems have completely ignored the legitimacy of the black culture, of which black language style is a highly integral part. Baratz and Baratz strongly support the recognition of an established black dialect in educational programs for black children.

Labov et al. (1968) performed a number of interesting studies on the language of poor black children. One of his major research concerns has been with the relationship between black dialect and standard English. Labov and his colleagues assume that black language constitutes a lawful, coherent system with a legitimate structure of its own.

Labov et al. (1968) cast doubt on the validity of the "deficiency theories" espoused by such writers as Bereiter and Engelmann (1966), who assert that poor black children cannot learn to read because their language is a deficient form of standard English. Labov's results indicate that black children possess a mature and socially efficient language; therefore, a simplistic "deficiency" hypothesis cannot explain the reading difficulties experienced by these children. Labov and his associates pointed out that there are limited instances of structural differences between non-standard English and standard English. However, these differences are not sufficiently numerous to explain reading deficiencies. Labov and his associates suggest that a major part of the problem is a conflict between the spontaneous use of black dialect and that form of speech required in the classroom. They see language as one factor in a cultural orientation that contradicts the values of the school. This conflict, not a deficient language, is primarily responsible for poor school performance on the part of poor black children.

The bulk of the research evidence seems to suggest that the language development of black children is, in most respects, not deficient or much different from the speech of middle-class children. There is also much cross-cultural evidence concerning this issue (Lenneberg, 1967; McNeill, 1970). The general conclusion of these studies is that the development of children's language is highly similar in form in various cultures and sub-cultures throughout the world.

At a recent conference, entitled "Cognitive and Language Development of the Black Child," a group of black scholars pointed out that the cultural-difference model contained more political and economic overtones than grammatical, phonological, or syntactical considerations. Very little clarification of the controversy involving the cultural-difference model has been demonstrated by using the difference-model approach. For example, what black English or nonstandard English really is has still not been resolved. Simpkins, Williams, and Gunnings (1971), Taylor (1973), Williams (1973), Beryl Bailey (1973), Gilliam (1973), Holt (1973), Smith (1973), Simpkins (1973), Smitherman (1973), Sims (1973), Covington (1973), in a barrage of criticisms, held that the concept of black English or nonstandard English contains deficit-model characteristics and therefore must be abolished. Following considerable discussion regarding the language of black people, the group reached a consensus to adopt the term "Ebonics" (combining ebony and phonics, or black sounds).[1]

Ebonics is defined as the linguistic and paralinguistic features on a concentric continuum that represent the communicative competence of West African, Carribbean, and United States slave descendants of African origin, including the various idioms, patois, argots, ideolects, and social dialects. Ebonics is thus the culturally appropriate language of black people and is not considered deviant. An example of Ebonics follows: "The Hawk is definitely not jiving outside today" ("It is uncomfortably cold today"). Contrary to popular belief, that sentence is not in slang or non-standard English form. Rather it is stated in the culturally appropriate and ingenious language of black people.

THE SCHOOL-AS-FAILURE MODEL

The third approach, referred to as the *school-as-failure model,* defines the locus of the difficulty as being in the school, in the curriculum, and in the staff, and charges that the schools do not respond to the needs of the child. The deficit is not so much within the child's resources. In this model, emphasis is placed on teacher training, retraining, increasing the teacher's sensitivity and knowledge about the child's culture, teaching resources, curriculum changes, and mutual communication between the community and the school.

Katz (1967) points out:

. . . children from low-income homes, most of whom are Negro, get more than their fair share of classroom exposure to teachers who are really unqualified for their role, who basically resent teaching them. . . . Summarizing my comments on teachers, their influences on Negro students' motivation may be considerable, particularly in the lower elementary grades when children are more emotionally dependent on adults. Apparently, many teachers inadvertently dispense strong, negative reinforcements in the form of personal disapproval and rejection, and studies of teachers' attitudes toward lower-class pupils suggest that the incidence of such teachers in predominantly Negro schools is relatively high (pp. 177–78).

In essence, the above explanations are given for the school-as-failure model. Acknowledging that there is discontinuity between home and school, the problem of education remains. What is needed is a curriculum model that responds to the educational needs of the child. Current models, for the most part, engage in what we call "backward learning," or going from the unfamiliar to the familiar. It would be more appropriate to reverse this process.

THE BICULTURAL MODEL

To survive the academic situation, black children are expected to know both black and white culture; that is, to become encultured in standard English and middle-class culture as well as to maintain black style. Valentine (1971), an anthropologist, is a leading proponent of this particular model. We call it a racist model because it does not require white children to become encultured to black culture. The model operates only in one direction. Survival for black children means the acquisition of two cultures. It negates a deep entrenchment in their own black culture (Simpkins, Williams, and Gunnings, 1971).

THE GENERAL-SYSTEMS MODEL

The fifth and final model defines the problem in terms of *general-systems theory*. Institutional racism is cited as the basic factor in the educational problems of the black child. From this perspective, the behavior of the child in a social system is related to his status and to the system's demands on him. The mother's and teacher's interactions with the child are seen as a reflection of the system's demands and expectations. Consequently, little is gained by attempting to change individual children through remedial efforts without employing programs designed to change the social structure or the social systems in which the child lives and the teacher works, especially since the structure establishes cultural and community values.

A DISCONTINUITY (MISMATCH) MODEL

What we are proposing here is a discontinuity or a mismatch theory to explain the black child's difficulties with tests and in classrooms. In general, many black children are prepared early in life to seek survival rather than academic success. Such preparation results in certain discontinuities for black children in traditional educational systems. Language usage constitutes one, if not the major, discontinuity experienced by the black child who enters the traditional classroom and undergoes standardized intelligence and achievement testing.

Hunt (1969) defines this problem as one of "match":

If encountering a given set of circumstances is to induce psychological development in the child, these circumstances must have an appropriate relationship to the information already accumulated in the child's mental storage from his previous encounters with circumstances (p. 129).

Applying Hunt's definition to the black child in particular, Williams (1972A) terms the situation as "the problem of mismatch," or the extent to which moderator variables (personal characteristics and test biases) are operative in influencing the relationship between predictor (tests) and criterion (scholastic achievement) variables.

Thus in light of the conceptual and methodological difficulties, we began to examine some basic factors associated with test performance and education. An initial step was to locate and examine the possible sources of common cultural biases in tests and classrooms. One very common finding was the language factor. Our observations led us to conclude that neither the cognitive processes nor the cognitive development of the black child is different from that of the white child, particularly by cognitive development we mean children's capacities to discriminate, recognize, identify, and manipulate the features and processes of the world around them.

Cognitive development or cognition refers to the process by which a child becomes aware of, knows, or learns to idenify, to label, and to interpret his or her world through mental processes. For the first two years of life, the cognitive processes of black and white children do not differ. For example, all infants learn to identify such diverse phenomena as hot, cold, up, down, and so on. Black babies learn these phenomena just as quickly and readily as babies of any other ethnic group. For example, a 2-year-old black boy is not going to fall down steps because of "cognitive deficits" or the lack of proper cognitive socialization. He may not "label" the objects with the same terminology a white child would use, but he is able to "understand" the direction of the danger involved. Nor is he going to touch a hot stove. He has learned the dangers involved in hot objects as well as in cold ones. In other words, he possesses the appropriate cognitions: he knows the difference between hot and cold.

Thus until approximately 2 years of age, we are positive that cognitive development is just the same in black children as it is in any group of children. We propose, however, that the *labeling* or the attaching of language to cognitions is different in black and white children because of their culturally different environments or backgrounds. The process by which black children attach labels to their cognitions is not different; however, the actual labels assigned to the cognitions are different. A child develops language-comprehension and language-production skills primarily as a result of the language model of his or her environment, a personal internal schematic organization, self-instruction, and those items that he or she differentially selects from the environment.

After 2 years of age, something very different happens. Children begin to label the events around themselves with language; that is, they label such objects as desks, chairs, and toys. They attach the same labels to these objects that they hear other people use. The black child is typically in a different labeling environment than the white child. Thus black children may not label their cognitions in the same way that mainstream children do. This does not mean that blacks are deficient in communications skills because they use different labels, nor does it mean that blacks have less language.

To test our hypotheses derived from discontinuity and mismatch theory, we conducted several initial studies to examine the differential effects of test instructions written in familiar versus standard language on the test performances of black children.

We divided 990 black kindergarten, first- and second-grade children into two groups of 445 each. Variables of race, IQ, age, sex, and grade were controlled by balancing the groups. We used the standard version of the Boehm Test of Basic Concepts (BTBC)[2] and a set of nonstandard questions that we developed. The BTBC consists of 50 pictorial, multiple-choice items that involve concepts of space, quantity, and time. Black teachers and graduate students translated the concepts and the objects into language *familiar* to the black children. Examples of standard and nonstandard versions of the basic concepts follow:

	Standard Version (Boehm)	Non-standard Version (Williams and Rivers)
1.	Space: Mark the toy that is *behind* the *sofa*.	Mark the toy that is *in back of* the *couch*.
2.	Quantity: Mark the apple that is *whole*.	Mark the apple that is *still all there*.
3.	Time: Mark the boy who is *beginning* to climb the tree.	Mark the boy who is *starting* to climb the tree. [Variations such as "about to" or "getting ready to" may be used.]

We are cognizant of the problem of standardization involved in changing test instructions. The essence of the study, however, was to determine how black children perform when the same test questions are worded differently.

The results showed clear-cut differences. The mean scores on the nonstandard version were significantly higher than those on the standard version (nonstandard mean = 35.59; standard mean = 32.26; $p = .05$). We examined this phenomenon further by comparing our findings with those of Boehm's original reliability sample. Boehm's 2647 children were from the same grade levels as the children in our sample. Boehm included children from low, middle, and high socioeconomic levels. Our children were all from the low-income level. When we compared the "standard-version" scores of Boehm's middle- and high-SES children with those of our children, her children scored significantly higher than ours. But when we compared the "nonstandard-version" scores of Boehm's and our children, no significant differences were found. In several instances, the nonstandard means of our groups exceeded those of Boehm's group.

These findings clearly suggest that language bias plays a significant part in reducing black children's scores on the Boehm Test. It is presumed that a similar factor operates on other standardized instruments, such as the Binet, Wechsler Intelligence Scale for Children (WISC), and Peabody Picture Vocabulary (PPVT). Thus when the test items are dialectically fair and culturally-specific, black children perform as well as their white counterparts. Williams (1972A) points out:

. . . A difference in labeling cognitions rather than a deficiency in language is to be found in the language of black children. That is, black children have developed a different or divergent language representation of persons, events, objects of the world about them, and have labeled these phenomena according to what meets approval in their environment (p. 2).

In describing the organization of cognitive patterns in children, Rivers (1969) points out that one of the most noticeable characteristics of developing cognitive behavior is the emergence of processes that involve the systematic transformation of direct sensory information from the environment into symbolic forms. Such transformations lead to an active interaction among learned symbolic responses. In some instances, this interaction can be somewhat detrimental, as when one verbal pattern interferes with the learning, understanding, retention, or production of another verbal pattern.

In many ways, standard English may not signal or activate the black child's linguistically-conceptual systems to the extent that systematic transformations are evoked to produce the expected cognitive responses. If the child is confronted with unfamiliar language stimuli, his or her cognitive transformational system will not adequately process the incoming stimuli. However, it is important to understand that this does not mean that the black child lacks the capacity for processing the standard language stimuli (verbal or written); what is implied is that the black child's "communication-intake gates" are not fully activated by the stimulus properties of standard English.

The following model seems appropriate to this state of affairs. Conceptually, two sensory input channel gates must be activated before a child can process information. Gate I is always open and receptive to incoming sensory information. However, for this information to enter the cognitive transformational channel of the system, it must activate Gate II. If the information does not meet certain specifications (that is, if it is unfamiliar, of insufficient amplitude, or just "noise"), it is returned to the source for better organization or for signals that meet system input specifications. If, on the other hand, the incoming information possesses familiar parameters, then Gate II is activated and the material is sent to the child's transformational system for further processing and decoding.

What is suggested by this research is that the teachers (1) become flexible and responsible to the child; (2) respond to where the child is; and (3) employ an appropriate teaching method to take the child from where he or she is to other goals (associative bridging). Simpkins (1973) defines associative bridging as a strategy to engage the student by using the verbal and nonverbal behavior s(he) has already acquired outside the classroom as a starting point and moving from the *familiar* to the *unfamiliar*.

The widespread belief, then, among white scholars that black children use restricted codes and show cognitive concreteness and rigidity, in our opinion, is false. To the contrary, black children must possess a great deal of cognitive flexibility to survive at all in urban schools and in society in general. They must be able to switch codes from "everyday talk" to "school talk." Everyday talk is a kind of familiar, informal language that is not rooted in phonology and syntax; it is getting over or just plain communicating. School talk or standard English is formalized and emphasizes grammar, diction, syntax, and so on. Black children are able to switch codes from everyday talk to school talk; perhaps their school talk is not as effective as white children's, but they do switch codes. If a child is put in a school system that employs a different language code, either the school must switch to that child's language system or the child must switch codes. Usually, the child is required to switch codes, suggesting cognitive flexibility rather than cognitive rigidity.

The model that we discuss here is certainly not a new one. It is similar to one proposed by Shannon (1948) some years ago. The essence of the information theory proposed by this researcher was that once a message has been selected by a source, it is *encoded* by a transmitter, sent over a communication channel, and then *decoded* by a receiver at the destination. How much of the information can be retrieved at the destination depends on the information available at the source and on whether the channel carries "noise" (signals from some other source that may interfere with the message under consideration). The activation of Gate II, of which we spoke earlier, depends on symbolic or abstract representations of objects, rules, and events rather than on concrete, rote, sensory properties. For the child to decode incoming linguistic messages properly, s(he) must first recognize, identify, and discriminate events from the standpoint of existing cognitive structures, and the message must be as free of "noise" as possible. For many black children, standard English is "noise"-laden stimuli, which, when presented, require them to switch codes from "everyday talk" to "school talk," or from nonstandard to standard English.

Present findings clearly mitigate against the less-language or deficiency hypothesis put forth by Bernstein (1961), Bereiter and Engelmann (1966), and Jensen (1969). What these results suggest is that the black child develops a different symbolic representation of concepts rather than a deficiency of concepts.

The basic contention here is that there is a problem of match (Hunt, 1969) or mismatch (Williams, 1972B) between black children's language background experiences and the language that they encounter in a standardized test situation. A discontinuity or mismatch occurs between the black child's cognitive linguistic system and the linguistic stimuli presented in test instructions and school curriculum. Psychological tests in particular may not adequately activate the cognitive linguistic processes of the vast majority of black children. To do so, it is necessary to accomplish a *match* by presenting the instructions and materials of psychological tests in ways that relate to the language backgrounds of black children.

NOTES

1. The term Ebonics was actually coined by one of the authors (Williams).
2. Published by the Psychological Corporation, 304 East 45th Street, New York, New York 10017.

REFERENCES

Bailey, Beryl. Disentangling the Language Web. Presented at the Conference on Cognitive Language Development of the Black Child, St. Louis, Mo., January 1973.

Baratz, J. C., and Shuy, R. W. (eds.). *Teaching black children to read.* Washington, D.C.: Center for Applied Linguistics, 1969.

Baratz, S. S., and Baratz, J. C. Negro ghetto culture and urban education: A cultural solution. *Soc. Educ.* (April 1969), 401–404.

Baratz, S. S., and Baratz, J. C. Early childhood intervention: The social science base of institutional racism. *Harv. Educ. Rev.* **40** (1970), 29–50.

Bereiter, C., and Engelmann, S. *Teaching disadvantaged children in the preschool,* Englewood, Cliffs, N.J.: Prentice-Hall, 1966.

Bernstein, Basil. Social class and linguistic development: A theory of social learning. In A. H. Halsey, J. Floud, and C. A. Anderson (eds.), *Education, economy, and society.* New York: Free Press, 1961.

Covington, A. Teachers' Attitudes Toward Black English Effects on Student Achievement. Presented at the Conference on Cognitive Language Development of the Black Child, St. Louis, Mo., January 1973.

Deutsch, M., et al. *The disadvantaged child.* New York: Basic Books, 1967.

Gilliam, A. Multicultural and Multilingual View of Black Language in the Americas. Presented at the Conference on Cognitive Language Development of the Black Child, St. Louis, Mo., January 1973.

Holt, G. Black English: Surviving the Bastardization Process. Presented at the Conference on Cognitive Language Development of the Black Child, St. Louis, Mo., January 1973.

Hunt, J. McV. *The challenge of incompetence and poverty.* Urbana: University of Illinois Press, 1969.

Jensen, A. R. How much can we boost IQ and scholastic achievement? Discussion: *Harv. Educ. Rev.* **39** (1969), 1–123.

Kagan, J. S., et al. How much can we boost IQ and scholastic achievement? Discussion: *Harv. Educ. Rev.* **39** (1969), 273–356.

Katz, I. The socialization of academic motivation in minority-group children. In D. Levine (ed.), *Nebraska symposium on motivation.* Lincoln: University of Nebraska Press, 1967.

Labov, W., Cohen, P., Robins, C., and Lewis, J. *A study of the nonstandard English of Negro and Puerto Rican speakers in New York City; Final Report.* U.S. Office of Education Cooperative Research Project No. 3288, New York: Columbia University, 1968 (mimeographed; 2 vols.).

Labov, W. The logic of nonstandard English. In F. Williams (ed.), *Language and poverty: Perspectives on a theme.* Chicago: Markham, 1970.

Lenneberg, E. H. *Biological foundations of language.* New York: John Wiley & Sons, Inc., 1967.

Loban, W. D. *The language of elementary-school children.* Champaign, Ill.: National Council of Teachers of English, 1963.

McNeill, D. The development of language. In P. J. Mussen (ed.), *Carmichael's manual of child psychology,* New York: John Wiley & Sons, Inc., 1970.

Rivers, L. W. The Stability of Patterns of Primary Mental Abilities in Children from Three Different Ethnic Groups. Unpublished doctoral dissertation, St. Louis University, 1969.

Shannon, C. E. A mathematical theory of communication. *Bell Syst. Tech. J.,* **27** (1948), 319–43, 623–56.

Shockley, W. Dysgenics, geneticity, raceology: Challenges to the intellectual responsibility of educators. *Phi Delta Kappan* **LIII**(5) (1972A).

Shockley, W. A debate challenge: Geneticity is 80% for white identical twins' IQs, *Phi Delta Kappan* **LIII**(7) (1972B), 136–43.

Simpkins, G., Williams, R. L., and Gunnings, R. What a culture a difference makes: A rejoinder to Valentine. *Harv. Educ. Rev.* **41** (1971), 535–41.

Simpkins, G. Reading Black Dialect and Associative Bridging. Presented at the Conference on Cognitive Language Development of the Black Child, St. Louis, Mo., January 1973.

Sims, R. Ollie and Leroy and the Language Arts. Presented at the Conference on Cognitive Language Development of the Black Child, St. Louis, Mo., January 1973.

Smith, E. Stylistic Features of Black English. Presented at the Conference on Cognitive Language Development of the Black Child, St. Louis, Mo., January 1973.

Smitherman, G. God Don't Never Change: Black English from a Black Perspective. Presented at the Conference on Cognitive Language Development of the Black Child, St. Louis, Mo., January 1973.

Stewart, W. A. On the use of Negro dialect in the teaching of reading. In J. Baratz and R. W. Shuy (eds.), *Teaching black children to read*. Washington, D.C.: Center for Applied Linguistics, 1969.

Taylor, O. T. Black Community Aspirations on the Black English/Standard English Controversy. Presented at the Conference on Cognitive Language Development of the Black Child, St. Louis, Mo., January 1973.

Valentine, C. Deficit, difference, and bicultural models of Afro-American behavior. *Harv. Educ. Rev.* 41 (1971), 137–57.

Williams, F. (ed.). *Language and poetry: Perspectives on a theme*. Chicago: Markham, 1970.

Williams, R. L. The Problem of Match and Mismatch in Testing Black Children. Presented at the Annual Meeting of the American Psychological Association, Honolulu, Hawaii, September 1972A.

Williams, R. L. The Struggle to Know, the Struggle to Survive. Presented at the Conference on Cognitive Language Development of the Black Child, St. Louis, Mo., January 1973.

Wolfram, W. A. The nature of nonstandard dialect divergence. *Elem. Engl.* 47 (1970), 739–48.

Drugging Children:
Child Abuse by Professionals

J. LARRY BROWN and
STEPHEN R. BING

Dr. Samuel A. Cartwright, a respectable Louisiana physician and a member of the American Medical Association discovered a new disease. During the social upheaval of the 1850s, Cartwright conducted a study on runaway slaves who had been caught and returned to their Southern owners. He applied his scientific skills to determine why they had run away. These slaves, Cartwright discovered, had drapetomania (*drapeto-*, the propensity to run; *mania-*, craze), a disease of the mind that caused them to abscond. In his written report to the Louisiana Medical Society, Cartwright expressed the concerns of the medical committee which he headed: "With the advantages of proper medical advice, strictly followed, this troublesome practice that many Negroes have of running away can be almost entirely prevented" (Cartwright, 1851, p. 707).

From a medical viewpoint, we may be fascinated at the extreme to which Cartwright cloaked racism in the garments of science, but it is sobering to realize that the disease drapetomania, is still listed in the respected *Taber's Medical Dictionary* (Thomas, 1970). However, our insight into Cartwright's discovery should make us wary of the more modern forms of "blaming the victim for the disease" that are cloaked in the same garments of science and technology. It is almost certain that those who view social and political phenomena through a medical model, designed to determine individual pathology, will discover a disease endemic to the victim.

History may record a modern form of drapetomania that presently victimizes our children. Hyperactivity, or minimal brain dysfunction (MBD), is attended by all the symptoms of a disease created by Dr. Cartwright himself. The "treatment" for hyperactivity or MBD is considered to be the

219

use of psychotropic drugs—strong chemical agents that act on the central nervous system to make rowdy children into calm ones, much as Cartwright sought to make runaway slaves into obedient servants. These drugs carry familiar household names such as Ritalin, Valium, and Mellaril. Collectively, they occupy a position on the behavior-control continuum far beyond Pavlovian modification, but not as far as the Orwellian spectre of genetic manipulation.

The use of such behavior-modifying agents gained national attention briefly during the 1960s, when controversy erupted over their use in Omaha, Nebraska. Following that incident, the drugging of children slipped from the national conscience, one of the many victims of Watergate, the economy, and other seemingly more important matters. But the diversion of public attention has not served children well. In the past ten years, the use of psychotropic drugs on children has grown rapidly— "zoomed," according to the experts.

Lacking conclusive data, estimates of children presently being treated with psychotropic drugs range from 300,000 to 2 million.[1] The potential pool is considered much larger, perhaps as many as 6 million. In some school districts, 10–15% of the children are given potentially dangerous drugs (Walker, 1974). In others, teachers and specialists estimate that 30% of the students are "suitable" candidates for drugging. Lest these estimates be discarded as Orwellian pipe dreams, consider the private physician in California who admits to treating more than 4000 children with Ritalin at the present time.[2]

The spiraling growth and continued use of psychotropic drugs on school children represents a major public-policy decision that has been made without adequate public debate or scrutiny. It is a decision arrived at by pharmaceutical manufacturers, researchers, and school managers, with the complicity of members of the medical community. It is a decision that, when examined in light of existing evidence, represents a technologically easy response to medical and social problems—without really addressing those problems.

DEARTH OF MEDICAL EVIDENCE

Available evidence indicates that the critical question to ask is not whether psychotropic drugs *are* effective, but whether they *should* be effective. A review of psychotropic drug studies reveals a predominant concern with two questions: Do the drugs work? If so, under what conditions? The researchers' preoccupation with these questions reflects the technological assumption, "If it works, it is good." But the rush to find something that "works" excludes the central issue: Is hyperactivity a medical problem? If so, is the use of psychotropic drugs an appropriate response to the problem?

During the past three decades, several hundred thousand children have been given psychotropic drugs by private physicians or researchers. The National Institute of Mental Health (NIMH) has poured millions of dollars into psychotropic drug research. Yet neither the money nor the research spanning nearly 30 years has produced one shred of "hard" medical evidence that MBD exists, let alone that it is a medical or a physiological phenomenon (Witter, 1971). This "disease" cannot be disclosed by a routine medical examination or by a specialized test such as an encephalogram. Belief within the medical community that MBD exists and is a specific medical problem, although totally unsubstantiated by "hard" scientific evidence—represents, in the words of Dr. Francis Crinella, a "fashionable form of consensual ignorance" (Witter, 1971, p. 31).

Without medical evidence to substantiate its existence, we can only conclude that behavior, and behavior alone, leads to a diagnosis of MBD. Dr. Cartwright himself accepted the behavior of running away from slavery as evidence of a medical disease. How can we be certain that we are not inflicting the same logic on our children?

Perhaps the most recent and well-known person to debunk the MBD-mania is Sidney Walker III, a private physician in California. A neuropsychiatrist, Walker applied his experience and training in neurology, surgery, neurosurgery, and psychiatry to the problem of hyperactivity. "In my medical practice," he reports, "I see many hyperactive children. I have never prescribed [psychotropic drugs] for these patients, and I never will" (Walker, 1974, p. 43). Utilizing sophisticated diagnostic tests to supplement his broad training, Walker has found that hundreds of MBD-diagnosed children actually do not have MBD at all. Walker also notes: "The hyperactive child's [real] problem can almost always be identified and treated if the physician is willing to take the time and trouble . . . ." (p. 43).

Clearly, what should be of foremost concern to physicians who prescribe drugs for hyperactivity is the evidence produced by Walker and other medical researchers that such drugs mask real physical problems and thereby actually jeopardize the health of their patients. The examples reported to date should generate concern even in the board chairmen of major pharmaceutical firms. Walker found one 5-year-old girl with a history of disruptive behavior, who was passed from doctor to doctor until it was finally found that she was not afflicted by the MBD menace but that she suffered from poor oxygenation because of a heart defect. Without a multidimensional approach to her diagnosis and corrective surgery, this girl would have borne the label "hyperactive" until she died from her cardiac condition.

Similarly, Walker found an 8-year-old boy, a tantrum-thrower for whom another physician had prescribed psychotropic drugs, to be prediabetic. The boy's abnormal glucose level, which influenced the function of his brain and nerve cells, resulted in his hyperactive behavior. With proper diagnosis and dietary intervention, his tantrums stopped; without a change in diet, his carbohydrate problem would have gone undetected. A host of other physical problems produce symptoms characteristic of the so-called MBD child. Two major ones are pediatric lead-paint poisoning and hunger. Either of these conditions—not uncommon in our nation—causes irritability and hyperactivity in children.

The crucial point underscored by such medical data is that in the absence of any evidence that such a thing as MBD exists, there is abundant evidence that real physiological problems cause hyperactive behavior in some children. The tragedy is that physicians who accept the MBD myth and who use the psychotropic drugs to treat hyperactive children, inadvertently mask the symptoms of real physical problems. Indeed, the technologically effective yet inappropriate action taken by these physicians may delay or prevent needed diagnosis and treatment and could actually jeopardize the lives of their young patients (Walker, 1974, pp. 44–48).

Aside from the danger of masking real physical problems, other dangers make the administration of behavior-modifying drugs to children a torturous decision for the physician. For many, prescribing these powerful chemical agents violates the medical dictum: "Start with the most conservative treatment." Doctors who fail to conduct extensive physiological tests or who do not take the time to talk with hyperactive children or to investigate their school situations cannot assert that they truly believe in that dictum.

But the effect of the actions of these physicians on children may violate an even more sacrosanct dictum, the cornerstone of the medical profession: "Do no harm!" In 1970, the Privacy Subcommittee of the U.S. House of Representatives, which investigated the use of psychotropic drugs on children, uncovered an astonishing fact. In 30 years of experience with psychotropic drugs and in spite of the millions of dollars spent in psychotropic drug research, not one study had been conducted to determine the long-term effects of these drugs on children.[3] The most benign conclusion that can be drawn from this discovery is that we cannot be certain what these long-term effects are. Yet in light of other discoveries, neither the public nor the medical community can take stock in that conclusion.

At the very least, we know that psychotropic drugs can cause a number of side effects: sleeplessness, nausea, irritability, depression, and acute psychosis. Recent research indicates that other serious consequences may result. Safer, Allen, and Barr (1972), for example, report that Ritalin suppresses normal growth (height and weight gains) in children. Yet even these data have not been sufficient to encourage the medical community to act to protect its youngest clients, to "do no harm." Advertisements of the manufacturer of Ritalin are still accepted in the *American Journal of Psychiatry*. In convoluted logic, they promote the drug for use in treating children, and simultaneously warn that "sufficient data on safety and efficacy of long-term use of Ritalin in children with MBD are not yet available."

With no evidence that psychotropic drugs are safe to use in treating children and with certain knowledge that these drugs present real physical dangers, their prescription by the medical community on a large-scale basis may represent a new era in the medical profession.

HYPERACTIVITY AND THE SCHOOLS

The public schools are increasingly active in the drugging of children. In Boston, for example, NIMH-funded researchers actually recruited in the schools for candidates for a psychotropic drug experiment. The symptoms the researchers told teachers to look for ranged from "shy" or "withdrawn" to "overactive," a behavior spectrum that unquestionably is subjective and encompasses the majority of school children (DiMascio, 1972).

Undoubtedly, many children exhibit hyperactive behavior in school and suffer actual physiological problems of the nature diagnosed by Dr. Walker. But all hyperactive behavior does not have a physiological basis. As Walker warns: "We must keep in mind that hyperactivity can be a convenient label for children who are hard to control for other reasons." In this regard, a blue-ribbon committee convened by the U.S. Office of Child Development concluded that hyperactivity is perhaps:

> . . . as much a problem of the kind of school room children have to adjust to rather than what is wrong [with the nervous system of the children]. . . . inattention and restlessness may be caused by hunger, poor teaching, overcrowded classrooms, and lack of understanding by the teachers. . . .[4]

If this is the case, relying on the judgments of school teachers and officials to determine whether children should be drugged is particularly insidious. Persons whose own actions and behavior may cause unusual stress and behavior among children are being called on to make informed judgments as to the cause of that behavior. Clearly, the assumption that errant behavior represents a problem endemic to the child rather than the school is frequently without merit. Sarason and colleagues (1966), for example, tested that assumption in an urban school system. Each time a child was labeled MBD or hyperactive by school officials, the researchers arranged for the child to be transferred to a new class and teacher. In almost every case, the move alone resulted in normalizing the child's behavior.

The experience of these researcher-clinicians, and of others, provides evidence that for some children, at least, hyperactivity is not as physiological as it is situational. Considering the joylessness of many schools with their authoritarian structures, it is fair to speculate that hyperactivity may be a "normal" response—indeed, even a healthy reaction—to an intolerable situation (Witter, 1971). The frenzied behavior of a child may actually be a sign of strength, a response to circumstances that affront his or her dignity and healthy development. But again, we find many making the uncomfortable comparison between the "pathological" behavior of Dr. Cartwright's slaves and hyperactive school children.

The damage to such a child is the permanent price paid for the assumption that hyperactivity is the fault of that child. The social cost, however, is that the use of drugs to treat school shifts attention from the faults of the school. Either schools cause misbehavior or they inappropriately responded to it. There can be no other alternatives. Yet by drugging children, school officials and the medical practitioners who rely on their assessments focus attention solely on the behavior of the child rather than on the real problem, be it physiological or situational. When drugs are used as a cheap alternative to school reform, then the practice of drugging children must be seen as a political action.

THE SOURCES OF ABUSE

Two forces, powerful and well-financed, are responsible for the present danger to children from psychotropic drugs: the pharmaceutical industry and certain agencies of the federal government. Neither of these forces could be so effective, however, without the complicity of certain segments of the medical community.

Government agencies are to be faulted on two counts: (1) the legislative and regulatory branches of the government fail to protect children from legalized drug abuse, and (2) government medical and research agencies conceive technological control techniques in response to political demands. In the past six years, HEW, NIMH, and other government agencies have directed their efforts toward tasks that would have been dismissed as Orwellian pipe dreams in another era. These agencies have considered camps to rehabilitate predelinquent (preschool-age) children; transistors implanted in the bodies of exoffenders to track their whereabouts; and national computerized registries of children and youth who have been accused, but not convicted, of drug offenses. Presently, federal monies are being spent on experimental brain surgery on so-called violent offenders, as well as on research to determine if aggressive persons have abnormal chromosome structures. We can no longer smile about the discovery of drapetomania, which these recent counterparts dwarf in significance.

Complementing the role of government agencies, and with their approval and support, pharmaceutical manufacturers overproduce amphetamines by the billions, many designed for hyperactive children. Without ever defining MBD, these companies manufacture drugs for this alleged disease, the symptoms of which any child may exhibit at one time or another.

The pharmaceutical industry literally blitzes the journals of the medical profession with pill-pushing ads that must make the careful observer wince. One, for example, displays the picture of a preschooler along with the caption: "Monsters? The dark? School?" The answer, a psychotropic drug, is displayed at the bottom of the page. While most parents and physicians know that such fears are normal in the young child, the drug represents a simplistic, time-saving remedy for the physician troubled by the parent or child who needs counseling.

Moreover, busy physicians frequently do not keep abreast of the current medical literature that conceivably could offset the intrusion of such unscientific advertisements into their profession. To compound the problem, sales-people from the drug industry bombard physicians with free samples of "easy cures." One nationally known manufacturer even provides physicians with an "MBD kit," complete with a plastic "MBD file folder." Under such a barrage, it is not surprising that thousands of physicians are prescribing psychotropic drugs for children, even in ways that have not been approved by the federal Food and Drug Administration.

As a consequence of actions and reactions, we are drugging hundreds of thousands of children: improperly diagnosed physiológical problems in children remain untreated, and inappropriate educational structures remain unaltered; the resulting hyperactivity in children leads to political and managerial demands for something that "works"; the pharmaceutical industry creates the technologically effective answer; and many medical practitioners, as Dr. Cartwright before them, legitimize the entire process.

PROTECTIONS NEEDED

The forces that encourage the drugging of children are too strong to anticipate an immediate termination of this practice. Moreover, the condition
of childhood in this nation is not accorded the protections that would be
provided were our national rhetoric about children to result in corresponding actions. Yet there are steps that can be taken on both state and national
levels to protect children from psychotropic drug abuse. Two examples in
Massachusetts are noteworthy.

In 1973, a coalition of parents and professionals succeeded in pressuring
the Human Rights Review Committee of the Massachusetts Department of
Mental Health to investigate a psychotropic drug experiment on children
in the Boston public schools. Researchers in that experiment, themselves
officials of the Mental Health Department, neglected to obtain informed
consent from the parents of children in the study. These parents did sign
a form, but the researchers failed to tell them of the possible side effects
of the drugs to be administered. Moreover, the study utilized children
solely as research subjects and provided no real services. The coalition
succeeded in bringing this experiment under public scrutiny. The Mental
Health Commission ordered the experiment terminated shortly after the
report of the Human Rights Review Committee. It is noteworthy that the
Commissioner's action was prompted not by public pressure but by facts
revealed through the process that could not withstand the test of public
review.

The same year, partially as a consequence of the above experiment,
Massachusetts adopted a model psychotropic drug law. The statute bans
the use of such drugs on school children for the purposes of clinical
research.[5] The law effectively excludes the public schools from participat-
ing in or from initiating any actions designed to treat children with drugs.
Additionally, the act limits the administration of psychotropic drugs to
individual instances when a physician attests that a specific drug meets a
legitimate medical need. Each case must then be forwarded to and certified
by the Massachusetts Department of Public Health. While limited, particularly in light of the other issues discussed in this chapter, the statute does
accomplish two important things: (1) it outlaws the use of children as
guinea pigs, and (2) it provides statistical data on the extent of psychotropic drug use on individual children in the state and identifies physicians
who may be the major prescribers. Moreover, the publicity attendant in
raising this psychotropic drug treatment as a public issue in the state serves
to warn and to educate parents about the dangers posed both by the drugs
and by those members of the educational and medical professions whose
actions jeopardize the health of their children.

SUMMARY AND CONCLUSIONS

The use of psychotropic drugs to control the behavior of preschool and preadolescent children in America is spiraling at an astonishing rate. These powerful chemical agents are prevalent, despite evidence that they present grave dangers to the healthy physical and psychological development of the children to whom they are administered. Moreover, the administration of these drugs on a large-scale basis by the educational and medical professions poses a clear threat to children and to childhood by the helping professions.

The practice of drugging children has no sound basis in law, medicine, or social policy. As such, it represents an ominous step along the Orwellian continuum of social control through psychotechnology. Strong actions are required by state legislatures and by civic organizations to monitor the abuse of children by professionals whose actions represent both a clear example of "blaming the victim for the disease" and a low point in professional ethics.

NOTES

1. See testimony presented to the Privacy Subcommittee of the U.S. House of Representatives, 1970, chaired by Congressman Cornelius E. Gallagher (D—New Jersey).
2. Reported to the authors in 1974 by a representative of National NBC News, New York, who interviewed the physician.
3. Ironically, funds for the first such study were awarded in 1970 to a researcher whose objectivity is not above question. Since 1967, he has received nearly half a million dollars in grants to test the effects of drugs on children. He is being paid currently, in part, to evaluate his own research.
4. Testimony presented to the Gallagher Privacy Subcommittee, U.S. House of Representatives, and contained in *Congressional Record* of the proceedings, September 29, 1970.
5. Massachusetts General Laws, Ch. 71, Sec. 54B.

REFERENCES

Cartwright, S. A. Report on the diseases and physical peculiarities of the Negro race. *New Orleans Med. Surg. J.* (May 1851).

DiMascio, A. *Drug treatment of behavioral disorders in children.* Boston: Massachusetts Department of Mental Health, 1972.

Safer, D., Allen, R., and Barr, E. Depression of growth in hyperactive children on stimulant drugs. *N. Engl. J. Med.* **8** (1972), 373–79.

Sarason, S. B., Levine, M. M., Goldenberg, I., Cherlin, D. L., and Bennett, E. M. *Psychology in community settings.* New York: John Wiley & Sons, Inc., 1966.

Thomas, L. L. (ed.). *Taber's cyclopedic medical dictionary* (12th ed.). Philadelphia: Davis, 1970.

Walker, Sidney, III. Drugging the American child. We're too cavalier about hyperactivity. *Psychol. Today* (December 1974), 43–48.

Witter, C. Drugging and schooling. *Transaction* **8** (July-August, 1971), 9–10, 31.

Treating Problem Children With Drugs: Ethical Issues

MARK A. STEWART

In the last ten years, physicians have relied heavily on psychotropic drugs in treating deviant behavior in children. Antidepressants are considered the best treatment for bedwetting; stimulants, the best treatment for learning disabilities and hyperactivity. Major tranquilizers are also given to many aggressive children, especially those living in institutions. The common use of drugs in dealing with difficult behavior in children is a natural extension of prescribing psychotropic drugs for the emotional and social problems of adults. The widespread nature of this practice is well illustrated by figures from a survey conducted in 1970 (Parry et al., 1973); across the country, 22% of all adults reported having used a psychotropic drug during the previous year.

Our society has been faced with similar problems in the past. Opiates, prescribed or bought over the counter, were taken by many people in the nineteenth and early twentieth century for psychological distress as well as for physical symptoms, and generations of fretful babies and toddlers were soothed in the same way (Terry and Pellens, 1928). Apparently, many physicians were ready to prescribe opiates for common pains (dysmenorrhea, for example) and for emotional stresses such as bereavement (Rush, 1812), and were reasonably blamed for a rate of addiction that may have reached 1% of the population (Terry and Pellens, 1928). What seems different today is the number of new drugs, the specificity of their actions, and the apparent lack of harmful side effects.

The ready availability of drugs to change people's feelings or behavior poses difficult questions. To what extent should we rely on such drugs for the relief of unhappiness or for the control of abnormal behavior? Have

229

intractable social problems been redefined as medical problems, because drugs have been found to provide immediate relief for them? As long as drugs reduce our discomfort over common behavior problems, will we actively look for psychological treatments that would be effective alternatives? Should physicians who are relatively untrained in dealing with psychological disorders be the ones who most commonly prescribe drugs that affect mood and behavior? Since tranquilizing drugs first appeared on the market in the 1950s, issues such as these have arisen; it is important to the health of our society to find the appropriate solutions.

The prescription of psychotropic drugs for children raises more pointed issues. In the first place, children are more objects of examination than willing subjects, because parents and teachers complain about children's difficult behavior—not the children themselves. Physicians are rarely able to observe children in their natural settings and therefore tend to base diagnoses of their problems primarily on the reports of parents and teachers. Such information is colored by what the parents and teachers consider normal behavior to be for a given child and by what they expect from their children in particular situations. In other words, the diagnosis of a disorder such as hyperactivity that is commonly treated with drugs may be based on a parent's or a teacher's subjective assessment of a child's behavior.

Children also tend to be objects rather than active participants in a drug-treatment program. Few children under the age of 12 are sufficiently introspective or far-sighted to judge whether they need treatment for hyperactivity or for school phobia, let alone what kind of treatment they should have. Most children need parents and professional adults to make these decisions, and would become anxious if they had to decide such questions for themselves. On the other hand, children can be actively involved in solving simple and immediate problems; the more they do so, the more likely it is that their treatment will be successful. For years, bed-wetting has been successfully treated by making informal contracts with children; more recently, it has become common for teachers to work out behavior and academic problems through individual contract with their students. Physicians, however, try to treat psychological problems such as hyperactivity as though they were diseases to be eradicated, rather than a set of deviant behaviors to be shaped one by one. As a result, it is difficult for a child to be involved in medical treatment, because the objectives are general rather than specific; for example, to stop being "hyperactive" rather than learn to concentrate on a school assignment for 15 minutes.

It would not be realistic to make drug treatment contingent on a child's consent, but the child should at least be told why the medicine is being prescribed, what is to be gained from taking it, and what side effects the drug can produce. Children should be encouraged to ask questions and to express their feelings about a plan of treatment, because they may not fully grasp the situation or they may be overawed and too anxious to talk naturally. With patience and encouragement, a child's assent to treatment can be obtained, so that s(he) will not feel like a pawn in the hands of adults. No one knows whether most physicians deal with children as openly as they should, but it is a fact that few articles written on drug treatment say anything about children's feelings and opinions on the subject.

The difficulty young children have in thinking about their own behavior or in discussing their feelings and experiences also makes it hard to obtain necessary information from them during follow-up visits. Judgments about the effectiveness of drug treatment are commonly based solely on the parents' reports, a situation that is doubly unfortunate. On one hand, it is difficult for parents to be objective in weighing the side effects that their child may experience, such as headaches and loss of appetite, against the benefits of the child's becoming more tractable at home and at school. On the other hand, parents cannot give a first-hand account of the drug's effects on their child's performance in school, and they do not talk freely or often enough with their child's teacher to truly know what is happening in the classroom. Few physicians consult their patients' teachers regularly to determine the results of drug treatment, let alone go to the classroom to observe for themselves, or even send an assistant to do so.

The vast majority of physicians who prescribe stimulant drugs or major tranquilizers for children with behavior problems have probably never themselves seen their patients' problem behavior in the classroom or the home, or the effects of drugs on behavior. These physicians must take parents' and teachers' statements at face value. It would be impractical for physicians to watch all children who have behavior problems at home and at school, but if they had observed children with such problems during their training as medical students or residents, they would be more skeptical about reports from untrained observers, more impressed with the role of the environment in causing the problems, and more cautious in prescribing drugs. Few medical schools or residency programs for pediatricians and family practitioners provide such experiences, or even any systematic training in the behavior and learning problems of children and the proper use of psychotropic drugs. Thus physicians with little or no training and experience in the field prescribe drugs for large numbers of children with unproved problems.

The naivete of physicians in diagnosing and treating behavior or learning problems in children could be developed ad nauseam. Otherwise responsible pediatricians and family practitioners may advise parents to let their child's teacher regulate the dose of stimulants, follow a child's course only once a year, prescribe doses three and four times the recommended maximum, prescribe drugs for 1- and 2-year-olds, and increase doses for children who already show signs of overdosage on the basis that their behavior has not improved or has actually worsened. The frequency with which such events are reported in specialized clinics suggests that physicians are generally unfamiliar with the risks of giving psychotropic drugs to children and that they are too easily swayed by pressure from parents and teachers. Few doctors question widely held but unproved ideas about the action of these drugs (for example, that stimulants have a paradoxical effect on hyperactive children that can be useful in making a diagnosis, or that stimulants can help hyperactive children to learn more effectively in school).

The same criticisms can be applied to physicians who write prescriptions for the psychotropic drugs consumed by adults in such vast amounts, but many of these doctors have at least had instruction in adult psychiatry and psychopharmacology as medical students; however, child psychiatry and its treatments are barely covered in medical school. This is not surprising as work with children is a specialty within a specialty. Moreover, attention to the problems of children has lagged behind for centuries; pediatrics did not separate from medicine until the sixteenth century, and child psychology and psychiatry did not become independent of their parent disciplines until the end of the nineteenth century. This may help to explain many physicians' ignorance of children's problems, but it hardly excuses such ignorance. We should expect those who prescribe powerful drugs (for example, amphetamines, phenothiazines, or antidepressants such as tricyclic amines) for children to know how to manage the treatment.

Clearly, the physician's lack of sophistication raises difficult social and ethical questions about the use of drugs to manipulate children's behavior, but there are also more basic questions to be raised on this subject. Some of these may be answered by research (for example, how appropriate is drug treatment to the nature of a behavior problem such as hyperactivity?). Other questions are more philosophical: "Does a child have a right to be hyperactive, if that is his or her natural behavior?" Beyond questions that chiefly concern the individual, there are issues of social policy: "Do we need hyperactive and other troublesome people? Are they assets more than problems?"

The question of whether a drug treatment is effective for a given problem usually takes precedence over the question whether such treatment is appropriate, as does the question of whether there is an alternative treatment. Data from a number of studies suggest that drugs often provide "symptomatic" relief for children who wet the bed, are afraid to go to school, or are unduly active, distractable, and impulsive. (In the last case, parents and teachers are relieved primarily; the children, only secondarily.) However, the long-term benefits from drugs or the benefits that persist after drugs are stopped seem to be insignificant, and we can reasonably conclude that drugs do not teach a child anything.

Psychological or social treatments are available for bedwetting and school phobia, and are being developed for impulsiveness, short attention span, and other components of the syndrome of hyperactivity. Although their effectiveness has not been fully established, some of these treatments result in cures (for example, the conditioning approach to bedwetting). Others remove painful symptoms, such as phobias, or help children develop their own controls over natural behaviors, such as impulsiveness and distractibility. These approaches to treatment shape a child's behavior, but it is unlikely that they fundamentally alter the child's personality in the way that drugs can. On the other hand, such treatments help a child learn to master stress and therefore tend to build self-respect. Needless to say, these treatments can only be effective if the child is an active participant.

Because effective psychological alternatives seem to exist, it is reasonable to ask how appropriate drugs are in the treatment of children's behavior problems. A central belief of physicians who endorse drug treatment of children is that difficulties ranging from hyperactivity to reading disabilities stem from subtle abnormalities in brain function. Biologic disorders do not have to be treated biologically instead of psychologically but if the concept of minimal brain dysfunction is valid, drug treatment becomes more intelligible. At present, however, this concept is not based on a solid foundation of facts, and it is now more than ten years old. So vague and inclusive an idea seems bound to follow the "Oedipus complex" and other unitary hypotheses to oblivion.

From their training and from their practice in dealing with sickness rather than health, physicians tend to assume that patients' symptoms reflect qualitative departures from normal function. Doctors seldom have the opportunity to see that the behavior troubling a mother or a teacher is within the range of "normal" child activity, assuming that normality is defined statistically rather than ideally. When we consider a child's behavior within a spectrum of normality, it may become obvious that the youngster's problems are social or educational and not medical. It would be silly to treat the learning problems of a child with a low IQ as a medical issue, except in a broad, humanistic sense. Treating hyperactivity or a reading disability as a medical disorder is also dubious. A reading disability is primarily a cognitive problem that hopefully will yield to psychological and educational advances, whereas hyperactivity is often a problem rooted in parents' and teachers' lack of skill in child management.

Clinicians' views of children's problems are limited in that they seldom learn the outcome of their involvement with many patients. Working with a host of immediate problems, they may never hear about the impossible child's success as an adult. Taking an unduly pessimistic view of children's problems, clinicians tend to employ more radical treatments than are necessary. In general, the validity of disorders such as hyperactivity has not yet been proved. The available data suggest that such traits as a high level of activity, a short attention span, impulsivity, and excitability persist into adult life, but these qualities may be advantageous in some walks of life (examples are saleswork, show business, and politics). If being hyperactive is an asset to an adult but a hardship for a child, then hyperactivity, in part, is a socially defined problem. Some physicians argue, however, that the condition is similar to diabetes and must be controlled with drugs throughout a person's life. It is true that some hyperactive children become adults with disturbed personalities, but it can still be argued that the wisest course of action is to learn why these children have problems and others do not, before advocating that all hyperactive children be treated as chronically diseased.

Regulating a child's behavior with drugs for periods of years raises ethical questions concerning long-term effects on children. Specialists see a number of young people who have taken stimulants every day of their lives from, say, ages 10 to 16, at which point both the children and their families are thoroughly dependent on a drug to maintain daily life. These children may have forgotten what their original personalities were, and they may feel quite uncomfortable about their natural behavior. They are in the dilemma of having to adjust to being different people if a psychiatrist recommends that they stop taking the drug, and their families are correspondingly troubled. Thus when these children are mature enough to decide for themselves whether or not to accept treatment with a psychotropic drug, they and their families may already be so conditioned to the drug's use that they are no longer free to choose.

The fact that drug-induced changes in behavior, such as being dry at night or doing more schoolwork, do not persist when the drug is stopped (Shaffer, Costello, and Hill, 1968; Weiss et al., 1975) is another drawback of drug treatment. Lennard and colleagues state the issue in general terms: "Drugs provide only effects, no learning, and it is learning and exercising the means of obtaining such effects that constitute a vital part of human life" (Lennard et al., 1972). For children the effects of drug treatment short-circuit their learning through experience and their own efforts to control their behavior and to master stress. In this sense, then, drugs tend to make children dependent, to undermine their self-respect, and to prevent them from building strength of character.

Prescribing stimulants to children seems to carry the risk of abetting drug abuse, but no study done so far answers the question of whether young people are more likely to misuse drugs if they have taken them as treatment in childhood. Undoubtedly, some older children experiment with their medicines or pass them on to friends, but how often that happens we do not know, nor do we know the consequences of these actions. We may also wonder whether giving some young people drugs to treat their behavior problems undermines society's message that teen-agers should not use drugs to solve personal difficulties. It may be, however, that our adolescents pay little or no attention either to this message or to its contradiction.

REFERENCES

Lennard, H. L., et al. *Mystification and drug misuse.* New York: Harper & Row, 1972.

Parry, H. L., et al. National patterns of psychotherapeutic drug use. *Arch. Gen. Psychiatr.* **28** (1973), 769–83.

Rush, R. *Medical inquiries and observations on the diseases of the mind.* Philadelphia: Kimber & Richardson, 1812.

Shaffer, D., Costello, A. J., and Hill, I. D., Control of enuresis with imipramine. *Arch. Dis. Child.* **43** (1968), 665–71.

Terry, C. E., and Pellens, M. *The opium problem.* New York: Committee on Drug Addictions, 1928.

Weiss, G., et al. The effect of long-term treatment of hyperactive children with methylphenidate. *J. Can. Med. Assoc.* **112** (1975), 159–65.

Needed: A Public Policy
for Psychotropic Drug Use
With Children

RODMAN McCOY and
GERALD P. KOOCHER

As the two preceeding chapters by Bing, Brown, and Stewart so aptly demonstrate, the issues involved in the use of psychotropic agents in the treatment of children are complex, wide-ranging, and hardly the subject of uniform agreement among professionals (let alone among parents, educators, and the children, themselves). These considerations make it necessary to raise potentially crucial questions about some of our most respected social institutions and our most commonly held attitudes. Virtually anyone who may have to deal with children in a supervisory capacity is likely to encounter these issues eventually, and professionals should be prepared to take an informed stand on the policy issues involved.

The expression "being prepared to take a stand" is often interchangeable with "formulating a policy." Considering the sheer number of people potentially involved in a child's drug-treatment program, it is not surprising to note the lack of consensus regarding drug therapy, given its subtlety and/or high degree of technicality. It is more than surprising, however, that there has been, and still is, an overwhelming absence of consensus among the very people who *would* play a professional role in the formulation and administration of any policy established to deal with the use of psychotropic drugs in the treatment of children with behavior problems. Yet it is indeed difficult to find a single instance in which a formal, de jure policy of this kind has been adopted by any group—from the American Medical Asssociation to the Highland Elementary School PTA. The lack of "policy-making behavior," particularly in an industrialized, largely centralized society like ours, should be regarded as evidence of the existence of an imminently dangerous situation—a situation that comes closer to critical mass as we consider (1) the delicate nature of the physical and psychological development of the child, and (2) the far- and wide-reaching effects, both known and unknown, of the variety of psychoactive drugs.

Thus it would be most constructive to prepare a set of antecedent criteria preceding the formulation of a specific public policy to ensure that the eventual policy is the safest, and most effective, considerate, consistent, and convenient means of enabling children with behavior problems to gain the fullest possible measure of whatever society has to offer. Four types of specific needs are apparent immediately:

1. The need for well-conceived psychopharmacological research.
2. The need for institutional reconciliation and communication.
3. The need for a comprehensive assessment protocol.
4. The need for parental consciousness-raising and involvement.

In elaborating on these criteria, we include our own perceptions of their fulfillment status at present. In the process, implications for more specific policy stances that might be taken by those who use psychotropic drugs in the treatment of children are indicated.

THE NEED FOR WELL-CONCEIVED PSYCHOPHARMACOLOGICAL RESEARCH

In the 38 years since Charles Bradley (1938) first tested Benzedrine on a group of 30 "behavior-problem children," well over 200 clinical investigations on the effects of a variety of psychotropic drugs for use in the treatment of children have been published. Focusing primarily on those drugs currently considered "treatments of choice" for the largest numbers of children who exhibit behavior disorders, we find amphetamine (Benzedrine), dextroamphetamine (Dexedrine), methylphenidate (Ritalin), and, to a lesser extent, the minor and major tranquilizers, including phenothiazine derivatives such as chlorpromazine (Thorazine). At first glance, the number of studies available seems to indicate a wide data base on which to justify subsequent usage of the drugs in question. Further buttressing this position, the clear majority of these experiments indicates at least some positive finding for the use of any of these drugs in the treatment of a variety of behavior problems. However, when we examine the research design and statistical methodology characteristic of these studies, as detailed by Eisenberg (1959), a glaring pattern of deficiency appears.

These are some of the reasons the need for *well-conceived* research is stressed. To date, no common protocol exists for testing the effectiveness or safety of using psychoactive drugs to treat children. For this reason, methodologically consistent replications of almost all the studies reviewed are nonexistent. Many individual studies suffer from at least one of the following deficiencies: subjects selected from nongeneralizable populations; lack of, proper, or any, control group; sample size too small to permit statistical tests of significance; ignorance of double-blind procedure; and nonuniformity of assessment across the sample. There are other deficiencies in this body of research as a whole that need correction before psychoactive drugs can truly be deemed safe and effective for treating children.

While it has been variously reported that dextroamphetamine and methylphenidate increase attention span and alertness, little is known of the effects that these drugs have on a cognitive structure such as memory, another important component of learning skills. The lack of longitudinality in many of the studies (for example, Bradley's 1938 experiment covers only a week in time) is a serious shortcoming when we consider that a child could be using one of these drugs for long periods of time with only minimal clinical follow-up. What about the well-known anorexic side effects of the use of stimulants of the central nervous system? Considering the balance of nutrition necessary to sustain maturation of the child, these "side effects" (known as the "main effect" when these drugs are prescribed as diet pills) have serious implications for the health of a large number of children.

Of the four antecedent criteria listed previously, the need for psychopharmacological research should be given top priority, largely because it constitutes the weakest link that holds together any proponent argument for the use of psychoactive drugs in the treatment of children's behavior disorders. We must be suspicious when pharmaceutical manufacturers are involved in a great deal of psychotropic drug research. While the Food and Drug Administration often plays a positive role in keeping suspect drugs (Thalidomide is an example the FDA is quick to use) off the market, the Administration is ill-inclined to pay such scrupulous attention to those drugs whose effects may be more subtle over a shorter time period and whose usage has a predominantly psychological effect. The status of this type of psychopharmacological research makes the prescription of many drugs for behavior disorders highly questionable. It is reasonable to suspect that a well-replicated, consistent, well-controlled, and statistically viable body of research will indicate much more limited use of these drugs than is presently operable. Any policy formulated that pertains to the psychopharmacological management of children's behavior disorders is negligent if it is established without questioning whether a drug "works" and is safe.

THE NEED FOR INSTITUTIONAL RECONCILIATION AND COMMUNICATION

The child with a behavior problem who is being considered for drug treatment does not fall into the bailiwick of one particular institution. S(he) is part of a family, goes to school, may have contact with the mental-health disciplines if s(he) is undergoing some sort of psychotherapy or assessment, and if drugs are prescribed, also has contact with a physician. Conducting a review of the available literature pertinent to the problem within its institutional context reveals differences in the perception of the problem that are potentially harmful to the children undergoing treatment. There seems to be a lack of information transfer across disciplinary lines. Finding a consensus is impossible and, again, not surprisingly so given the differences in training. What is disheartening is that individual disciplines pay so little attention to the concerns of other fields, preferring apparently to channel expertise incisively. The lack of an overview bodes ill for the child who comes into contact with a variety of institutions. This lack of communication may result from the prejudices that cause one professional to disregard out-of-hand the opinions of a professional in another field. But, to be fair a discussion of these prejudices would have to include almost every aspect of human behavior and would be far too lengthy to include here. Only a few of the points normally involved in such a discussion are well documented from an empirical viewpoint, although the contrasts between the two preceeding chapters serve to illustrate these differences to a degree. Hopefully, it is sufficient to say that these attitudinal differences do exist; that they are sometimes conditioned by aspects of professional experience that, at best, bear little relevance to the problem at hand; and that it would be most helpful to the child if they could be overcome to the degree that neither jeopardizes integrity nor oversteps the limits of sound, careful, scientific examination. The professional who is involved in the management of children with behavior disorders, whether teacher, physician, psychologist, psychiatrist, or school administrator, is better qualified if sensitized to the issue and aware of the interdisciplinary approach necessary to investigate all aspects of the child's problems.

The antecedent criterion implicit in the criticism of the institutional roles played in the treatment of children's behavior disorders is the greater interdisciplinary cooperation of the professionals involved. Such cooperation is a necessary precedent to the fulfillment of the following criterion as well.

THE NEED FOR A COMPREHENSIVE ASSESSMENT PROTOCOL

More recent references indicate much less prediliction to ascribe universal etiologies to specific behavior disorders. Since Lehtinen and Strauss (1947) declared the existence of hyperactivity in a child "sufficient itself to make the firm diagnosis of brain damage, even in the absence of other neurological evidence," some progress has been made toward apprising the spectrum of professionals of the variety of etiologies that can cause a child to exhibit some behavioral anomaly. Leon Eisenberg (1969) has devoted much of his attention toward achieving an understanding of hyperkinesis, but his recognition of the shortcomings of earlier organic/experiential diagnosis is perhaps generalizable to the range of childhood behavior disorders. Eisenberg is not the only person to recognize the necessity of comprehensive assessment, but he does raise questions about considering the resources of the community when formulating an assessment protocol. In other words, it is fine to suggest that a child with a behavior problem be exposed to a variety of assessment modalities, such as an electroencephalogram, medical-history scrutinization, neurological examination, questionnaires/rating scales given to parents and teachers, or even some of the more sophisticated mechanical observation methods, such as the ballistocardiographic chair (Werry and Sprague, 1970); if these resources are not readily available, the eventual treatment may not be appropriate. Making these resources available should be a priority; failing to do so penalizes the poor and uninformed and can expose the child (by the prescription of psychotropic drugs without adequate assessment) to unnecessary danger, as Stewart notes in the preceding chapter. Coordinating comprehensive assessment makes the previous point about institutional cooperation all the more valid. We must draw on the various resources of educators, administrators, psychologists, psychiatrists, and general practitioners to administer a comprehensive assessment as soon as possible after a behavior disorder becomes pronounced enough to cause a complaint to be issued. Four equally important areas of investigation need to be incorporated into eventual policy regarding assessment:

1. *Psychological/psychiatric review*: An analysis of cognitive and interpersonal strengths and weaknesses that could be instrumental in influencing the child's behavior.

2. *Total environmental review*: This should include interviews with teachers, the child, and the parents and an investigation of their respective resources to determine the conditions under which the child is expected to function. Although it may overlap somewhat with psychological/psychiatric review, total environmental review is intended to be a broader and more integrated approach to the child's world than the normal "office assessment" would imply.

3. *Medical history review*: This workup should include as detailed a study as possible of medical events from birth records to the present status of the child. Only in this way can the effects of prenatal influences, birth accidents, childhood infections, and sundry other conditions with possible behavioral correlates be fully integrated so that the child's behavior can be completely understood.

4. *Neurological examination*: This should include an electroencephalogram, as well as the usual reflex, postural, and motility studies.

It is absolutely necessary that any policy dealing with the chemical treatment of childhood behavior disorders specify these four areas of study and guarantee that they are tested. It is also necessary, especially when such studies indicate drug treatment, that the approval of the parents, a physician (implicit in the writing of a prescription), and those responsible for making prior assessments are secured. Last, but certainly not least in importance, the use of medication should be discussed realistically with the child and his or her feelings should be incorporated in the overall treatment plan, as Stewart suggests in the preceding chapter.

THE NEED FOR PARENTAL CONSCIOUSNESS-RAISING AND INVOLVEMENT

Parents who give informed consent for a treatment to be administered to their child must be prepared to face a certain amount of disillusionment that may be engendered by the lack of a specific policy related to their child's behavioral disorder. Currently, much of this disillusionment is probably overcome by the sheer faith and trust that many parents have in their family physician or medical-care system. Most people have only one doctor and usually do not seek corroborating medical opinions. This tendency is likely to increase if the school system places the onus for seeking help on the parents, as it usually does. If the school does offer to refer the child, it may be to a physician or a school psychologist who is salaried by the school system. In our review of the literature, it is noteworthy that a bias appears to exist toward assuming an etiology of brain damage (term of choice, minimal brain dysfunction) among those writing in the educational context (Cruickshank et al., 1961). Because education cannot be expected to cure brain damage, the child is shunted to the social institution of medicine that suffers from its own biases. Parents should be aware of the relative noninvolvement of the school in treating the behavior disorders of their children. At this point, school functionaries act as monitors (initial complaint, feedback, procedure, making sure the child takes the pill, and so on), and often display little concern for the child with the problem in the face of his or her disturbance of classroom routine. It might be more constructive for parents to agitate to encourage the educational institutions to make a statement of policy and thereby to cooperate and become involved with mental-health and medical institutions that now play a more active role in determining treatment models and enacting assessment procedures. Parental involvement must be expanded by the adoption of therapeutic treatments that make less use of psychoactive drugs, so that any policy that incorporates comprehensive assessment (and thus likely to turn up a variety of etiologies and possibly indicate treatment modalities that preclude the use of drugs) also emphasizes active parental involvement and not mere consent.

SUMMARY AND CONCLUSION

In conclusion, the lack of formalized inter- or intra-institutional policy designed to deal with the large numbers of children with behavior disorders is a serious problem that must be resolved if we are to achieve equality of opportunity. Naturally, the establishment of a policy does not necessarily mitigate the realities as they existed before the policy was written. The ability of a policy to change realities depends on the clout of the policymakers, and it is difficult to see who would have enough clout to overcome the particular barriers that must be removed or at least eroded before a policy can even be formulated. If we could ensure institutional cooperation, if we could establish a comprehensive, uniform assessment plan, if we could acquire greater parental input, and if we could base our policy on a statistically strong body of psychopharmacological research, we could be more certain of a subsequent reduction in the usage of psychoactive drugs to treat children with behavior problems. It seems likely that we could find other strategies more effective, safer, more considerate, and just as convenient as many of us now view the use of drugs. Perhaps we have settled too quickly for technological solutions at the expense of both our philosophy and the rights of our children.

REFERENCES

Bakwin, H., and Bakwin, R. M. *Clinical management of behavior disorders in children.* Philadelphia: Saunders, 1966.

Bradley, Charles. The behavior of children receiving Benzedrine. *Am. J. Psychiatr.* 94 (1938), 577–85.

Chess, S., and Thomas, A. W. *Annual progress in child psychiatry and child development.* New York: Brunner/Mazel, 1968.

Christensen, D., and Sprague, R. Reduction of hyperactive behavior by conditioning procedures alone and combined with methylphenidate. *Behav. Res. Ther.* II 3 (1973), 331–35.

Cruickshank, W. M., et al. (eds.). *A teaching method for brain-injured and hyperactive children.* Syracuse: Syracuse University Press, 1961.

Eisenberg, Leon. Basic issues in drug research with children. In S. Fisher (ed.), *Child research in psychopharmacology.* Springfield, Ill.: Thomas, 1959.

Eisenberg, Leon. The management of the hyperkinetic child. *Dev. Med. Child Neurol.* 8 (1969), 593–98.

Fisher, S. (ed.). *Child research in psychopharmacology.* Springfield, Ill.: Thomas, 1959.

Lehtinen, L. E., and Strauss, A. A. *Psychopathology and education of the brain-injured child.* New York: Grune & Stratton, 1947.

Lesser, L. Hyperkinesis in children: An operational approach to management, *Clin. Pediatr.* 9 (1970), 548–53.

Sroufe, L. A., and Stewart, M. A. Treating problem children with drugs. *N. Eng. J. Med.* 289 (1973), 407–13.

Stewart, M. A. Hyperactive children. *Sci. Am.* (April 1970), 94–98.

Werry, J. S., and Sprague, R. L. Hyperactivity. In Costello, C. G. (ed.), *Symptoms of psychopathology.* New York: John Wiley & Sons, Inc., 1970.

Epilogue:
"But We Always Do It That Way!"

FREDA G. REBELSKY

Twenty years ago, the ocean floor was supposedly a relatively flat surface covered with silt, made of the materials of sunken continents. But discoveries in the last few years show mountains and gaping chasms lying deep under the ocean—and these discoveries have radically changed our ideas about the formation of the earth and allowed us to "see" what scientists had either ignored or mislabeled for centuries. So, too, the knowledge that babies can distinguish between forms immediately after birth has led us to notice capabilities in the infant that were always present but were long ignored. How many millions of people looking at babies had not "seen" that they were looking back!

An equally gigantic change must be made in our present stereotypes about children, so that those of us who care about children's rights can begin to examine why we do what we do to children. This book attempts to change some "mental sets," some labeling procedures. It is no longer meaningful or in the best interest of the child to bow to the historical precedent "But we've always done it that way." It's time for a change *now*.

My basic assumptions are that we do *not* know what produces optimal human growth and development. We do not know what we want people to achieve in the long run—and even if we did, we would not know how to help them reach those unknown goals.

However, I do believe that all organisms are smart and that they do their best, given their view of the circumstances they are in. Children are different from adults, with very different cognitive and emotional abilities. This makes our task of understanding what they do and why they behave the way they do even more difficult.

A little anecdote may serve as an illustration here. I found my 4-year-old son carefully spreading toothpaste over a wooden cocktail table. When I asked him why he was doing this, he replied that the toothpaste had cleaned his teeth so well that he wanted to clean the table for me! I could have considered only the behavior itself, but, as an adult, I know that I must consider motivation as well. If I had punished the behavior, what would I have taught the child?

The adult's and the child's perspectives are different: there is a different sense of self. To pretend, as we repeatedly do, that children are like adults is to miss significant data about the nature of children and childhood.

It helps adults to label a child "dyslexic," "hyperactive," "troubled"— but it doesn't help the child, whose behavior is then no longer viewed as valid and differentiated. The most "hyperactive" child does not behave the same way throughout each day and in all circumstances. As adults, we have the ability and must take the responsibility to consider the reasons for the child's behavior, to distinguish between what induces quieter and more active behaviors, and to differentiate among the behaviors we have lumped under any one label.

It is up to us, then, to force ourselves to be reflective in areas where we have previously been certain—and that is a very difficult task. It was difficult enough to do about ocean bottoms and infant vision; it is even more difficult to do about children, because here our own sense of competence is at stake.

People who are different from us often scare us; we want to change them, put them away, or ignore them. Children scare adults by reminding us all of childish ways, and adults often act "childishly" with children. (A mother in a supermarket yelling, "Stop your screaming!" is an obvious example.) Adults, who know how to look at motivation, often focus on behavior instead (just as children do). Adults, who know about differentiation, often group and label in an undifferentiated way (just as children do). Adults, who understand that process is as important for teaching as content, often focus on content (just as children do).

I think we will be less frightened of those who are different from us when we recognize how much they frighten us and when we recognize in ourselves those feelings that others stir up in us. We can then, at the very least, have some respect for our own abilities to reflect.

My bias is that when we stop pretending we know things we do not know and when we stop doing things the way they have always been done, we will all be better able to aid our children and ourselves—to feel smart, secure, confident, and knowledgeable. The process of inquiry and discovery, both of ourselves and of those we seek to help, will, I am sure, lead to a more genuine respect for our own abilities and for the abilities of others. Then, and only then, will we have less need to worry about "rights" of any kind.

Name Index

247

Subject Index